ATLAS OF THE HUMAN BRAIN

ATLAS
OF THE HUMAN BRAIN

by DONALD H. FORD

STATE UNIVERSITY OF NEW YORK, DOWNSTATE MEDICAL CENTER,
BROOKLYN, NEW YORK

and J. P. SCHADÉ

CENTRAL INSTITUTE FOR BRAIN RESEARCH
AMSTERDAM (THE NETHERLANDS)

ELSEVIER PUBLISHING COMPANY / *Amsterdam London New York* / 1971

ELSEVIER PUBLISHING COMPANY
335 Jan van Galenstraat P.O. Box 211, Amsterdam, The Netherlands

ELSEVIER PUBLISHING CO. LTD.
Barking, Essex, England

AMERICAN ELSEVIER PUBLISHING COMPANY, INC.
52 Vanderbilt Avenue New York, New York 10017

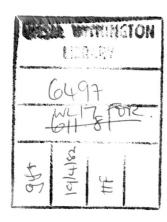
FIRST EDITION 1966
REPRINTED 1967
SECOND REVISED EDITION 1971

Library of Congress Card Number: 74–135480
ISBN 0–444–40890–8
With 145 illustrations

PRINTED IN THE NETHERLANDS

Preface

An understanding of Neuroanatomy is to a certain extent dependent on the ability to visualize the nervous system in a three-dimensional manner. While this is certainly true for Gross Anatomy as well, the incorporation of many details into the relatively small mass of the central nervous system appears to make this region more difficult to comprehend.

The following Atlas is based on illustrative material and demonstrations used in the Department of Anatomy of the Downstate Medical Center, University of New York (Brooklyn), and in the Central Institute for Brain Research at Amsterdam which have been found useful in permitting a ready comprehension of the structure of the brain. All material used is photographic and unretouched. The illustrations have been divided into the following subgroups: I. Anatomy of the Brain and Spinal Cord; II. Gross Anatomy; III. Vessels; IV. Gross Dissection; V. Sectional Anatomy in the Coronal, Horizontal and Sagittal Planes, and VI. A Pal–Weigert Atlas of 30 μ Thick Sections stained for Myelin.

A text is included with the intent of providing a Method for grasping the details of the anatomy of the human brain and of the interrelationships of nuclear groups and nerve tract or fiber systems.

The nomenclature used is based mainly on the Editions of the *Nomina Anatomica* approved by the Sixth and Seventh International Congresses held in Paris, 1955, and in New York, 1960. The naming of structures in the Pal-Weigert Atlas is based on the *Nomina Anatomica* whenever possible. These terms are then supplemented with those given in Brain Stem Atlases by Olszewski and Baxter (1954), and Riley (1960).

Contents

SECTION I

Anatomy of the Brain and Spinal Cord

Anatomy of the Brain and Spinal Cord

One of the aims of teaching the anatomy of the CNS is to provide a background for the understanding of the important neuronal pathways and their relation to function. In order to achieve such an understanding it is necessary for the student to become familiar with the structure of the brain. Familiarity with structure is helpful in visualizing and retaining the routes taken and connections made by nerve impulses. Structure then provides a concrete basis of function.

A sound strategy for learning the anatomical components of the CNS is to begin with the gross features and proceed toward a greater differentiation of the different parts. The student's objective should be to form a concept of the three-dimensional structure of the brain. Once such a concept is achieved, the appreciation of the subsequent discussion of functional systems should be greatly facilitated.

This laboratory guide is deliberately organized to aid the student in acquiring such an understanding. The major divisions and subdivisions of the CNS are first outlined, aids in gaining a three-dimensional concept of the brain are then provided; the blood vessels of the brain are discussed so that the student can learn them in relation to the structure which they supply and with which he has become familiar; the ventricular system is outlined in relation to its adjacent brain components; and finally, the functional systems are treated in what seems to be a meaningful order to the authors.

The physical organization for study of the gross brain may be planned in many ways. An arrangement which has served ideally is for students to work in groups of four, each having two and a half formalin-fixed brains for study. The half brain should be utilized for gross consideration of the lobes, gyri, sulci, etc. One whole brain may then be used for sectional studies and the remaining brain used for study of the distribution of the vascular system and for final review.

The laboratory instruments which are most useful include: scalpel, fine forceps and scissors.

In most courses of neuroanatomy, it is not possible to start the study at the autopsy table. Whenever possible, however, this is an instructive beginning as it provides for an appreciation of certain relationships between brain, meninges and skull which is not as readily obtained after removal of the brain from the skull cavity. Such an exposure of the brain *in situ*, starting with the outer dural surface after removal of the skull cap is demonstrated in Figs. 1–8. In Fig. 2, one half of the dura has been reflected to demonstrate the underlying cerebral hemisphere. At this point, perhaps the most prominent structures are the *venae cerebri superiores* which are usually congested at death. Note that the more caudal veins tend to arch sharply forward toward the rostral pole prior to emptying into the *sinus sagittalis superior*. This later sinus may be dissected at this time, or it may be done prior to reflecting the dura. The next step is to remove the hemisphere of one side (Fig. 3), which reveals the *falx cerebri* in the mid-sagittal plane and the *tentorium cerebelli* in the horizontal plane. The latter serves to separate the cerebral and cerebellar hemispheres. Note the free edge of the tentorium (*incisura tentorii*) where this dense dural membrane arches forward around the mesencephalon toward its attachments to the clinoid processes.

Removal of the other hemisphere (Fig. 4) permits one to look down upon the cavities of the anterior and middle cranial fossae. The posterior fossa containing the *metencephalon* and *myelencephalon* is roofed over by the tentorium cerebelli. The mesencephalon is encircled by the free edge of the tentoria. The points of exit of the *nervi olfactorius* (I), *opticus* (II) and *oculomotorius* (III) may be observed.

As is apparent in Fig. 4 and 5, the mesencephalon seems somewhat compressed by the edges of the incisura tentorii. This is obviously not normal; nor is it necessarily pathological. After death, a large amount of the cerebrospinal fluid in the *cavum subarachnoideale* is resorbed by the brain, causing it to swell. This edema is frequently aggravated by pulmonary and cardiac congestion just prior to death. Thus, when viewed at autopsy the brain is frequently distended. This sort of edema should not be confused with that caused by disease.

Removal of one half of the tentorium cerebelli (Fig. 6) demonstrates the superior surface of the cerebellum and four additional cranial nerves, the *trochlearis* (IV), *trigeminus* (V), *abducens* (VI) and *vestibulocochlearis* (VIII). At this time the primary branches of the trigeminus and their common ganglion can be readily dissected and studied in relation to the *sinus cavernosus*, oculomotor, trochlear and abducens nerves. By depressing the mesencephalon and pons towards the basi occiput, the *arteria basilaris* at the base of the pons comes into view (Fig. 7). In this instance the *arteria labyrinthi* which enters the *meatus acusticus internus* together with the vestibulocochlear nerve may be seen. Finally, the entire cerebellum, pons and medulla may be removed to expose the emptied posterior cranial fossa with the *medulla spinalis* projecting up through the *foramen magnum* (Fig. 8).

At this time the exit of the remaining cranial nerves (*facialis* (VII), *glossopharyngeus* (IX), *vagus* (X), *accessorius* (XI), and *hypoglossus* (XII)) may be observed.

3

The Gross Divisions and Subdivisions of the CNS

The study of the gross features and boundaries of the brain can be carried out by using one half brain (Figs. 9, 11, 14–19) cut only in the mid-sagittal plane and a whole brain cut in coronal sections (Figs. 63–72). An improved three-dimensional conception is obtained of the relationships of the deep nuclear structures to each other and to the ventricular system by utilizing brains cut in the horizontal (Figs. 73–76) and sagittal planes (Figs. 77–82). For the benefit of those who are unfamiliar with the terms for planes of section or terms of relative position, a brief description is given here. There are three common planes in which a brain may be cut: the sagittal, coronal and horizontal planes. Terms of relative position commonly used are rostral, caudal, dorsal, ventral, medial and lateral. The understanding of these terms depends on the knowledge of the anatomical position which is applicable to all animals, including man. A man supporting himself on all four extremities with his line of vision parallel with the floor (head raised) is in an anatomical position comparable with that of all four-legged vertebrates. In this position his back and the top of the scalp are most dorsal, his adbomen and chin are most ventral, his buttocks are most caudal, his forehead and nose are most rostral, his midline is most medial and his ears are the most lateral part of his head. A plane which bisects him into right and left halves is the mid-sagittal plane. Planes parallel to the mid-sagittal plane are para-sagittal planes. Any plane parallel with the floor on which the man supports himself is a horizontal plane in the brain and his spinal cord is to be considered to be parallel with the horizontal plane. Any plane perpendicular to the sagittal and horizontal planes simultaneously is a coronal plane. On this basis, the ventral aspect of the brain is inferior (but ventral is not synonymous with the anterior, as it is with the abdominal wall). The dorsal aspect of the brain may also be considered as the superior surface (but dorsal is not synonymous with the posterior surface, as it is in relation to the back). In the human forebrain the term posterior refers to the occipital or caudal end, and the term anterior refers to the frontal or rostral end.

Clean away the pia–arachnoid of the half brain (as seen in Fig. 9) with the mid-

4

sagittal surface exposed and study the surface morphology. Separate the rostral part or forebrain (telencephalon–diencephalon) and mesencephalon from the hind brain (metencephalon–myelencephalon). This is done by cutting through the brain stem at a plane identified as the isthmus rhombencephali. This plane represents the line of separation between the rhombencephalon and the metencephalon in the embryonic brain. In the adult, it is represented by a plane which passes dorsoventrally at right angles to the long axis of the brain stem starting just caudal to the inferior colliculus on the dorsal surface. Ventrally, it passes just rostral to the pons. The outline of the brain and spinal cord which appears below should guide you in defining the essential components.

The CNS is divided into its major divisions and subdivisions in the following discussion. First identify the major parts I–VI, then the major subdivisions A..., and then lesser subdivisions 1..., etc. Such a procedure will prove ample opportunity for review.

I. Telencephalon (cerebral hemispheres, Figs. 10–16, 18–20)

This comprises the two large hemispheres which are connected by the *corpus callosum* (see mid-sagittal section of the brain). The anterior bend of the corpus is known as the *genu*; the posterior bulge is the *splenium*. The cerebral cortex forms the outer cellular layer of the cerebrum. The cerebral hemispheres are marked by grooves (*sulci*) end elevations (*gyri*). Some of the major sulci are the boundaries of the major lobes (Figs. 10 and 13).

A. Neo-cortical areas

Almost all the exposed area of the cerebrum is formed of neo-cortex. Neo-cortex is defined as that portion of the cerebral cortex which is recent from the standpoint of evolution and development. This cortex occupies a relatively vast area of the brain.

1. Lobus frontalis (Figs. 10, 11–15)

Rostral portion of cerebrum which is bounded by the *sulcus centralis* caudally and laterally, and the *sulcus lateralis* ventrally (Fig. 15). The lobe extends onto the medial mid-sagittal surface as well, and is bounded ventrally by the rostral half of the corpus callosum. Its exact caudal limit on the medial side is discussed in the description of the *gyrus cinguli* below.

a. *Gyrus precentralis* (Fig. 14). Lies between the *sulcus precentralis* and the *sulcus centralis* (Fig. 15). The sulcus centralis usually does not quite reach the sulcus lateralis and does not show more than an indentation on the dorsal aspect of the

5

medial surface. The sulcus precentralis, which lies rostral to the sulcus centralis, is not usually continuous dorsoventrally, being interrupted by a small unnamed gyrus.

b. *Gyrus frontalis inferior* (Figs. 14 and 15). Lies between the sulcus lateralis ventrally and the sulcus frontalis inferior dorsally. Its caudal border is the ventral third of the *sulcus precentralis.*

(*1*) *Pars opercularis.* Portion which lies between the sulcus precentralis and the ramus ascendens of the sulcus lateralis.

(*2*) *Pars triangularis.* Portion which lies between the ramus ascendens and a horizontal ramus of the sulcus lateralis.

(*3*) *Pars orbitalis.* This remaining portion of the gyrus frontalis inferior is adjacent to the orbital cortex and overlies the bony partition separating the cranial from the orbital cavities.

c. *Gyrus frontalis medius* (Figs. 14 and 15). Lies between the *sulci frontalis superiores* and *inferiores.* The middle third of the *sulcus precentralis* marks its caudal end.

d. *Gyrus frontalis superior* (Figs. 14 and 15). Lies between the *sulcus frontalis superior* laterally and the *sulcus cinguli* medially, and, therefore, exists on both the lateral and medial aspects of the frontal lobe. Laterally, its caudal end is marked by the dorsal third of the sulcus precentralis and medially its caudal border reaches the *lobulus paracentralis* (a junction between the gyrus precentralis and postcentralis around the short extension of the sulcus centralis onto the medial surface).

On the medial surface (Figs. 11, 16–19):

e. *The anterior half of the gyrus cinguli* (Figs. 16, 18 and 19). This gyrus is wrapped around the anterior (rostral) part of the *corpus callosum.* The sulcus cinguli is dorsal and rostral to it. Ventrally, the gyrus curves back under the genu of the corpus callosum, ending in a region termed the *area subcallosa* (Fig. 19). Dorsally, it extends back over the corpus callosum, passing under the *lobus paracentralis.* Caudal to this point (in that part called the lobus parietalis), this gyrus is less distinct.

f. *Area subcallosa* (Fig. 19). A small area of cortex which lies rostral to the *lamina terminalis* which separates the ventriculus tertius from the cavum subarachnoideale. It is continuous with the gyrus cinguli rostro-dorsally.

g. *Gyrus subcallosus.* The gyrus is a thin elongated bulge closely applied to the undersurface of the *rostrum corporis callosi* and it is frequently very small or impossible to see on the surface. It appears to be grossly continuous with the thin *paraterminal gyrus* which runs from the *substantia perforata anterior* to the *lobus frontalis* in a region just rostrally adjacent to the lamina terminalis. Contained within the gyrus paraterminalis is a bundle of fibres known as the *diagonal band of Broca.*

6

On the ventral surface (Figs. 13 and 20–22):

h. Gyrus rectus. A small straight, elongated gyrus lying between the midline and the *sulcus olfactorius*. The *bulbus olfactorius* (Fig. 13) and tract lie in the sulcus olfactorius.

i. Gyri orbitales. The ventral surface of the lobus frontalis overlies the orbit, hence the remaining gyri of the frontal lobe are termed the orbital gyri.

2. *Lobus parietalis* (Figs. 10–12, 14–16)

This lobe lies between the caudal boundary of the *lobus frontalis* and *sulcus parieto-occipitalis* on the medial surface. On the lateral side, it lies between the sulcus centralis and an imaginary plane extending ventrally from the *sulcus parieto-occipitalis* to the *incisura preoccipitalis* (Figs. 10 and 15). The lobe extends ventrally only as far as the imaginary line extending between the parieto-occipital boundary plane and a second imaginary line extending from the caudal tip of the sulcus lateralis in a plane which is a few degrees from the horizontal as it progresses toward the polus occipitalis. This boundary also separates the parietal from the temporal lobe.

a. Gyrus postcentralis (Figs. 14 and 15). Lies between the *sulcus centralis* and *sulcus postcentralis*. Dorso-medially it communicates with the gyrus precentralis through the lobulus paracentralis. Ventrally, it is bounded by the sulcus lateralis.

b. Lobulus parietalis superior (Figs. 14 and 15). Lies between the *sulcus postcentralis* and the *parieto-occipital boundary*. The most dorsal-medial surface of the brain is its dorsal boundary and its ventral boundary is the highly variable *sulcus interparietalis*.

c. Lobulus parietalis inferior (Figs. 14 and 15). This constitutes the remainder of the lobulus parietalis which is inferior to the sulcus interparietalis.

(*1*) *Gyrus supramarginalis* (Fig. 14). The most rostral portion of the lobulus parietalis inferior. It forms a marginal boundary around the dorsally directed terminal end of the sulcus lateralis.

(*2*) *Gyrus angularis* (Fig. 14). The middle portion of the same lobule. It is wrapped around the dorsally directed terminal end of the *sulcus temporalis superior*.

(*3*) *Gyrus parietalis posterior*. This is the most caudal portion of the inferior lobule and it lies between the *gyrus angularis* and the *parieto-occipital boundary*. It is frequently absent because the caudal border of the gyrus angularis is often identical with the parieto-occipital line.

On the medial surface (Figs. 16–19):

d. Precuneus (Fig. 16). Lies between the *pars marginalis* of the *sulcus cinguli* and *sulcus parieto-occipitalis*. At its dorsal border it is continuous with the *lobulus parietalis superior* and at its ventral border it is bounded by the *sulcus cinguli*.

7

e. Gyrus cinguli (pars posterior) (Figs. 16, 18, and 19). Extends caudally from the fronto-parietal boundary (*sulcus centralis*) to the area just overlying the *splenium* around which it is wrapped. It is bounded dorsally by the *sulcus cinguli* and ventrally by the *corpus callosum*. After passing around the caudal aspect of the *splenium corporis callosi*, it appears to be passing in a ventral rostral direction into the lobus temporalis. This part is termed the *isthmus gyri cinguli*.

3. Lobus occipitalis (Figs. 10, 15, 18–20)

Separated from the rest of the cerebrum by an imaginary plane running through the *sulcus parieto-occipitalis* and the *incisura preoccipitalis* (Figs. 15 and 16).

On the lateral surface:

a. Gyri occipitales laterales (Figs. 15 and 16). A group of small variable gyri occupying the entire lateral surface of the occipital lobe.

On the medial surface:

a. Cuneus (Fig. 16). Lies dorsal to the *sulcus calcarinum.*

b. Gyrus occipito-temporalis medialis (Figs. 16 and 19). Lies ventral to the *sulcus calcarinum* with a tongue-like extension into the *lobus temporalis*, which often appears connected by a gyral bridge to the *isthmus gyri cinguli.*

4. Lobus temporalis (Figs. 10, 11, 13–16, 18–20)

Bounded by the *lobus occipitalis* caudally and the *sulcus lateralis* and *lobus parietalis* dorsally.

On the lateral surface:

a. Gyrus temporalis superior (Figs. 14 and 15). Bounded by the *sulcus lateralis* dorsally and the *sulcus temporalis superior* ventrally.

b. Gyrus temporalis medius (Figs. 14 and 15). Bounded by the *sulcus temporalis superior* dorsally and the *sulcus temporalis medius* ventrally.

c. Gyrus temporalis inferior (Figs. 14, 18, and 10). Bounded by the *sulcus temporalis medius* dorsally and the *sulcus temporalis inferior* ventro-medially. The ventral border frequently lies in the curvature of the basal surface of the temporal lobe.

On the basal surface (Figs. 18–21):

d. Gyrus occipito-temporalis lateralis (Figs. 18–20). A fusiform-shaped gyrus lying between the *sulcus temporalis inferior* and the *sulcus collateralis.*

e. Gyrus parahippocampalis (Figs. 18–20). This is the most medial gyrus and it lies between the *sulcus collateralis* and the *hippocampal fissure*. The *uncus*, a medially located hook at the rostral end of the gyrus parahippocampalis is part of the paleocortex.

Gyri within the sulcus lateralis (Figs. 52–56):

f. Gyri temporales transversi (Figs. 53, 55). On spreading the lips of the *sulcus lateralis*, one or two gyri may be seen on the dorsal surface of the *gyrus temporalis superior*. They pass obliquely caudally into the sulcus lateralis and terminate just caudal to the gyri which comprise the insula.

5. Insula (Figs. 53 and 54)

The spreading of the lips of the sulcus lateralis (the lips are collectively known as the *opercula*) also reveals the cortex which is hidden in the most medial aspect of the sulcus. The *gyri breves insulae* are at the rostral end and the *gyrus longus insulae* is at the caudal end.

B. Paleocortical areas

With respect to phylogeny and ontogeny this area develops earlier than the neo-cortex. It is in juxta-position to the archicortex which will be described subsequently. It receives numerous connections from the olfactory system and is composed of (1) the uncus (Figs. 18 and 19) and (2) the immediately surrounding pyriform cortex, plus (3) the entire olfactory cortical area (Fig. 21). This includes the olfactory gyri (or striae), nuclei in the substantia perforata anterior and parts of the amygdaloid nucleus.

C. Archicortical areas

From the point of view of evolution and embryological development, these areas are even older than the paleocortex.

1. Hippocampus

This structure cannot be seen unless the *cornu inferior* of the *ventriculus lateralis* is opened up during a dissection of the *lobus temporalis* (Figs. 61 and 62). It may also be visualized on coronal sections. It forms the medial ventral wall of the *cornu inferius* of the lateral ventricle and can be seen in that position on the gross coronal sections (Figs. 69–72). The cells of this structure give rise to a continuous band of fibers, commencing as the *fimbria fornicis* (Fig. 62).

The *fornix* can be seen in the mid-sagittal section arching over the diencephalon (Figs. 16–19). The fornix terminates partly in the *septal area* close to the region of the *commissura anterior*. The remainder of the fornix curves caudal to the *com-

missura to terminate in the *hypothalamus* and *thalamus* with a few fibers reaching the *mesencephalon*.

2. *Gyrus dentatus* (Figs. 70 and 71)

Lies between the *fimbria fornicis* and the *gyrus parahippocampalis* within the *sulcus hippocampi*. It is visible as a thin, tooth-like structure when viewed from the medial aspect. The boundary of the gyrus dentatus and hippocampus is seen much more clearly in cross section, particularly when viewed with some magnification. Despite the anatomical distinction between the hippocampus and the gyrus dentatus, the two are usually considered together as being a part of the same functional entity. The *gyrus dentatus* (dentate fascia) is continuous caudally with the *gyrus fasciolaris*, a structure which swings caudally and dorsally and is closely applied to the caudal, external surface of the splenium of the corpus callosum.

3. *Hippocampal rudiment*

This consists of two thin parallel bands of grey matter on the dorsal surface of the corpus callosum. The *striae longitudinalis medialis* and *lateralis* are small longitudinally directed fiber bundles running within this film of cortex. They continue rostrally over the *corpus callosum* to the *septal area*, serving to connect it with the *hippocampal rudiment* and *gyrus dentatus*.

D. Deep nuclei of the telencephalon

1. *Nuclei of the septem pellucidum*

These nuclei are within the base of a double membrane, the *septum pellucidum* (Figs. 16–19) which is located between the anterior portions of the lateral ventricles. It extends from the *fornix* to the *corpus callosum*.

2. *Basal nuclei (basal ganglia)*

These structures may be best visualized by utilizing brains sectioned in the coronal and horizontal planes (Figs. 63–76). Reference to sections cut in the sagittal plane often helps to develop a better three-dimensional concept (Figs. 77–82). One of the whole brains assigned to a student group may be used for the exercise. Sections about 1 cm thick should be cut with a sharp long-bladed knife.

   a. Lenticular nucleus. This aggregation of cells lies deep to the *insula* and lateral to the *capsula interna* (a stout group of fibers connecting the cerebral cortex with various subcortical regions). The actual lateral border of this nucleus is the *capsula interna* (a thin sheet of fibers surrounding the lateral aspect of the nucleus which contains fibers interconnecting various cortical areas). The lenticular nucleus is composed of the *globus pallidus* and the *putamen*.

(*1*) *Globus pallidus.* In fresh specimens this is seen as a pale somewhat fibrous structure forming the ventral and medial part of the lenticular nucleus. It is divided into medial and lateral nuclear masses which are separated by a thin fibrous structure, the *lamina medullaris medialis.*

(*2*) *Putamen.* In fresh specimens, the putamen is much darker, larger, and runs further rostrally and caudally than does the globus pallidus. At its rostral extent, it is connected by cellular bridges with the *caput* of the *nucleus caudatus,* creating striations in the rostral end of the capsula interna. The *nucleus caudatus* and the *putamen,* surrounding the striated portion of the capsula interna, form the *corpus striatum.* The *putamen* is separated from the globus pallidus by fibrous membrane, the *lamina medullaris lateralis.*

b. *Nucleus caudatus* (see also Fig. 50). This is a large curved mass, with a large rostral head (caput) and a long, slender, curved body (corpus) and elongated tail (cauda). It lies in the lateral wall of the *ventriculus lateralis* and extends from the *cornu anterius* into the *cornu inferius* where it is found in the roof of the ventricle. The head of the caudate can be seen from the mid-sagittal surface if the septum pellucidum is cut through to expose the cavity of the ventriculus lateralis.

c. *Claustrum.* This thin plate of cells lies between the insula and putamen encapsulated by the *capsula externa* medially and the *capsula extrema* laterally.

d. *Corpus amygdaloideum.* This nuclear mass is oval in shape and lies within the substance of the *gyrus parahippocampalis* in the region of the *uncus.* It lies dorsal and rostral to the tip of the *cornu inferius* of the *ventriculus lateralis* and the *pes hippocampi.* In coronal section, it can be seen ventral to the *globus pallidus,* and it is in close nuclear juxtaposition with the *putamen* as well as with a surface, cortical component (Fig. 66). Among the deep nuclei are those often termed the septal area. These nuclear groups consist of the *nuclei of the septum pellucidum* and the neurons within the *gyrus paraterminalis.*

II. Diencephalon (Dorsal Thalamus, Hypothalamus, Metathalamus, Subthalamus and Epithalamus, Figs. 17, 18, 20, 31, 32, 39, 69)

The ventriculus tertius is a narrow midline space which separates the paired diencephalic nuclear masses. A longitudinally oriented sulcus (the *sulcus hypothalamicus*—Fig. 17) arising from the *aqueductus cerebri* separates the upper 2/3 (*thalamus*) from the lower 1/3 (*hypothalamus*). A small bundle of fibers, the *stria terminalis* runs in a groove on the dorsolateral surface and denotes the dorsal lateral boundary between the thalamus and nucleus caudatus. The thin membraneous *lamina terminalis* at the rostral end of the ventriculus tertius is the boundary between the diencephalon and the telencephalon. A plane which passes caudal to the *corpora mammillaria* and just rostral to the *colliculus superior* indicates the approximate boundary between the *diencephalon* and *mesencephalon*. Such a plane actually represents a rather arbitrary separation, since the nuclear groups of the diencephalon and mesencephalon overlap each other. However, the separation is useful in terms of gross anatomical and pathological observation. The large white capsula interna forms the lateral boundary of the diencephalon, and can be clearly distinguished in coronal sections (Figs. 63–72). A cellular bridge (*massa intermedia* or *adhesio interthalamica*) crossing the ventriculus tertius usually serves to join the two thalamic masses.

1. Dorsal thalamus

This is the bulk of the thalamus that remains when the other parts to be described immediately below are identified as separate entities.

2. Metathalamus

This is comprised of the geniculate bodies which are at the caudal end of the diencephalon. They are tucked under the posterolateral margin of that part of the thalamus known as the *pulvinar*.

  a. Corpus geniculatum laterale (Figs. 23, 70, 73, 78). The *tractus opticus* may be followed into this area on the gross coronal or horizontal sections, as well as on mid-sagittal specimens. When the nucleus is cut through, it characteristically has a triangular shape and curved striations may usually be seen traversing this dark nucleus. A small bundle of fibers passes medially from the structure into the rostral mesencephalon. This is the *brachium colliculi superioris*.

  b. Corpus geniculatum mediale (Figs. 23, 31, 32, 80). This small elevation may be found just slightly caudal and immediately medial to the *corpus geniculatum laterale* and is not distinguished by internal striations. A small bundle of fibers (*brachium colliculi inferioris*) may be seen entering it from the mesencephalon.

3. Epithalamus

A superficial, medially located appendage of the diencephalon comprised of:

  a. Stria medullaris thalami (Figs. 17, 18). This is a bundle of fibers arising in part from the septal area which may be seen traversing the dorsomedial aspect of the dorsal thalamus arching dorsally over the adhesio interthalamica. This stria provides an attachment for:

  b. The epithelial roof of the ventriculus tertius. This is an epithelial membrane (frequently pulled away when the brain is cut through the mid-sagittal plane) stretching from the stria medullaris thalami of one side to that of the contralateral side. It contains the *plexus chorioideus* of the ventriculus tertius and forms its roof.

  c. Trigonum habenulae (Fig. 32). The stria medullaris projects caudally into the *nucleus habenulae* which underlies the *trigonum*, as seen from the dorsal aspect. The nuclear areas are, of course, paired and are connected with each other through a bridge, the *commissura habenularum*. Do not confuse this commissure with the stouter *commissura posterior* (Fig. 17) which lies immediately ventral to the habenular commissure and is the plane which roughly marks the caudal junction of the diencephalon with the mesencephalon.

    d. Corpus pineale (epiphysis). The small unpaired midline structure which attaches to the habenular area is the pineal body, now considered as possessing some ill-defined endocrine function.

4. *Subthalamus* (Fig. 69)

This structure lies at the ventro-caudal border of the diencephalon and it is lateral to the caudal part of the hypothalamus. It can be seen in the gross coronal sections. Its borders are the *capsula interna* ventrolaterally, the *nucleus ruber* caudally, the *hypothalamus* medially and rostrally, and the *dorsal thalamus* dorsomedially. It contains:

    (a) *The Nucleus subthalamicus*. A lens-shaped nucleus found tucked against the *capsula interna* as it borders on the mesencephalon.

    (b) *The Fields of Forel*. H (pre-rubral), H_1 (fasciculus thalamicus), and H_2 (fasciculus lenticularis). These are projection fiber systems: the first is concerned with the ascending projections from the *lower brain stem* and *medulla spinalis*, while the H_1 and H_2 are concerned with projections from the *basal nuclei*.

    (c) *Zona incerta*. A nuclear area inserted between the H_1 and H_2 fields of Forel (Figs. 111–113).

5. *Hypothalamus* (Figs. 17, 18, 20, 21, 39, 68)

The hypothalamus is limited by the following boundaries: dorsally, the *sulcus hypothalamicus*; rostrally, the *lamina terminalis*; caudally, the plane of separation between the mesencephalon and diencephalon in which the *commissura posterior* may be found; and laterally, the *capsula interna* and *subthalamus*.

    In addition to the nuclear masses which exist in the walls of the ventriculus tertius, the hypothalamus has the following additional anatomic parts:

    a. Chiasma opticum. The region of partial decussation of the optic nerves at the base of the ventriculus tertius. (This is not a functional part of the hypothalamus).

    b. Corpora mammillaria. A pair of spherical structures at the caudo-ventral border of the hypothalamus.

    c. Tuber cinereum. A conical protrusion between the chiasma opticum and the corpora mamillaria.

    d. Infundibulum (pituitary stalk). This slender structure provides for a neural connection to the *neurohypophysis* and a vascular connection to the *adenohypophysis* from the tuber cinerum. Properly, the neurohypophysis may also be considered as part of the hypothalamus.

III. Mesencephalon (Midbrain, Figs. 4, 17, 23, 31, 32)

A cross sectional plane passing through the *commissura posterior*, being just caudal to the *corpora mamillaria* defines the rostral limit of the midbrain. The caudal limit is defined by a similar plane passing through a region just caudal to the *colliculi inferiores* and just rostral to the rostral border of a large ventral bulge on the brain stem, the *pons*. This latter plane passes through what was the point of juncture between mesencephalon and rhombencephalon in the embryonic brain, the isthmus rhombencephali.

A. Tectum mesencephali (Figs. 11, 17, 20, 23, 31, 32)

This is the portion of the midbrain which lies dorsal to the *aqueductus cerebri*. It includes the *colliculi* (little hills).

1. Colliculus superior

The rostral pair of elevations: each receives fibers from the *corpus geniculatum laterale* via fiber bundles passing medially, dorsal to the *corpus geniculatum mediale*. The bundles form the *brachium colliculi superioris*.

2. Colliculus inferior

The caudal pair of elevations. A tract visible on the lateral surface of the midbrain runs from each colliculus inferior to the ipsilateral *corpus geniculatum mediale*. This is the *brachium colliculi inferioris*.

3. The dorsal half of the periaqueductal grey matter

B. Crus cerebri

The ventral portion of the midbrain is formed by two broad tracts which represent a continuance of the descending fibers passing through the *capsula interna*. Each bundle has indentations medially and laterally, which are called the *sulci medialis et lateralis cruris cerebri*. A plane drawn through the pair of sulci on each side defines the dorsal boundary of the crus cerebri throughout the short length of the mesencephalon. The *nervus oculomotorius* may be seen exiting through the *sulcus medialis cruris cerebri*.

14

C. Tegmentum mesencephali

The portion of the mesencephalon which lies between the tectum and the crus cerebri. The spherical *nucleus ruber* is found within the tegmentum as are the various nuclear groups of the mesencephalic *formatio reticularis*, and the motor nuclei and *nervi oculomotorius* and *trochlearis* and the ventral half of the periaqueductal grey matter.

D. Substantia nigra (Figs. 20, 69, 70, 80)

A nuclear mass which lies at the border of the *tegmentum mesencephali* and *crus cerebri*. It is defined anatomically as being a part of the crus cerebri. However, it is functionally associated with the nuclear masses of the tegmentum. This region will appear quite dark in adult brains due to the presence of *melanin* within the nerve cells.

IV. Metencephalon (Pons and Cerebellum, Figs. 23–32, 83–88)

A. Cerebellum

This is a large multifolded lobular structure found astride the dorsal aspect of the brain stem and located just ventral to the *polus occipitalis* of the cerebrum, from which it is separated by the *tentorium cerebelli* in the cranial cavity. This prominent foliated structure is anatomically continuous across the midline through a median constriction referred to as the *vermis*. The following constitutes a simplified functional division of the cerebellum. The cerebellar cortex and white matter is subdivided into anterior, posterior and flocculonodular lobes. The posterior lobe contains deep nuclear structures which relay corticofugally the influence of the cerebellar cortex.

1. Lobus anterior

   a. Anterior lobe. Contains all those parts of the cerebellum, both hemispheric and vermian, which are rostral to the *fissura prima* (Fig. 24). The vermian components are called the *lobulus centralis* and the *culmen*.
   b. The declive, folium and tuber vermis constitute the parts of the vermis which are located between the *fissura prima* and *fissura prepyramidalis*. This part of the vermis, while developing at the same time as the anterior lobe, has the gross appearance of interconnecting the two halves of the posterior lobes which constitute the largest part of the corpus cerebelli.
   c. Pyramis. This is an entirely midline structure within the vermis which is no

more than a quarter of an inch in width which lies between the *fissura prepyramidalis* and the *fissura postpyramidalis*.

d. Uvula. This also is an entirely midline vermian structure similar to the pyramis which is between the *fissura postpyramidalis* and *fissura posterolateralis*.

2. Lobus posterior

That part of the *hemisphericum cerebelli* which is caudal to the *fissura prima*, including the tonsils of both sides. This is, by far, the largest part of the cerebellum.

3. Lobus flocculonodularis

This most primitive part of the cerebellum consists of the *nodulus* and both *flocculi* (Figs, 24, 29) which are attached to each other by means of the fibers running through the *velum medullare inferior*. These fibers form part of the *pedunculus flocculi*. A second group of fibers extends from the flocculus into the *area vestibularis* (Fig. 30) at the ponto-medullary junction, establishing connections with the vestibular nuclei. The nodulus appears anatomically as a part of the vermis.

4. Deep nuclei

The *nucleus fastigii* is located close to the midline in the cerebellar white matter, at the apex of the *recessus fastigii* of the *ventriculus quartus* and is intimately related functionally to the flocculonodular lobe. The *nucleus globosus* and *nucleus emboliformis* are intermediate functionally and anatomically between the dentate and fastigial nuclei. The *nucleus dentatus* (Figs. 32 and 88) is located within the white matter of the cerebellum and intimately related to both anterior and posterior lobes. Of the deep cerebellar nuclei, only the nucleus dentatus may be visualized in gross sectional material. Identification of the other three nuclei requires a Pal–Weigert preparation (Fig. 94) or some other histological method.

5. Laminae albae

Cerebellar white, as viewed on the mid-sagittal section, may be seen to be made up of 5 thin arms (Fig. 24), each of which undergoes some secondary branching. One arm goes to the anterior lobe and breaks up into 2 secondary branches for the culmen and lobulus centralis of the vermis. The second primary arm goes to that part of the vermis associated with the posterior lobe, with secondary arms being directed into the declive, folium and tuber vermis. The third branch goes to the pyramis, while the fourth goes to the uvula and the fifth to the nodulus.

6. Pedunculi cerebelli (Figs. 23, 29, 84–88).

The cerebellum is attached to the brain stem by three large brachia or peduncles.

a. The pedunculus cerebellaris superior (brachium conjunctivum) extends rostrally from under the anterior lobe into the substance of the mesencephalon. The *velum medullare superius*, which forms the roof of the rostral portion of the ventriculus quartus, is suspended from the medial aspect of the two superior brachii.

b. *The pedunculus cerebellaris medius* (brachium pontis) extends dorsally into the *hemispherium cerebelli* from the pars basilaris pontis. The brachium pontis is differentiated from the more ventral pons proper by the presence of the exiting fibers of the *nervus trigeminus* (V) which provide a convenient external anatomical landmark between the two structures. The nervus trigeminus, if not removed during autopsy, can be seen to have two roots. The large major root (*radix sensoria*) is sensory and the smaller minor root (*radix motoria*) is motor in function. The sensory root connects with the large *ganglion trigeminale* from which three branches emerge peripherally. The minor root is rostromedial to the sensory root and has no connection with the sensory ganglion and finally becomes associated with the mandibular division peripherally.

c. *The pedunculus cerebellaris inferior* (restiform body) extends from the dorsolateral aspect of the *medulla oblongata* into the substance of the cerebellum. It also forms the lateral wall of the caudal end of the ventriculus quartus.

B. Pons

This is the large bulbous structure on the ventral aspect of the brain stem. The rostral border is at the junction with the mesencephalon. It is at the dorsal surface of this border (*isthmus rhombencephali*) that the *nervus trochlearis* (IV) emerges, just caudal to the *colliculus inferior*. The caudal border of the pons is marked ventrally by the *sulcus bulbopontinus* and dorsally by the *striae medullares ventriculi quarti*. The latter is a faint series of striations running transversely on the floor of the ventriculus quartus. They may not always be visible in gross preparations. The *nervus abducens* (VI) may be seen emerging from the bulbopontine sulcus to extend rostrally on the ventral surface of the pons, while the *nervus facialis* (VII) and *nervus vestibulocochlearis* (VIII) emerge from the dorsolateral aspect of the sulcus. The bulging ventral portion of the pons (*pars basilaris pontis*) is distinct from the *pars dorsalis pontis* or tegmentum which lies below the floor of the ventriculus quartus. Thus, the pons consists of two major parts.

1. Pars basilaris pontis

This is the large bulging ventral portion of the pons which forms the externally visible enlargement with fibers projecting dorsally into the cerebellum. In cross section (Figs. 83–86, 96–106), the enlargement can be seen to be formed of clusters of cells and many compact fibers running longitudinally and transversely.

2. Pars dorsalis pontis (tegmentum)

This central core of the pons is bounded by the *pars basilaris* ventrally, the *pedunculus cerebellaris medius* laterally, and the floor of the ventriculus *quartus* dorsally. A number of landmarks appears on the floor of the fourth ventricle which may conveniently identify the position of underlying structures.

a. Eminentia medialis. The floor of the fourth ventricle is rhomboidal and contains a longitudinal groove (*sulcus medianus*, Fig. 30) which divides it into two symmetrical halves. Between the sulcus medianus and the lateral border of the floor, another groove (*sulcus limitans*) may be seen. The ridge which lies between these two grooves on either side of the midline extending rostrally from the *stria medullaris* to the opening of the *aqueductus cerebri* is formed by underlying nuclear structures. This ridge is the *eminentia medialis*.

(*1*) *Colliculus facialis.* The slightly rounded prominence which forms the caudal third of the *eminentia medialis* is the *colliculus facialis*. Its slight elevation is caused by the underlying genu of the *nervus facialis* (VII) as it curves around the *nucleus n. abducentis* (VI).

b. Fovea superior (trigeminal fovea). This is a deep depression in the *sulcus limitans* rostral to the *stria medullaris* and is associated with underlying trigeminal nuclear structures. A shallow groove extends rostrally from the fovea superior to the aqueductus cerebri. This overlies the *locus coeruleus*, which has a rather dark color due to the presence of pigmented nerve cells in the nucleus beneath the groove.

V. Myelencephalon (Medulla Oblongata, Figs. 22–29)

The *medulla oblongata* is the most caudal portion of the brain stem and is continuous with the *medulla spinalis* (spinal cord) caudally. Various surface sulci of the spinal cord extend up onto the surface of the medulla.

The medulla may be grossly separated from the rostrally located pons by the *sulcus bulbopontinus* (ventrally) and the *stria medullaris* (dorsally). The latter, as noted above, is in the floor of the ventriculus quartus. At its caudal end, it may be distinguished from the spinal cord by the presence of two decussating fiber bundles, the *decussatio pyramidum*, which are found on the ventral surface. Like the pons, that part of the medulla in the floor of the *ventriculus quartus* is split into symmetrical halves by the *sulcus medianus*.

A. Structures at the pontomedullary junction and the caudal portion of the floor of the ventriculus quartus

1. Fovea inferior (vagal trigone)

The *sulcus limitans*, seen on the floor of the ventriculus quartus in the pontine region continues caudally into the medulla where it divides into medially and laterally directed branches. The *fovea inferior* is at the rostrally directed apex of the triangle formed by these branches. The area embraced by the arms of the fork constitutes the *vagal trigone* (*ala cinera*), since the dorsal autonomic nucleus of the *vagus nerve* (X) underlies this area.

2. Trigonum nervi hypoglossi

The *sulcus medianus* in the floor of the ventriculus quartus defines the medial limit of the *hypoglossal trigone* while the medial branch of the *sulcus limitans* forms its lateral border. The rostral end of the inferior fovea defines the approximate rostral extent of the trigonum nervi hypoglossi. Cells of the hypoglossal nucleus (XII) underlie the trigone.

3. Area vestibularis (acoustic trigone)

The *sulcus limitans* lies at the medial base of this trangle, the *fovea superior* is the rostral angle of the trigonum, the *fovea inferior* forms its caudal angle while the *acoustic tubercle* (*nucleus cochlearis dorsalis*) provides for the lateral angle of the trigone. The acoustic tubercle may be located in the floor of the lateral foramina of Luschka (*apertura lateralis ventriculi quarti*) and marks the position of the dorsal cochlear nucleus where it overlies the pedunculus cerebellaris inferior. The cochlear division of the *nervus vestibulo cochlearis* (VIII) enters the CNS at this point. The medial part of the acoustic trigone overlies the *vestibular nuclei*. The stria medullaris divides the trigone into rostral pontine and caudal medullary components. Note that this trigone is found in both the pontine and medullary regions of the floor of the ventriculus quartus.

4. Nervus facialis (VII)

The nerve emerges just medial to the *nervus vestibulocochlearis* at the *pontomedullary junction*. The *nervus intermedius* (sensory and parasympathetic portion of VII) lies between the VIIth and VIIIth nerves.

5. Nervus abducens (VI)

This nerve emerges at the pontomedullary junction, a short distance lateral to the ventral midline, and extends rostrally (Fig. 6).

B. Structures identifiable on the outer surface of the medulla, from the dorsal aspect to the most ventral

1. Tuberculum nuclei gracilis (clava)

This is the enlarged rostral end of a ridge on the caudal dorsal aspect of the medulla lying between the *sulcus medianus posterior* and the *sulcus intermedius posterior*. The ridge, which extends rostrally from the spinal cord, is formed by the underlying *fasciculus gracilis*. The rostral bulge is caused by the *nucleus gracilis* which lies adjacent to the caudal border of the ventriculus quartus.

2. Tuberculum nuclei cuneati

A second small enlargement on the caudal dorsal surface of the medulla is caused by the terminal nucleus at the rostral end of the *fasciculus cuneatus*. This bulge is called the *tuberculum nuclei cuneati* and results from the underlying nucleus cuneatus. The ridge formed by the fasciculus cuneatus lies between the *sulcus intermedius posterior* and the *sulcus lateralis posterior* and is laterally adjacent to the fasciculus gracilis.

3. Trigeminal eminence

The trigeminal eminence is found just lateral and inferior to the tuberculum nuclei cuneati and may cause such a small elevation as to be virtually indistinguishable. It is formed by the underlying *nucleus et tractus spinalis nervus trigemini*. This descending tract of the fifth nerve is actually within the *sulcus lateralis posterior*, which becomes greatly expanded by the bulk of these fibers.

4. Pedunculus cerebellaris inferior (restiform body)

The restiform body lies just rostral to the *tuberculum nuclei cuneati* on the dorso-lateral aspect of the medulla and it is also dorsal to the trigeminal eminence in the rostral part of the medulla. It passes under the *acoustic tubercle* and then turns dorsally quite sharply to enter the cerebellum. At this point, the *restiform body* and the *acoustic tubercle* form the floor of the *apertura lateralis ventriculi quarti* (lateral foramina of Luschka). The rostral margin of the foramina is formed as the fibers of the restiform body turn dorsally. In the medulla, this fiber bundle is just dorsal to where the *sulcus lateralis posterior* would be if it could be visualized on the medulla. It appears grossly as a rostro-dorsal projection of the fibers in the *fasciculus cuneatus*. Despite this superficial gross appearance, the fibers forming the restiform body come from quite a different source. *Nervi glossopharyngeus* (IX), *vagus* (X), and the *radices craniales of the n. accessorius* (XI) emerge at the lateral inferior border of the restiform body in such a way that IX is most rostral, X is intermediate with many roots, while the accessory portion of XI is most caudal. The *radices spinales* of the *nervus accessorius* arise from the cervical cord and join the accessory

portion at this point. The cochlear division of the eighth nerve embraces the restiform body in such a way that the *nucleus cochlearis dorsalis* is dorsal and the *nucleus
cochlearis ventralis* is lateral to the fiber bundle. The vestibular division of the
eighth nerve passes through or ventral to the restiform body to enter the medulla.
The roof of the ventriculus quartus with its plexus choroideus is suspended in part
from the restiform body (Fig. 29). The roof continues posteriorly and becomes
continuous with the *velum medullare inferius* (Figs. 29 and 32).

5. Oliva

This is a prominent olive-shaped elevation seen at the ventrolateral aspect of the
medulla. It is caused by the underlying presence of a large, much folded nuclear
structure, the (inferior) *nucleus olivaris*. Its posterior margin is about 2 to 3 mm
ventral to the exiting roots of *nervi glossopharyngeus, vagus et accessorius*. It is
surrounded by the *sulcus postolivaris* dorsally and the *sulcus preolivaris* ventrally.
These two sulci join at the caudal end of the olive to continue caudally as the
sulcus lateralis anterior. The *nervus hypoglossus* emerges medially through the
preolivary sulcus with a number of rootlets.

6. Pyramis

A prominent pair of fiber bundles may be seen as the most ventral and medial
surface structures of the medulla. They are separated by the *fissura mediana anterior*.
They extend from the pontomedullary junction to their decussation (*decussatio
pyramidum*), which marks the caudal limit of the medulla. Most fibers cross over at
this point and disappear deep into the substance of the *medulla spinalis* (spinal
cord). The rootlets of the emerging *nervus hpoglossus* are lateral to the pyramis,
and thus emerge from between the pyramis and the oliva.

VI. Medulla Spinalis (Spinal Cord, Figs. 33–38)

The *medulla spinalis* possesses the same meningeal coverings as the brain. However, the spinal dura is sufficiently thin for the spinal vessels to be visualized through
it (Fig. 33). There is a rather well developed modification of the pia of the cord in
that it forms a series of lateral projections between the radix dorsalis and the radix
ventralis which attach laterally to the dura mater. This is the *ligamentum denticulatum* (Fig. 36).

The medulla spinalis extends caudally from the *decussatio pyramidum* down
through the spinal canal formed by the vertebrae. It terminates in the adult at the
level of the intervertebral space between the first and second lumbar vertebral
bodies. There are two areas of enlargement in the spinal cord, each of which is

associated with the peripheral plexuses of nerves concerned with innervation of the extremities. The more rostral is the *intumescentia cervicalis* which extends from about the fourth cervical segmental level to the first thoracic level (provides for the *plexus brachialis*). The second more caudal swelling starts at about the twelfth thoracic segment and extends down to the fifth lumbar or first sacral level. This is the *intumescentia lumbalis* which provides for the nerves entering the *plexus lumbosacralis*. At the terminal, or caudal end, the cord tapers down to a small cone, the *conus medullaris*. A thin threadlike extension, the *filum terminale* continues caudally from the conus to become attached to the periosteum of the *coccyx*. This thread is accompanied by all three meningeal layers (*dura mater, arachnoidea* and *pia mater*). The numerous nerve roots which extend caudally in the spinal canal below the conus medullaris until they exit through the appropriate foraminae form the *cauda equina*. At the rostral end of the medulla spinalis the radices spinales of nervus accessorius may be seen exiting between the dorsal and ventral spinal nerve radices. These nerve fibers then ascend through the foramen magnum.

The spinal cord is grooved by six sulci, the *sulcus medianus posterior*, a pair of *sulci laterales posteriores* and a pair of *sulci laterales anteriores*. There is then a prominent groove along the anterior surface, the *fissura mediana anterior*. At the rostral, cervical level, an additional sulcus appears, the *sulcus intermedius posterior*. Nerve rootlets (radices) may be seen entering the sulcus lateralis posterior throughout the length of the spinal cord. These are the afferent or sensory nerves, each of which has a *ganglion spinale* associated with it. These ganglia are aggregations of the cell bodies of the neurons forming the sensory nerves. A similar series of the rootlets may be seen leaving the spinal cord through the *sulcus lateralis anterior*. These are the motor neurons which provide for innervation of both somatic and autonomic structures.

The various sulci and fissures divide each half of the spinal cord longitudinally into three large bundles of nerve fibers (Figs. 90–92). Thus, there is a dorsally situated *funiculus posterior* between the *sulcus medianus posterior* and *sulcus lateralis posterior*, a laterally placed *funiculus lateralis* between the *sulcus lateralis posterior* and *sulcus lateralis anterior* and a *funiculus anterior* between the *sulcus lateralis anterior* and the *fissura mediana anterior*. All of these funiculi contain ascending and descending fiber tracts which serve to interconnect various levels of the spinal cord and transport information to and from various brain structures.

The central portion of the spinal cord consists of a long nuclear mass, H-shaped in cross section, which extends throughout the entire length of the cord. This is the site of the nerve cell bodies of the cord. As viewed in cross section, the H of grey or substantia grisea can be seen to consist of a *cornu anterius*, a *cornu laterale* in the thoracic and upper lumbar regions, a *cornu posterius* and a pars intermedia (Figs. 90–92).

VII. Nervi Craniales (Cranial Nerves)

The term cranial nerves is reserved for twelve pairs of peripheral nerves whose origin or termination occurs in the brain. They are concerned with non-specialized motor and sensory functions of somatic and visceral structures as well as the more specialized functions of olfaction, vision, audition, equilibration and taste. The peripheral distribution of these nerves is usually covered in courses of gross anatomy; the central origin or termination of the nerves falls within the neuroanatomical province. Two of these nerves, the olfactory (I) and the optic (II) are not true nerves but are extensions of the brain itself and may be considered tracts which exist outside the structural limitations of the CNS. Three nerves, the oculomotor (III), abducens (VI) and hypoglossal (XII) emerge from the ventral aspect of the brain stem. One nerve, the trochlear (IV) arises from the dorsal aspect of the brain stem and the remaining nerves, the trigeminal (V), facial (VII), vestibulocochlear (VIII), glossopharyngeal (IX), vagal (X) and accessory (XI) all arise or enter the brain stem at its lateral surface in an area which coincides roughly with the position which might be occupied by the sulcus lateralis posterior of the spinal cord, if such a sulcus was present on the brain stem.

1. Nervus olfactorius (I, Figs. 3–5, 13, 20–22)

The true olfactory nerves are receptor cells in the dorsal nasal mucosa whose central processes are grouped into about 20 bundles which pass through the *cribriform plate* to terminate in the *olfactory bulb*. Sheaths of the brain meninges ensheath these bundles as they pass through the cribriform plate. Thus, the pia becomes continuous with the neurolemmal sheaths of the nerve bundles and the dura is continuous with the periosteum of the bones of the nasal cavity. At this point the intracranial cavum subarachnoideale becomes related to the lymphatic drainage of the nasal cavity.

The *olfactory bulb* and the tract (*tractus olfactorius*) which connects the bulb to the brain represent an extension of the telencephalon. The bulb and tract may be seen on the ventral surface of the *lobus frontalis*, just lateral to the mid-sagittal plane, lying in the *sulcus olfactorius*. The narrow gyrus medial to the tract is the *gyrus rectus*. Caudally, the tract bifurcates into two well developed bundles, the *striae olfactorii medialis et lateralis*. The medial stria terminates in the *medial gyrus olfactorius* while the lateral stria is directed into the *gyrus parahippocampalis* in the neighbourhood of the *uncus hippocampi* (*prepyriform cortex* and *amygdala*). The triangular area, encompassed by the two stria, represents the *substantia perforata anterior* through which pass vessels supplying the basal nuclear structures (putamen, globus pallidus and part of caudate).

2. Nervus opticus (II, Figs. 3–6, 13, 21–23, 39)

The optic nerve, like the olfactory, is not a true nerve, but an extension of the brain itself, and it appears as a tract of fibers extending from the retina into the diencephalon. The retina itself develops as an evagination from the ventral diencephalic wall. It carries with it the primitive ependymal layer which provides for neuroblasts and spongioblasts within the entire CNS and for the visual receptor, relay nerves and supporting cells of the retina. In the retina, the rod and cone cells, which are the first receptors for visual input, may be considered the true optic nerves. The subsequent pathway via the bipolar and then the ganglion cells may then be considered the afferent pathway transmitting the sensory signals to the diencephalon.

The optic nerve runs in an occipital direction from the orbit through the *canalis opticus* to enter the cranial cavity. At this point the *chiasma opticum* is formed just rostral and ventral to the hypothalamic portion of the diencephalon (see figures). A partial decussation occurs at this point. The further continuation is via the *tractus opticus* and now contains information coming from both eyes. The optic tracts continue on an occipital course, arching around the *crus cerebri* to terminate in the *corpus geniculatum laterale* at the caudal inferior aspect of the diencephalon (Fig. 23).

3. Nervus oculomotorius (III, Figs. 3–6, 17, 21)

The third cranial nerve is concerned with the motor innervation of four muscles (medial, inferior, and rectus superior muscles, as well as the inferior oblique muscle) within the orbit and the levator palpebrae muscle of the upper eye lid. There is also a parasympathetic division which accompanies the somatic motor elements into the orbit and provides for the innervation of the ciliary muscle and the pupillary sphincter muscle. The nerve can be seen leaving the inferior aspect of the brain stem as a large nerve trunk passing through the *sulcus medialis cruris cerebri* of the mesencephalon. The nerve trunk passes between the *arteria cerebellaris superioris* and *arteria cerebri posterioris* and then proceeds rostrally through the wall of the *sinus cavernosus* and then past the lateral aspect of the *arteria carotis interna*, and finally through the *fissura orbitalis superior* into the orbit.

4. Nervus trochlearis (IV, Figs. 6 and 23)

This nerve, like the oculomotor, provides for the intraorbital innervation of somatic musculature, in this instance of only one (superior oblique) muscle. The trochlear nerve is the only cranial nerve exiting from the dorsum of the brain and may be observed doing so just caudal to the *colliculus inferior* in the region known as the *isthmus rhombencephali*. The nerve is small in diameter and difficult to see as it is somewhat covered over by the rostral edge of the corpus cerebelli. The peripheral course of the nerve follows the oculomotor once it reaches the wall of the sinus cavernosus.

5. *Nervus trigeminus* (V, Figs, 6, 7, 26, 27 and 41)

The trigeminal is the large nerve for somatic sensory information arising from the face, with three main branches (*mandibular, maxillary* and *ophthalmic*). These three sensory nerves from the face sh are a common ganglion (*ganglion trigeminale*) which is enclosed in a dural sac adjacent to the *sinus cavernosus*. This dural sac can be readily dissected (Fig. 6) to show the ganglion resting in a small groove, the *impressio trigemini* on the medial end of the petrosus portion of the *os temporale*. The central stem, arising from the ganglion, passes caudally to penetrate through the fibers of the pons in order to terminate in central nuclei in the brain stem. The point where the trigeminal fibers pass into the pons has been used arbitrarily as a point of anatomical reference to separate the ventrally located *pars basilaris pontis* from the more dorsally placed *brachium pontis*.

A motor component is also associated with the trigeminal nerve. This *radix motoria* is small and in a rostromedial position relative to the sensory fibers as it exits from the pons. In its peripheral course it accompanies the mandibular ramus to innervate the *temporalis, masseter, pterygoid, tensor tympani* and *tensor veli palatini muscles*.

6. *Nervus abducens* (VI, Figs. 6, 7, 22, 27)

This is also a nerve supplying intraorbital somatic musculature, the *lateral rectus muscle* of the eye. The fibers leave the brain stem at the ventral aspect of the ponto-medullary junction just lateral to the midsagittal plane and then proceed rostrally to pierce the dura close to the *nervus trigeminus* and finally enter the orbit through the *fissura orbitalis superior*. It also has a course through the wall of the *sinus cavernosus*. The nerve is frequently described as passing between the *arteria cerebelli inferior anterior* and the *arteria labyrinthi* just after arising from the brain stem. This relationship, however, appears rather infrequently as the arteria labyrinthi is commonly a ramus arising somewhat distally from the arteria cerebelli inferior anterior.

7. *Nervus facialis* (VII, Figs, 13, 22, 25–27, 29)

This is the important nerve providing for motor innervation of the *muscles of facial expression*. Its origin from the brain stem is at the dorsolateral aspect of the *bulbopontine sulcus*, just inferior to the *apertura ventriculi quarti (foramen of Luschka*, Fig. 27). It is also just ventral to the *vestibulocochlear nerve* at this point. While the facial nerve is largely constituted of motor fibers for striated musculature, it also contains motor fibers to such visceral structures as the lacrimal gland, submaxillary and sublingual glands and mucus and serous glands of the oral and nasal mucosa. Afferent fibers transmitting taste and visceral afferent sensations from the oral and nasal pharynx are also associated with the seventh nerve. All the general visceral afferent and special afferent (taste) fibers plus those of the parasympathetic motor outflow for salivation, lacrimation, etc. are found in the division of the seventh nerve known as the *nervus intermedius*. This rather small nerve may be observed between the larger trunks of the *nervus facialis* and *nervus vestibulocochlearis* as the three nerves exit from the dorsolateral aspect of the bulbopontine sulcus. After leaving the brain stem all three nerves follow a short course directly laterally to enter the *meatus acusticus internus*. The facial and intermediate nerves then enter the *canalis facialis* in the petrous portion of the *os temporale*. The facial nerve itself exits at the *stylomastoid foramen* to form a plexus in the parotid gland before its final distribution of the facial muscles.

8. *Nervus vestibulocochlearis* (VIII, Figs, 6, 7, 13, 22, 25, 27)

This may be considered as a compound sensory nerve subserving two specialized functions, *hearing* and *equilibration*. The *cochlear portion* (auditory) terminates in a nuclear swelling on the dorsolateral surface of the rostral end of the medulla and in a grossly indistinct collection of cells just ventral to the rostral end of the *pedunculus cerebellaris inferior*. The more dorsal elevation is the acoustic tubercle (Fig. 30). The vestibular portion passes directly under the *pedunculus cerebellaris inferior* to reach nuclear structures within the medulla. In its peripheral course, the eighth nerve parallels the laterally directed course of the nervus facialis to enter the *meatus acusticus internus*.

9, 10, 11. *Nervi glossopharyngeus, vagus et accessorius* (IX, Figs. 22, 27–29)

These three cranial nerves all exit or enter the *medulla oblongata* just below the inferior margin of the *pedunculus cerebelli inferior*. While no clearly developed sulcus is apparent at this point, the region is in a position comparable to that of the *sulcus lateralis posterior* of the medulla spinalis. The nerves are arranged in descending order: IX, X and XI. The vestibulocochlear nerve (VIII) may be seen entering at the dorsolateral angle of the bulbopontine sulcus just rostral to the nerve IX.

The intracranial course of all three nerves is short as they pass in an antero-inferior direction toward the lateral margin of the basi-occiput to enter the *foramen jugulare*. The nervus accessorius (XI) has two separate origins, one of which consists of the *radices craniales* seen here at the medulla. The other origin is the cervical portion of the spinal cord which provides for the *radices spinales*. The cranial portion shares a common origin with the nervus vagus (X) in the medulla and a more or less common peripheral distribution. Indeed, it may be asked whether or not this is truly a separate cranial nerve. The spinal roots which ascend within the spinal cord, enter the skull through the foramen magnum (Figs. 8, 37), and join with the cranial portion to travel with them for a short distance. These spinal contributors to the cranial nerve then have a final peripheral distribution distinctly different from the vagus, terminating in the *sternocleidomastoid muscle* and part of the *trapezius* muscle.

The glossopharyngeal nerve provides *taste fibers* to the posterior 1/3 of the tongue, *visceral afferents* to the nasal, pharyngeal and palatal mucosa, afferents to the carotid sinus, *secretory fibers* to the parotid gland, and *motor fibers* to the stylopharyngeus muscle.

The vagus (X) and medullary portion of accessorius (XI) should be considered together as nerves providing for a wide variety of sensory and motor fibers to viscera, as well as for the motor innervation of the muscles of the pharynx. Because of the widespread afferent and efferent distribution of all three nerves to such visceral structures as the carotid sinus, heart, lungs, liver and upper gastrointestinal tract, and because of the central connections made in the medulla, these nerves are concerned with the many important visceral reflexes.

12. Nervus hypoglossus (XII, Figs. 22, 27, 28, 29)

The last of the cranial nerves is the motor nerve to the *intrinsic muscles of the tongue*. It exits from the ventral aspect of the medulla between the pyramis and the oliva. There is a faint sulcus at this point which is frequently referred to as the *preolivary sulcus*. The fibers follow a short antero-inferior course before entering the *canalis hypoglossi* which is just lateral to the *foramen magnum* in the floor of the posterior cranial fossa.

VIII. Substantia Alba (White Matter, Figs. 32, 55-59, 63, 90)

Beneath the cortex of the cerebral hemispheres and the cerebellum, surrounding the medulla spinalis and intermixed with nuclear regions in the brain stem are accumulations of nerve fibers which appear white in fresh or unfixed brain because of the accumulations of myelin which sheath the nerve fibers so prominently in these areas. These areas of fiber pathways form the white matter of the brain, often referred to as the *substantia alba*. These bundles interconnect various areas of cortex and regions of the brain to each other. There are (1) long ascending or descending tract systems of the spinal cord, (2) short arching fibers connecting adjacent cortical gyri, (3) longer arching fiber bundles interconnecting the different cerebral lobes, (4) commissural fiber systems which cross the midline to comparable areas on the other side, and (5) projection systems arising from the cortex which descend to the thalamus and lower centers, and projections arising from the thalamus to reach the cerebral cortex.

(1) The long ascending and descending fiber systems of the medulla spinalis (spinal cord) are perhaps best visualized in sections in which the myelinated fibers are stained (Figs. 90–92). (Note that in these preparations the grey matter is light in appearance and the stained white matter is black). It will be noted that there are three primary columns, the *posterior, lateral* and *anterior funiculi* on each side of the cord. Within these large bundles there are numerous subdivisions into more specialized groups in which the ascending units are more peripherally disposed in the anterior and lateral columns (*tractus spinocerebellaris, fasciculus anterolateralis*), while the posterior columns are made up of essentially ascending fibers. The descending fibers tend to be grouped more around the grey matter (*tractus corticospinalis lateralis* and *anterior*, and the *reticulospinal, vestibulospinal, rubrospinal* and *tectospinal tracts*).

(2) If one peels off the surface cortex of the cerebral hemisphere, one finds that there are short bundles which interconnect the adjacent cortical areas to each other (Fig. 56). The precise function of these short *arcuate* fibers as well as the longer fiber bundles interconnecting the various lobes within a hemisphere is uncertain.

(3) In the process of pulling away the mantle of cerebral cortex covering over the white matter, the white matter also becomes torn away in sheets. With some experience various bundles may be demonstrated extending between the various lobes. Thus, there is the *fasciculus longitudinalis superior* which arches around the insula, receiving and giving off fibers throughout its course (Fig. 56) and which appear to interconnect all the major lobes. The *fasciculus uncinatus* (Fig. 57) serves to establish connections between the orbital and polar regions of the lobus frontalis with the rostral lobus temporalis. One long bundle, the *fasciculus occipitofrontalis inferior* extends from frontal to occipital pole (Fig. 57), passing just beneath the insula and nucleus lenticularis. The most inferior of these long bundles of white matter is the *fasciculus longitudinalis inferior*. On the medial surface of the hemisphere a long bundle with contributions being made into it along its course arches over the *corpus callosum*, extending from the white matter within the gyrus *parahippocampalis* through the *gyrus cinguli* down over the genu of the corpus callosum to reach the *area subcallosa* (Fig. 58). This is the *cingulum*. If the grey matter within the *sulcus calcarinus* is scrapped away, an underlying arcuate bundle of fibers may be seen extending between the cuneus and the gyrus occipitotemporalis medialis. The bundle is called the *calcarinum*.

(4) There are several commissural bundles in the brain. The largest is the *corpus callosum* which can be seen in the midsagittal plane. It has been divided into a rostral knee-shaped portion (*genu*), a middle body (*truncus*), and a caudal region (*splenium*). Fibers passing through this structure are believed to interconnect with

the homologous cortical areas for every part of the neocortex. The *commissura anterior* is also apparent in the sagittal plane. It is just rostral to the *columna fornicis* and caudal to the *gyrus paraterminalis*. It extends between the olfactory bulbs rostrally and the area of cortex around the uncus caudally. The *commissura fornicis* is a small commissure under the caudal part of the *truncus corporis callosi* interconnecting the *hippocampus*. A small commissural bundle may be seen just dorsal to the commissura posterior. This is the *commissura habenularum*, which interconnects nuclei of the two habenular areas. The last major commissural structure is the *commissura posterior* found at the junction of the diencephalon and mesencephalon at the caudal superior end of the ventriculus tertius. It interconnects various nuclear masses at the rostral end of the mesencephalon. There are other smaller commissural bundles associated anatomically with the hypothalamus, but which have functional relationships with the basal nuclei which are difficult to see in gross preparations.

(5) A great mass of fibers in the brain is included in the projection group. Thus, there are numerous fibers leaving the cortex of all lobes which descend through the capsula interna to terminate in the thalamus, mesencephalon, metencephalon, medulla oblongata and medulla spinalis, terminating on associative nuclei and various motor or relay nuclei. They pass in large part through the crus cerebri, down through the pons and finally a part of them continue along the ventral surface of the medulla oblongata as the pyramis which undergoes partial decussation before penetrating into the medulla spinalis. There are, in addition, ascending projection fibers arising from the thalamus which reach the cerebral cortex via the capsula interna. The *fornix* is also a projection system containing fibers arising from cells in the hippocampus which go into the *hypothalamus, septal area* and *mesencephalon* (Fig. 58). The *stria medullaris, stria terminalis* (not illustrated) and the *fasciculus mamillothalamicus* may be considered as minor projection units between nuclear subgroups or cortex and nuclei of the diencephalon or basal nuclei.

IX. Ventricular System (Figs. 17, 24, 28–30, 32, 49, 50, 60–62)

In the early embryologic stages, the brain of man is a hollow tubular structure. This internal cavity is filled with fluid (cerebrospinal fluid) and will be found in all the major parts of the adult brain, though much modified from its early state. A large *ventriculus lateralis* is present in each cerebral hemisphere. The largest choroid plexus is present in this particular ventricle. This intrahemispheric ventricle connects medially via the *foramen interventriculare* (foramen of Monroe) with the *ventriculus tertius* which is a small narrow cavity oriented vertically between the two diencephalic masses. It is frequently bridged by a thalamic nuclear mass, the *adhesio interthalamica* (massa intermedia). A small opening may be seen at the caudal dorsal aspect of the ventriculus tertius, just under the *commissura posterior*. This is the rostral opening of the *aqueductus cerebri* which runs caudally through the mesencephalon to the *ventriculus quartus*. This latter ventricular cavity is flattened dorso-ventrally and possesses a somewhat rhomboidal shape. It opens laterally through the *apertura lateralis ventriculi quarti* (foramen of Luschka) into the *cavum subarachnoideale*. A caudal midline opening is sometimes described, the *apertura mediana ventriculi quarti*, whose function is open to discussion. The spinal canal (*canalis centralis*), which runs through the center of the grey matter of the spinal cord, represents the caudal extent of the ventricular system. It runs from the caudal end to the ventriculus quartus.

1. Ventriculus lateralis

The lateral ventricle may be divided into a *cornu anterius*, a *cornu posterius* and a *cornu inferius*. These are associated with the frontal, occipital and temporal lobes respectively. A *pars centralis* interconnects the three horns. All subdivisions have a close relationship with the corpus callosum. An appreciation of these relationships as well as of the other structures bounding the ventricle may be obtained from the dissection illustrated by Figs. 49, 50, and 60–62. The coronal and horizontal planes of section are also useful for determining the various relationships of the ventricle.

2. Ventriculus tertius

The third ventricle communicates with the lateral ventricle through the *foramen interventriculare*. The anterior margin of this foramen is formed by the *columna fornicis* and the caudal margin is formed by the *nucleus anterior thalami* (Figs. 17, 18, and 75). The third ventricle itself lies between the two diencephalic masses and may be bridged by the *massa intermedia* of the thalamus. It is roofed by the *tela choroidea ventriculi tertii*. Its floor is marked by two recesses, the *recessus opticus* and the *recessus infundibuli* (Figs. 17 and 67). At its caudal dorsal apex the ventricle drains into the *aqueductus cerebri* (Fig. 17) which is in the center of the *substantia grisea centralis of the mesencephalon*. It is roofed over by the tectal plate of the colliculi, while the tegmentum mesencephali is ventral to it (Figs. 83–85).

3. Ventriculus quartus

The rhomboidal shaped fourth ventricle has for its floor the *pars dorsalis pontis* rostrally and the *dorsum* of the *medulla oblongata* caudally (Figs. 24, 30). This floor surface has many surface markings which are indicative of the underlying structures. The roof of this ventricle anteriorly is the *velum medullare superius* (Figs. 24 and 32) which arches up into the cerebellum toward the fastigial nuclei in the midline (Fig. 24). Just below the fastigial nuclei, the *velum medullare superius* meets the *velum medullare inferius* (Figs. 24 and 29) at a point called the *recessus fastigii*. As indicated previously, the fourth ventricle drains laterally via the *recessus lateralis ventriculi quarti* into the *cavum subarachnoideale* (Fig. 28).

Vascular Supply (Figs. 39–51)

A. The arteries (Figs. 39–46)

The blood supply to the CNS is critical since no cerebral cortical neurons can survive a loss of their source of oxygen for more than 5–6 minutes at normal body temperatures. Cells of the basal ganglia appear capable of surviving periods of anoxia of up to 10 minutes, while Purkinje cells are more comparable to cerebral cortical cells in this respect. Motor cells of the cord and brain stem are the most resistant to oxygen deprivation and may survive after periods of circulatory arrest as long as 15 minutes. Therefore, any general or local diminution in supply may in many instances be shortly followed by clinical indications of CNS damage. Indeed, the various forms of CNS vascular disease (aneurism, hemorrhage, thrombosis, arteriosclerosis, etc.) are responsible for the largest part of the neurological disorders seen. A thorough knowledge of the anatomy of these vessels and their neuroanatomical relationships is necessary for the interpretation of many neurological disorders resulting from these vascular problems.

For this part of the laboratory study, a brain should be used in which the leptomeninges and their contained vessels are still intact. As much as possible, attempt to relate the vessels to the neighboring neuroanatomical structures. Compare distribution, origin and size of the vessels in several brains, noting the variations, particularly in the vessels forming the *circulus arteriosus cerebri* at the base of the brain.

The brain and its stem are supplied from two main sources: 1. the *vertebral–basilar complex* which serves the hind- and midbrain and the posteroinferior-medial (occipital lobe) aspect of the hemispheres, and 2. the *arteriae carotides internae* which supply the remainder of the hemisphere, the basal nuclei and the diencephalon. At the caudal end of the diencephalon the two sources overlap.

1. The two arteriae vertebrales

These can be seen joining to form the arteria basilaris at the ventral aspect of the brain stem. Before joining, however, each gives off a medical branch. These branches fuse to form the *arteria spinalis anterior* which then descends along the anterior surface of the medulla spinalis in the *fissura mediana anterior*. Numerous collaterals (medullary arteries) from the *intercostal segmental arteries* join the anterior spinal artery at lower levels. The vertebral arteries also give off an important lateral branch before joining. This is the *arteria cerebelli inferior posterior* which in turn frequently gives off the *arteria spinalis posterior* (a caudally directed branch on the posterior surface of the spinal cord which also receives collateral connections from the intercostal and other segmental arteries). The arteria spinalis posterior may, however, arise directly from the arteria vertebralis. The arteria cerebelli posterior inferior supplies the caudal part of the inferior aspect of the corpus cerebelli and provides perforating rami for the deep cerebellar nuclear masses. This vessel encircles the medulla oblongata in its course from the arteria vertebralis to the cerebellum. As this occurs it provides the important perforating rami for the dorsolateral aspect of the medulla.

The first large branch of the *arteria basilaris* (starting from the caudal end) is the paired *arteria cerebelli inferior anterior* from which the smaller *arteria labyrinthi* usually arises. The inferior anterior cerebellar artery, as its name implies, supplies the anterior or more rostral portion of the inferior surface of the corpus cerebelli. Frequently both inferior cerebellar arteries arise from a common stem which may spring from either the arteria vertebralis or arteria basilaris. The sixth cranial nerve is usually observed passing just rostral to the arteria cerebelli inferior anterior. The *arteria cerebelli superior* is given off at the rostral end of the arteria basilaris. This vessel commonly splits into 3 subdivisions (*pars medius, intermedius* and *lateralis*) on the dorsal surface of the cerebellum. Again a perforating ramus is given off for the deep nuclei. The arteria basilaris finally terminates by branching into the two *mesencephalic stem arteries of the arteriae cerebri posteriores*. A group of smaller vessels or a single vessel arise near the origin of this mesencephalic stem vessel and encircle and supply the mesencephalon at this same site. These are the *rami ad tectum mesencephali*. Note the prominent oculomotor nerve passing between the arteria cerebelli superior and the mesencephalic stem of the arteria cerebri posterior. A large cluster of small vessels arise from the rostromedial surface of the mesencephalic stem of the arteria cerebri posterior near its origin. They penetrate deeply into the mesencephalon by passing through the *substantia perforata posterior* of the *fossa interpeduncularis*. These are the *rami ad tegmentum mesencephali* which also supply the caudal end of the *corpus mamillare*. The distal portion of the arteria cerebri posterior supplies the inferior aspect of the temporal lobes and medial aspect of the occipital lobes, including the important visual cortices. The proximal segment of the distal portion of the arteria cerebri posterior also gives off a *choroidal–diencephalic ramus*. The choroidal vessels are directed to the choroid plexuses of both the third and lateral ventricles. The diencephalic vessel supplies the caudal inferior end of the thalamus and the metathalamus.

2. *The arteria carotis interna*

This artery splits into four main branches: The *a. cerebri anterior* and *a. cerebri media*, the *a. choroidea anterior* and the *a. communicans posterior* (proximal stem of the arteria cerebri posterior). The anterior arteries are connected via the *a. communicans anterior* and supply most of the medial surface of the hemisphere. Just distal to the arteria communicans anterior a large recurrent branch, the *ramus centralis* (medial recurrent artery of Heubner) is given off. This passes laterally and caudally, giving off perforating branches to the corpus striatum (head of caudate, rostral putamen, and adjacent part of the capsula interna). Just before the arteriae cerebri anteriores are joined to each other by the communicating artery, each gives off numerous caudally directed perforators to supply the rostral hypothalamus and preoptic areas. The arteria cerebri media passes laterally through the *limen insula* superior to the rostral part of the temporal lobe which may be partially removed to facilitate visualization of the vessel. It branches out into a 'candelabra' of vessels over the surface of the insula and then undergoes further arborization on the lateral surface of the hemisphere with many collateral branches joining to the other main arterial stems. Perforating vessels arise from this plexus to supply the cortex. As the arteria media passes laterally towards the insula, many perforating vessels to the *basal nuclei* (putamen and lateral part of the globus pallidus and the rest of the caudate nucleus) are given off which penetrate through the *substantia perforata anterior*. These are the rami centrales of the arteria cerebri media (lenticulostriate arteries or arteries of 'stroke').

The third ramus, the *arteria communicans posterior* connects the carotid and basilar systems. It also gives off a supply for the rostral end of the diencephalon (thalamus and hypothalamus) and connects with the mesencephalic stem of the posterior cerebral artery. This vessel, by connecting the components of the basilar and carotid arteries just beneath the hypothalamus, forms the *circulus arteriosus cerebri* (Fig. 39) surrounding the mamillary bodies and the tuber cinereum of the hypothalamus.

The fourth artery of major importance is the *arteria choroidea anterior* which arises from either the arteria cerebri media, the a. carotis interna, or a. communicans posterior as a single vessel or as a cluster of vessels. It follows the pathway of the tractus opticus laterally and caudally, providing a supply to the *uncus* and *choroid plexus* of the cornu inferius of the ventriculus lateralis. It also supplies the *medial part of the globus pallidus* and the ventral anterior and lateral part of the *thalamus*, and the *hippocampus*.

B. The Veins (Figs. 47–51)

The veins drain into the prominent venous sinuses within the cranial dura mater. An attempt should be made to separate the arteria cerebri media from the accompanying veins, which have much thinner walls. Do this by blunt dissection, starting at the origin of the artery and progressing distally. Note the veins on the dorsal aspect which drain toward the *sinus sagittalis superior*. These are the *venae cerebri superiores*. A set of *venae cerebri inferiores* drain into the *sinus transversus*. Attempt to locate the *vena anastomotica superior* (vein of Trolard) and *vena anastomotica inferior* (vein of Labbé). The veins draining the dorsal aspects of the basal nuclei and dorsal thalamus drain primarily into the *vena cerebri interna* (seen on the medial surface of the hemisected brain). The branches contributing to the *vena cerebri interna* are the *vena septa pellucidi*, *vena thalamostriata*, *vena choroidea* and *venae subependymales* which are on the surface of the caudate nucleus. The two internal cerebral veins then drain into the *vena magna* (of Galen) which in turn enters the *sinus rectus*. At this point, the venae basales (Fig. 51) draining the inferior aspect of the midbrain and diencephalon enter into the system (Fig. 48). The ventral parts of the deep telencephalic nuclei and ventral diencephalon drain into the *vena basalis* (of Rosenthal). The vena basalis is formed by the joining of the *vena cerebri media profunda* and the *vena cerebri anterior*.

Functional Mechanisms

Traditionally, the study of the functional pathways within the spinal cord and brain stem is accomplished, in part at least, by the use of the brain and cord sections stained to show the myelin covering of the nerve fibers. With this technique, areas which contain large amounts of myelinated fiber appear quite dark, while regions rich in nerve cell bodies or unmyelinated neurons take up relatively little of the stain and hence appear very light. There are, of course, various regions with admixtures of cell bodies and myelinated fibers which will demonstrate intermediate densities of staining.

While studying the functional pathway, it is good to relate them to the surface structures already learned. Attempt to visualize the effects which masses (bone from a fracture, tumors or large blood clots) capable of applying pressure, might have on the underlying pathways in the cord and brain stem. Before following each functional pathway through the pictures of the Pal–Weigert series, identify as many parts of the pathway in the whole brain and cross sectional brain preparations as possible!

Another approach which is frequently successful and which may be done in conjunction with the study of stained sections, is to make up a set of 8 × 10-inch cards on which are drawn diagrammatic representations of the brain and spinal cord sections represented in Figs. 90 through 118 (see also Figs. 132–145). These are then mounted on a 6-ft. board with a slot to hold each card. Then, as the tract systems are studied, colored string or yarn can be drawn through the cards in the appropriate places for each tract. While this may seem almost a grade school approach to the problem of placement and understanding the relationships of the different tracts, it is often useful with students who have difficulty with 3-dimensional conceptualization.

A. Somatic sensations from the body

Sensory information arising from various types of receptors with endings in the skin, muscles and joints may be divided into two major categories: *1.* the primitive sensations of pain and temperature, itch, tickle and light touch, and *2.* sensations which are generally considered to provide more specific informations, i.e. conscious proprioception (the knowledge of position of the parts of the body, or change in position), 2-point discrimination (the ability to distinguish between being stimulated by two sharp points close together and a stimulus applied by only one stimulating source), exact tactile localization, and probably vibratory sense (ability to distinguish the vibrations of a tuning fork applied to a bony prominence). The various modalities of sensation in category *2* summate in some way, possibly at cortical levels, to provide information regarding the size, texture and weight of objects held in the hand. The cell body of the primary neuron for both categories of somatic sensation from the body is in the dorsal root ganglion. The cells for pain and temperature etc. of group *1* are thought to be smaller and more darkly staining than those of group *2*.

1. Pain and temperature, etc. from the body

Spinal cord

Primary neuron

In the dorsal root ganglion.

Central process

Enters spinal cord via the *lateral division* of the dorsal root where fibers enter the *fasciculus posterolateralis* (tract of Lissauer) and divide into short ascending and descending limbs which extend only about one segmental level (Figs. 90–92).

Synapse

On secondary neurons in the *substantia gelatinosa*, the *nucleus posteromarginalis* or the *nucleus proprius*, after giving off collaterals. Synapses may be at the level of entry or at a segment above or below the level of entry.

Cells in the nuclei posteromarginalis and substantia gelatinosa may synapse on the intercalated neurons which activate motor neurons in the anterior horn at the same level. Synaptic connections from these nuclei are also made on the cells of the nucleus proprius whose axons cross in the *commissura alba* (anterior) and ascend in the ventrolateral part of the spinal cord white matter as the *lateral spino-reticular-tectal* and *thalamic system* (*lemniscus spinalis, fasciculus anterolateralis*).

Medulla

At this level the fibers of the *fasciculus anterolateralis* (*lemniscus spinalis*) are located just dorsal to the *nucleus olivaris* (Figs. 93, 94, 133–145) and ascend in the ventro-lateral reticular formation (tegmentum) dorsal and lateral to the *lemniscus medialis*.

Terminals

a. Synaptic terminations occur on cells of the *lateral* and *medial reticular nuclei* and *dorsal accessory olive*.

b. At the pontomedullary junction, some fibers terminate in the *nucleus raphe pallidus*. Other fibers of this group decussate and appear to join fibers going to the contralateral nucleus raphe pallidus. Exact terminations of these decussating fibers are not clear, however.

c. On the cells of the motor nuclei of the *Vth* and *VIIth nerves*. These are most prominent in lower species.

d. On cells of the *nucleus subcoeruleus* (*pars ventralis*).

Pons

The fibers of the spinal lemniscus may be identified in the caudolateral aspect of the *pars dorsalis pontis* (pontine tegmentum) at the angle between the *lemniscus medialis* and *lemniscus lateralis*. At this point exact lines of demarcation between the three ascending fiber systems are obscure. Terminals occur on cells in the *lateral reticular formation* and are fairly wide spread.

Mesencephalon (Fig. 104, isthmus rhombencephali, Figs. 106–110)

Those fibers still remaining in this ascending pathway (many having terminated at lower levels) are still to be shown ascending in a position between the medial and lateral lemnisci and are at this level laterally placed near the surface of the mesen-cephalon. At the rostral end of the mesencephalon all the ascending pathways have more or less blended together with fibers arising from or passing through the *nucleus ruber*. All travel rostrally into the thalamic structures in a region which has been called the '*prerubral field*' or the '*tegmental field*' or the '*H-field of Forel*'. Numerous terminals are made in the lateral part of the *substantia grisea centralis* and to the *superior colliculus* from the ascending pathway. The latter fibers con-stitute what is frequently termed the *spino-tectal tract*. Crossing fibers of this sys-tem are also present in the *posterior* and in the *tectal commissures*. The decussating fibers are thought to terminate in the *intralaminar thalamic nuclei*.

Additional terminations are made in the *magnocellular portion* of the *corpus geniculatum mediale*.

Dorsal thalamic terminations (Figs. 111, 112)

At least two fiber groups end in this area, one to the *nucleus ventralis thalami posterior lateralis*, and the other to the *intralaminar nucleus*. Some information terminating on thalamic cells is undoubtedly relayed to the *postcentral gyrus* (primary sensory cortex) of the lobus parietalis via the posterior limb of the *capsula interna*.

2. Conscious proprioception, 2-point discrimination, etc. from the body

Primary neuron

In the dorsal root ganglion.

Central process

Enters the spinal cord via the *medial division* of the dorsal root (Figs. 90–92). There is a prominent ascending ramus which enters the *funiculus posterior* which may ascend as far as the caudal medulla (Figs. 132–137); many fibers terminate at lower levels. A descending ramus also enters the funiculus posterior. While most of these fibers are relatively short, some may descend as far as ten or more segments. These elements are probably mainly concerned with reflex responses to the sensory input at the appropriate cord levels. Collaterals of primarily the descending ramus terminate on *internuncials* or on motor neurons in the ventral horn. This system provides for the classical two-neuron arc which constitutes the pathway of the stretch reflex.

The ascending fibers (*fasciculus gracilis* and *cuneatus*) constitute the bulk of the posterior funiculus. Sensory fibers from sacral levels enter most inferiorly and become placed most medially in the posterior funiculus. Other components entering the cord at higher levels become positioned just lateral to those which entered the cord just caudal to them. Thus, cervical units will be most lateral in the posterior funiculus and thoracic units just medial to them, etc.

The ascending fibers terminate in relay nuclei at the caudal end of the closed medulla. Sacral, lumbar and lower thoracic fibers terminate in the medial nucleus, *nucleus gracilis*. Upper thoracic and cervical fibers terminate in the laterally placed *nucleus cuneatus*. Decussating fibers (Figs. 134–139) arise from these nuclei and cross the midline at several levels and come to occupy a more ventral position on the opposite side, just medial to the *nucleus olivaris*. The crossing fibers are the *internal arcuate fibers* and they become what is termed the *lemniscus medialis* which forms a large bundle easily followed through subsequent pontine and mesencephalic sections. From its medial position in the medulla it moves somewhat dorsolaterally in the pons to occupy a position at the anterior (ventral) edge of the *pars dorsalis pontis* (Fig. 97). In the mesencephalon it slowly shifts further laterally (Fig. 104) until at the mesencephalo-diencephalic junction it has almost attained a dorsolateral position. At this point it enters into the *tegmental field* and the fibers enter the dorsal thalamus and terminate in the *nucleus ventralis thalami posterior lateralis* (Fig. 111). The tertiary relay neurons of this nucleus project the somatic sensory information via the posterior limb of the *capsula interna* to the *somatic sensory cortex* (postcentral gyrus, areae 3, 1, 2) to the cortical side which is ipsilateral to the projecting neurons from the thalamus but controlateral to the side of the body from which the stimulus arose.

B. Somatic sensations from the face

Nervus trigeminus V (Figs. 94–99, 132–145)

The trigeminal nerve provides for the somatic sensations arising from the face and conveys the same two categories of information (*1*) pain, temperature, etc., and (*2*) 2-point discrimination, vibratory sense etc., from the face as have just been discussed for the body. There is an additional motor component which travels with the mandibular ramus of the nerve to innervate the muscles of mastication.

Primary neuron

In the ganglion trigeminale.

Central process

Fibers enter the *pars dorsalis pontis* via the proximal root of the nervus trigeminus (Fig. 100). This root passes through the large fiber mass of the *pedunculus cerebellaris medius* before reaching the deeper nuclear part of the pons. These entering fibers may provide neurons which only descend in the brain stem, or which bifurcate and possess either ascending or descending limbs. Terminals are established in a wide variety of nuclei: (1) nucleus of the *tractus solitarius*, (2) in the *dorsolateral reticular formation* of the medulla and lower *pars dorsalis pontis*, (3) the *nucleus spinalis* of V, (4) the *nucleus sensorius superior* of V, and (5) in the various motor nuclei of cranial nerves, associated with reflex responses to facial stimulation, (i.e. III, VI, VII, IX, X and XII). These connections may be accomplished indirectly.

Primary trigeminal terminals on secondary neurons

1. Descending fibers

Non-bifurcating type conveying pain and temperature, etc. from face and scalp to terminate on cells in the:

a. Nucleus spinalis, which is divided into the subnuclei *oralis, interpolaris* and *caudalis*. Subnuclei interpolaris and caudalis give rise to the crossed *ventro-central trigeminal tract* which transmits pain and perhaps temperature to higher levels. The rostral part of the nucleus oralis and the ventral portion of, the *nucleus sensorius superior* of V form a functional unit concerned with the discriminative somatic sensations.

(*1*) *Ophthalmic fibers*; are most ventral and descend most caudally.

(*2*) *Maxillary fibers*; are more dorsally placed than (*1*).

(*3*) *Mandibular fibers*; are most dorsally placed and descend only a short distance from their point of entry and terminate in only the rostral end of the nucleus spinalis.

b. Nucleus of tractus solitarius.

c. Dorsolateral pontine and *medullary reticular formation, motor nuclei, salivatory nuclei*, etc.

2. *Bifurcating fibers*

a. The descending component probably conveys light touch, providing for a tactile (non-specific) component which runs along with pain and temperature. The descending fibers travel with the *tractus spinalis* of V and terminate in *reticular nuclei* or in the *nucleus spinalis* of V.

b. Ascending fibers are probably concerned with proprioception, 2-point discrimination, etc. and terminate in the:

(*1*) *Nucleus sensorius superior* of V.

(*2*) *Nucleus mesencephalicus* of V (contains unipolar cell bodies whose fibers share a peripheral distribution with the Vth nerve. This is not a synaptic center).

Secondary fibers arising from the nuclei of the trigeminal nerve

1. Nucleus spinalis of the trigeminal nerve

a. Subnucleus caudalis—provides for crossed and uncrossed ascending fibers. In the medulla these fibers cross in the area between the hypoglossal nucleus and the pyramidal tracts. In crossing these fibers establish connections with the *XIIth motor nucleus, medial magnocellular portion of the reticular formation, VIth* and *VIIth motor nuclei*. The ascending tract formed from the decussating and non-decussating fibers is the *tractus trigeminalis centralis ventralis* which is believed to be diffusely scattered along the dorsomedial edge of the *nucleus olivaris*. In the pons this tract occupies a somewhat indistinct position along the medial anterior margin of the pars dorsalis pontis. As it ascends, it tends to shift laterally throughout the pons until it is near the lateral margin of the brain stem at the rostral end of the mesencephalon where it blends in with the other ascending fibers present in the tegmental field.

Collaterals of this tract go to the *substantia grisea centralis, colliculus superior, regio pretectalis, intralaminar nuclei of thalamus, subthalamic area* and the *nucleus ventralis thalami posterior medialis.*

2. Ventral portion of nucleus sensorius superior and subnucleus oralis of the nucleus spinalis of V

a. Primarily crossing fibers forming the *tractus trigeminus dorsalis* for discriminative sensations which terminate in the *nucleus ventralis thalami posterior medialis.*
b. Cerebellar connections.

3. Dorsomedial portion of the nucleus sensorius superior

From here, ipsilateral fibers enter the *tractus trigeminalis dorsalis.* This tract is found just ventro-lateral to the *substantia grisea centralis mesencephali* and lateral to the *fasciculus longitudinalis medialis.*

C. The olfactory pathway (Figs. 13, 20)

Although the olfactory sense is sometimes considered a visceral afferent system because it is associated with some visceral functions such as taste and because the olfactory nerve innervates a mucosa, it is better to consider it a somatic afferent system. The olfactory mucosa is of ectodermal origin with primary olfactory neurons as distance receptors which analyze the external environment, and which are capable of making fine discriminations among odorants. It is, therefore, being considered here among the somatic sensory systems. Olfaction is a phylogenetically primitive sense, being well developed in all the vertebrate classes.

1. The primary olfactory neurons

These are located in the olfactory portion of the nasal mucosa; their axons penetrate the *cribriform plate* and end in the *olfactory bulb* which contains the secondary cell bodies.

2. The secondary axons

These axons pass caudally through the *tractus olfactorius* and then through the olfactory striae to terminate in various tertiary olfactory areas.

3. Tertiary terminals

(a) in the grey matter of the *olfactory stalk* and *olfactory* trigone;

(b) some secondary axons pass medial to the trigone in the medial olfactory stria and terminate in a very small zone of cerebral cortex known as the *anterior continuation of the hippocampus* which lies on the medial olfactory gyrus.

(c) Most of the secondary fibers enter the *lateral olfactory stria* and terminate in the cerebral cortex of the *lateral olfactory gyrus*, the lateral edge of the *anterior perforated space* (Fig. 21), the *limen insulae* (Fig. 54), the prepyriform cortex and anterior amygdaloid nuclear region. The latter two are often considered the primary *olfactory cortex*.

The total area occupied by the tertiary olfactory zone is only a few square centimeters and small compared with the formidable array of names used to describe it. This region is usually hidden from view because it conforms to the ledge formed by the lesser wing of the sphenoid bone. It should be possible to identify some of the named zones also on the Pal–Weigert preparations. The fibers of the lateral olfactory stria are observable grossly and under the microscope, and can serve as a guide for the principal olfactory pathway. The commissura anterior which interconnects the olfactory bulbs and some tertiary zones, is easily located on the sections (Figs. 116, 117). Some secondary olfactory fibers enter this commissural pathway and terminate in the neighborhood of the contralateral olfactory bulb but their ultimate destination is not precisely known.

D. The visual pathway (Figs. 109–113)

Identify the *nervus opticus* on the gross brain and begin following the optic pathways caudally from the *chiasma opticum* on the gross brain and brain stem sections to the *corpus geniculatum laterale*.

1. Pathway to the visual cortex

Identify the tractus opticus adjacent to the lateral border of the *crus cerebri*. The tract of one side enters the ipsilateral *corpus geniculatum laterale*. Optic radiations leave the lateral geniculate body and pass laterally through the *radatio optica*. The optic radiations (radatio optica) can be seen in the gross brain coronal sections as a broad fiber bundle (somewhat darker than other areas of white matter) cut transversely and lying lateral to the *cornu inferius, cornu posterius* and *antrum (trigonum collaterale)* of the *ventriculus lateralis*. There is a thin layer of myelinated fibers between the ventricular cavity and the optic radiations which consist of fibers which have passed through the corpus callosum. This is the *tapetum* which is best seen in relation to the cornu posterius of the ventricle. It will appear whiter than the optic radiations in coronal sections and darker in horizontal sections. (The relative degree of whiteness of myelinated fiber tract bundles depends on the plane of section through the fibers. When cut in cross section, fiber bundles usually appear darker than when they are cut longitudinally). These fibers terminate on cells in the calcarine cortex, which is an area of cells situated in the cortex surrounding the *sulcus calcarinum*. The cortical area is marked by a myelinated layer of fibers running parallel to the surface of the cortex (*line of Gennari*) which can be readily visualized in gross coronal preparations. Accordingly, the area is given the name *striate cortex*.

2. Pathways to brain stem structures (Figs. 108–110)

A portion of the *tractus opticus* bypasses the *corpus geniculatum laterale* to form the *brachium colliculi superioris*, whose fibers enter the *pretectal area* and the *colliculus superior*. Some fibers of this bundle also arise in the corpus geniculum laterale. Fibers leave the pretectal area and the superior colliculus to enter into the pathways essential for visual reflexes being mediated through such structures as the *oculomotor nucleus*, the *trochlear* and *abducens nerve nuclei*, via the *fasciculus longitudinalis medialis* and the *tractus tectospinalis*. Note the nucleus of *Edinger–Westphal* (Fig. 109) which is that part of the oculomotor nuclear complex which is associated with the parasympathetic innervation of the muscles of accommodation. The nuclear masses of the pretectal region are interconnected through the commissura posterior (Fig. 110). Other connections of the superior colliculus are of a more general nature, contributing to the *substantia grisea centralis*, the *cerebellum* and the *formatio reticularis* of the tegmentum mesencephali. Another contribution of the visual system is made through the central grey and midbrain reticular formation to the nonspecific thalamic projection nuclei which project to the cerebral cortex. Direct retinal–thalamic connections have also been demonstrated physiologically in some mammalian forms. Thus, it can be seen that the visual stimulus contributes specific cortical and nonspecific subcortical projections. The situation is analogous to somatic projections.

E. The auditory system (Figs. 93–110)

The auditory system can be divided into a specific cortical projections system and a nonspecific brain stem–diencephalic projection system, through which numerous brain stem reflex connections exist.

1. Auditory projections to the cortex

The specific projection system follows the outlined path:
The primary neuron in the auditory afferent path is found in the *organ of Corti*. The proximally directed fibers enter through the cochlear division of the *vestibulo-*

cochlear nerve. At the point where the auditory fibers reach the pontomedullary junction there is a bulge caused by the *nucleus cochlearis ventralis* (Fig. 94) which can generally only be seen in the brain stem series. Other fibers continue to the *nucleus cochlearis dorsalis* (Fig. 93) which can be seen in the brain stem series and on the gross brain as an elevation on the dorsal surface of the *pedunculus cerebellaris inferior* (restiform body). Many axons arising from the secondary neurons in either the dorsal or ventral cochlear nucleus cross to the other side of the brain stem via the fibers of the *corpus trapezoideum* (Figs. 96, 97) and then ascend rostrally. Some fibers also ascend on the ipsilateral side. The trapezoid body is a fairly circumscribed accumulation of fibers at the ventral aspect of the caudal end of the pars dorsalis pontis. It contains not only decussating fibers of the auditory system, but ascending fibers of the medial lemniscal system which are passing through the auditory projections at this point. It is the coalescence of these two fiber systems which causes this region to be so prominent when stained to demonstrate myelin. Some fibers belonging to this system actually cross the brain stem at much more posterior levels in the substance of the pars dorsalis pontis.

The ascending auditory fibers coalesce into a fiber bundle known as the *lemniscus lateralis* which commences at the level of the *nucleus olivaris* (*superior*) and is visible just lateral to the next rostral nuclear structure, the *nucleus subcoeruleus* (Fig. 99). Fibers extend rostrally in the lateral lemniscus to terminate in part in the *nucleus colliculi inferioris*. Tertiary fiber projections arise from the inferior colliculus to form the *brachium colliculi inferioris*. Contributions to this brachium are also made by those fibers of the lateral lemniscus which bypass the colliculus inferior. The brachium courses superficially ventrolateral to the colliculus superior to reach the *corpus geniculatum mediale* (Figs. 108, 109). The colliculus inferior, its brachium and the corpus geniculatum mediale are identifiable on the gross brain as well as in Pal–Weigert sections. Fibers then extend from the medial geniculate body to the *gyri temporales transversi* on the dorsal surface of the *lobus temporalis*, within the *sulcus lateralis*. This specific projection system in the cortex makes possible the appreciation of the position of sound patterns.

2. *Auditory contributions to the brain stem*

Direct or collateral connections from the primary auditory path are made to the nuclei of the *corpus trapezoideum*, the *nuclei of the lemniscus lateralis* and *colliculus inferior*, and possibly to the *nucleus olivaris superior* which provide the substrate for the establishment of reflex connections which are made along the course of the same pathways previously described for the auditory projection system.

Additional crossed connections exist from the nuclei of one lemniscus lateralis through the substance of the tegmentum mesencephali to the other lemniscus lateralis. These connections cannot be seen in the brain stem series. The reflexes subserved by these brain stem stations include adjustments of tension on the ear to compensate for changes in loudness (reflex via Vth and VIIth nerves).

Any of the brain stem pathways of the auditory system are in an excellent position to contribute to the formatio reticularis. Indeed, reciprocal connections exist between the auditory receptors and the reticular system. The contribution to the reticular system provides for that component of auditory projection which may be designated the *non-specific projection* which includes some projection to the non-specific projection of the thalamus. The auditory system is capable of powerfully alerting the organism, as illustrated by the startle reaction which ensues from sudden loud sounds. Thus, the auditory system conforms with the previous afferent projection systems in that it possesses both specific and non-specific components.

F. The vestibular system (Figs. 93–110, 139–145)

The other component of the vestibulocochlear nerve, the *vestibular* (arising from the *canales semicirculares, maculae et sacculi*) contributes primary afferents whose connections in the brain stem are better known than its cortical projection. The brain stem connections of the vestibular systems are profuse. Two general categories of subcortical function exist.

1. First, a *non-specific component* which contributes to the *reticular system* in a manner similar to that of the other sensory modalities, providing for a series of complex reflex connections. In general, these reflexes are concerned with maintaining upright posture and appropriate eye to head and head to body positions. Righting reflexes also depend upon the vestibule, while other reflexes correct for swaying to one side. It can be seen from the complexity of such adjustments that a rather elaborate system of connections is required. These exist and can be traced anatomically. The final explanation of how these reflex adjustments occur is not clear but many connections are suggestive for functional interpretation. For example, the connections with the pretectal area and the third, fourth and sixth nuclei, suggest an involvement in the reflex control of the eyes by stimuli arising from the vestibular apparatus.

2. The second category of vestibular connections deals with those which penetrate the brain stem deep to the pedunculus cerebellaris inferior to make connections with four different vestibular nuclei: the *nuclei medialis, lateralis, superior* and *inferior* (spinal) which can be readily identified on the brain stem series (Figs. 93–97). These nuclei underlie the *area vestibularis* (acoustic trigone). Direct connections are also made to the most primitive part of the cerebellum: the *flocculus* and *nodulus* and their associated nuclei, the *nuclei fastigii*. The connections are

accomplished through the *juxta-restiform body* (identifiable on the slides) and the *uncinate fasciculus* of Russell (not clearly distinct in Pal–Weigert slides). Other connections are made through the *fasciculus longitudinalis medialis* which may be traced up and down the brain stem (Figs. 93–110, 139–145) and can be considered as linking the vestibular system with the motor nuclei which influence eye movements. This fasciculus can also be followed caudally into the spinal cord as the *tractus vestibulospinalis medialis*. The *tractus vestibulospinalis lateralis* proceeds caudally from the lateral vestibular nucleus. The latter tract, however, cannot be followed in the brain stem series. These two tracts may well serve to coordinate neck, shoulder and upper trunk with eye movements.

The vestibular system makes connections with the reticular system, which cannot be seen clearly.

G. Cerebellar pathways

The vestibular system provides an admirable introduction to the cerebellar system. It is clear from the complexity of righting and postural reflexes that a high degree of synergy and coordination of movement is required, which depends considerably upon the cerebellum.

In view of the common need for all vertebrates to maintain a proper posture, particularly during locomotion, it is to be expected that the portions of the cerebellum involved would be those common to all vertebrates, and would be among the most phylogenetically ancient cerebellar structures. This part of the cerebellum is medially situated and functionally concerned with axial structures. Prominent vestibular connections with this part of the cerebellum might also be anticipated due to the prominent role played by the vestibular system in equilibration. Phylogenetically newer parts of the cerebellum are more laterally placed, have little vestibular input and seem largely concerned with the extremities.

The cerebellum, of course, has its own afferent and efferent connections. These are the connections which are essential for the regulation of synergy, muscle tone and postural background.

1. Cerebellum afferents other than vestibular

The cerebellum receives information from the *medulla spinalis*, the *brain stem* and the *telencephalon*.

a. Projections from the medulla spinalis (Figs. 90–92). When somatic receptors send afferents into the spinal cord, they give rise to three possible routes toward the cerebellum. The most primitive route is by way of fibers which ascend via rather ill defined pathways and synapse first in the lateral reticular formation of the rostral *medulla oblongata* which then relays the impulse to the *ipsilateral cerebellar cortex*. A second route is by way of the *tractus spino-cerebellaris posterior*. The fibers conveying proprioception which enter the spinal cord via the medial portion of the dorsal root give off collaterals which synapse on the cells of Clarke's Column (nucleus thoracicus) which can be identified in the ventromedial part of the dorsal horn (Figs. 90, 91) from the first thoracic to the third lumbar segmental level. The fibers terminating here are largely ipsilateral in origin and the nucleus thoracicus which receives them contributes axons which ascend ipsilaterally, forming the *tractus spinocerebellaris posterior*. Follow the tract up the cord into the *pedunculus cerebellaris inferior* (restiform body, Fig. 93) which projects to the anterior lobe and vermis of the cerebellum and provides for an "unconscious' projection of proprioceptive information to the cerebellum. The third route taken is by way of the *tractus spino-cerebellaris anterior*. This tract arises when collaterals from proprioceptive somatic afferents terminate on cells of the *substantia intermedia lateralis* in the spinal cord grey matter (Figs. 90, 91). The axons of cells in this column ascend bilaterally. Those which decussate do so through the *commissura alba anterior*. The anterior spinocerebellar tract enters the cerebellum in part by way of the *pedunculus cerebellaris superior* (brachium conjunctivum). Most of the fibers in this tract join with the posterior tract in the rostral cervical cord and enters the cerebellum by way of the restiform body.

b. *Brain stem projection* (Figs. 93–100, 140–145). The *reticular system* has abundant connections with the cerebellum. *Olivocerebellar* fibers exist and can be clearly seen as crossed fibers emerging from the hilus of the *nucleus olivaris* (inferior) projecting into the contralateral restiform body. The *nucleus arcuatus* sends internal and external *arcuate fibers* to the cerebellum, also via the restiform body. Part of this system is represented by the *stria medullaris acoustica*. The external fibers proceed ipsilaterally, while the internal fibers enter into the contralateral cerebellar cortex.

c. *Telencephalic projections*. The principal outflow from the neocortex to the cerebellum is achieved by fibers which descend through the *capsula interna* to terminate in the *pars basilaris pontis* (*tractus corticopontino-cerebellaris*). Other contributions are made by *corticobulbar* and *corticospinal motor fibers* which give off collaterals to the same nuclei. The *cerebral peduncles* (crus cerebri) convey corticopontine fibers which terminate ipsilaterally on cells in the *pars basilaris pontis*. The cells of the pons then project to the cerebellar cortex through the contralateral *brachium pontis* (*pedunculus cerebellaris medius*) (Figs. 96–100). These constitute the neocortical contributions to the neocerebellum. The development of neocortex, pons and neocerebellum (posterior lobe) parallel each other phylogenetically. An outflow from the *globus pallidus*, *nucleus subthalamicus* (representing the primitive telencephalic motor outflow), and the *substantia grisea centrale mesencephali* also reaches the cerebellum. The route for these connections probably depends upon associations with the *formatio reticularis*. The outflow from these structures cannot be traced in the Pal–Weigert preparations beyond the H and tegmental fields of Forel. The secondary projection from mesencephalic reticular centers is probably mediated through the *tractus tegmentalis centralis* (Fig. 96–105) which terminates on the *nucleus olivaris inferior*. Thus, the olive may be considered as the relay nucleus for subcortical projections to the cerebellum.

2. Efferents from the cerebellum (Figs. 94–109)

The cerebellar efferents arise chiefly from the deep cerebellar nuclei whereas the afferent fibers are directed largely to the cerebellar cortex. The cortex is, of course, connected with these deep nuclei. Identify the *nuclei dentatus, emboliformis, globosus* and *fastigii* (Figs. 94). The brachium conjunctivum (*pedunculus cerebellaris superior*) is chiefly formed of fibers arising from the nucleus dentatus although the other deep nuclei have been shown to contribute to it as well. Follow the brachium conjunctivum rostrally through to its decussation (*decussatio pedunculorum cerebellarium superiorum*). It terminates in the *nucleus ruber* and the mesencephalic *formatio reticularis* as well as in the *nucleus ventralis thalami intermedius* (lateralis) (Figs. 113–116). The latter receives fibers from both the nucleus ruber and the brachium itself. In turn, the nucleus intermedius sends its fibers to the motor and premotor cortex. Recent evidence indicates that there are projections to the intralaminar thalamic nuclei as well. The connections of the brachium with the mesencephalic tegmentum (reticular system) can influence lower motor nuclei through *reticulospinal fibers*. In addition, the brachium conjunctivum appears to possess a descending limb which travels through the brain stem toward the spinal cord, establishing connections in the *nucleus olivaris inferior, formatio reticularis* and *spinal cord*. The descending limb is not clearly visible as a separate entity.

There are, in addition, fibers which leave the cerebellum through the restiform body. It is likely that these connect with the medial reticular formation in the medulla and also send stimuli to the cord. The *nucleus fastigii* appears as the chief source of these efferents.

H. Pathways of the primary motor system (Pyramidal system)

The *pyramis* of the medulla is called such because of its characteristic shape in cross section. Accordingly, an anatomical pyramidal system was so named. The contained fibers were found to originate, for the most part, in the cerebral cortex. Clinical cases existed which pointed to involvement of the anatomical pyramidal system when certain motor deficiencies and signs appeared. It was easy to assume, therefore, that the functional and anatomical pyramidal systems were the same. The term 'pyramidal system' was used interchangeably for either the anatomical or the physiological concept. However, detailed analysis of this system reveals many complexities and contradictions which do not fit into such a simple concept.

The pathway which is traced here is the anatomical one. There is no question but that the described anatomical pathway is important in motor regulation, particularly the kind of motor regulation which appears later in phylogeny. The motor functions involved are those closely associated with what is described as 'voluntary movement'. However, it should be borne in mind that the primary motor system is superimposed on a more primitive or secondary motor system and a clear separation is impossible. The primitive motor system certainly makes a contribution to the grace and ease of voluntary movement and may duplicate much of the function of the primary system in certain circumstances.

The anatomical pyramidal system may be traced as follows (Figs. 90–119): Contributions arise from the *sensory-motor* and *premotor cortex* which enter the *capsula interna* (Figs. 111–119). Contributions from the rest of the cerebrum also occur, but to a lesser degree. Fibers destined to pass through the *crus cerebri* traverse the *crus posterius capsulae internae*, wherein there is some topographic organization. The capsular fibers concerned with innervation of neurons pertaining to motor function next enter the crus cerebri mingled with corticopontine fibers (Figs. 107–111). Corticospinal fibers then penetrate the *pars basilaris pontis* in fascicles whereas corticopontine fibers end on pontine cells (Figs. 96–107). Cortico-bulbar fibers leave the pathway to end in the vicinity of the proper cranial nerve nuclei. Although the path taken by these fibers to the cranial nerve nuclei can not be seen on the Weigert figures, it is worthwhile at this time to identify all the cranial nerve motor nuclei (Figs. 93–109, 138–145). Pay particular attention to the nucleus of the *nervus facialis* and the peculiar course of its fibers around the nucleus of the *nervus abducens*. Also note the exiting fibers of the *nervus trochlearis* decussating at the *isthmus rhombencephali* (Figs. 104, 105).

The 'final common pathway' neurons for control of the vocal cords depend upon the cells of the *nucleus ambiguus* (Figs. 135–137). The latter nucleus cannot be seen clearly in these slides but its location can be approximated by estimating its position in the ventrolateral reticular formation of the upper medulla. The nucleus contributes fibers which form the *recurrent laryngeal nerve*.

The corticopontine fibers make it possible for the telencephalon to enter into an interchange with the cerebellum which has been previously outlined.

The corticospinal fibers continue into the cord via the *medullary pyramids* (Figs. 134–145). After almost completely decussating at the caudal end of the medulla (Figs. 132, 133), two caudally directed tracts exist on each side of the cord, the crossed *tractus corticospinalis lateralis* and the *tractus corticospinalis anterior*, which is uncrossed. Trace the tracts in the cord (Figs. 90–92). The fibers in the anterior tract are believed to cross over finally just before terminating. They end principally on interneurons which, in turn, end on the ventral horn motor cells.

In addition to these straightforward 'obvious' connections of the primary motor system, connections are made with components of the secondary motor system. Among the latter are such important areas as those parts of the *reticular formation* which possess *downstream connections*. The connections with the reticular formation are to both medial and lateral subdivisions and include particularly those in the *mesencephalon* and in the *nucleus reticularis pontis oralis* (Figs. 102–105). Connections are also made with the *nucleus gigantocellularis* (Figs. 96, 97) of the medulla. The latter connections are probably principally from *area 6* (premotor cortex) and the *nucleus caudatus*. The cortical connections to the reticular systems are not only anatomical structures but physiologically active components of the nervous system. The anatomical connections with the secondary or primitive motor system are not obvious in the slide series.

I. Secondary or primitive motor system

Quadrupedal progression, emotionally-triggered movements of body and face, complex self-scratching and licking, shivering and movements involved in stretching and yawning depend mainly upon the operation of the secondary motor system.

The term 'extrapyramidal' was originally coined to refer to all motor pathways which exist outside the pyramidal pathways. Anatomically, it is a waste basket category for motor pathways not included in the pyramidal system. Inasmuch as clinical cases were well known in which motor impairment of a peculiar stereotyped nature existed associated with lesions outside the pyramidal system, it was natural to attribute functional unity to an *'extrapyramidal'* motor system.

In the following discussion identify, locate and relate to each other the various structures mentioned. Use either sections of the Gross Brain or the Weigert preparations.

We will begin with the *midline* and *ventral anterior nuclei* of the thalamus (*nucleus ventralis thalami anterior*)—Figs. 113, 117. These nuclei receive from both the reticular system, and from the primitive sensory system; the midline nuclei receive from both systems while the ventral anterior nucleus is reported to receive from the reticular system. The midline nuclei possess an outflow to the hypothalamus and connect reciprocally with the *nucleus amygdaloideum* (Fig. 112) through the *ansa peduncularis* (Fig. 114). The midline nuclei, therefore, are in a position to convert primitive sensory and reticular input into such primitive motor functions as described above (scratching, licking, emotional, etc.). The changes may be seen to take the form of somatic and visceral motor responses associated with emotional or other compelling reactions consequent to considerable reticular activation or to primitive sensory input. It is known from experimental evidence that direct hypothalamic or amygdaloid stimulation results in such responses.

Primitive motor reactions (they are primitive in the sense of being basic but not in the sense of being poorly executed) require considerable coordination. It has been stated that the cerebellum is implicated in smooth synergy and coordination, and would be expected to take part in these primitive reactions. An interaction of the midline nuclei with the cerebellum can be demonstrated anatomically as follows: the *midline nuclei* have an outflow to the *mesencephalic reticular core*. The region lying close to the *griseum centrale mesencephali* (Figs. 107–109), an anatomical continuation of the thalamic midline nuclear region into the mesencephalon, gives rise to a considerable number of fibers which contribute with other fibers to the formation of the *tractus tegmentalis centralis* (Figs. 96–106). This tract, as previously indicated, terminates in the *nucleus olivaris inferior* along its lateral surface where the fibers form what is called the *amiculum*. The inferior olive has already been described as sending its fibers to the contralateral cerebellum via the restiform body. The cerebellum sends its fibers via the *superior peduncle* to the *nucleus ruber* and the *intralaminar* and *midline thalamic nuclei* among other regions. Accordingly, the midline nuclei constitute a link for the confluence of compelling primitive sensory input and rapid motor output associated with cerebellar regulation. The cerebellar regulation does not end simply with the mentioned link. The cerebellum, in addition, has been described as being connected with the *nucleus ventralis intermedius* (lateralis). Both the anterior part of this nucleus and the *nucleus ventralis thalami anterior* mentioned earlier connect reciprocally with the *globus pallidus* primarily through the *fasciculus thalamicus* (H_1, Fig. 113). The globus pallidus, in turn, contributes to the *formatio reticularis* (through the H field of Forel) to the *subthalamic nuclear areas* (via collaterals from the fasciculus lenticularis—H_2). The subthalamic nuclear areas have been shown to contribute to the pacing of quadrupedal progression. All the above nuclei and fiber bundles may be considered as being part of the 'extrapyramidal' system. A cortical component may also be considered. This would include those fibers concerned with the cortico-ponto-cerebellar-rubro-thalamo-cortical circuit. When the complex system of connections in the primitive motor system is disturbed, it is not surprising to find that the individual shows an absense or abnormality of primitive motor functions. The abnormalities may take the form of (1) lack of emotional facial expression, (2) lack of well-coordinated quadrupedal progression (in human beings the difficulty appears as failure of the arms to swing in rhythm with leg movement and a difficulty in starting or stopping walking movements), (3) abnormal yawning movements, (4) trembling at rest, (5) flinging movements, (6) contorted postures, (7) uncontrolled writhing movements, (8) autonomic disturbances, and (9) slowing of voluntary movement. Numbers 1, 2, 3, 4, 8, and 9 are symptoms of *paralysis agitans*. The symptoms are not necessarily all seen in the same patient, nor is any particular region in the extrapyramidal system always associated with a particular group of clinical signs. The other disturbances are seen in other diagnostic categories.

J. The central portion of the autonomic outflow

It is appropriate to follow a discussion of the primitive motor system by a discussion of the autonomic outflow. It has already been indicated that the primitive motor system is closely integrated with hypothalamic function. The *hypothalamus* has been spoken of as the *head ganglion of the visceral motor system*. One would expect that primitive motor adjustments of a somatic nature would be integrated with appropriate visceral adjustments. Thus, an animal in a resting posture or state might be expected to show a great degree of effective digestive function, which is facilitated by the parsympathetic outflow, particularly by that portion controlled by the vagus nerve. On the other hand, the animal responding to danger by well-coordinated quadrupedal progression or to pain by a well-coordinated counter-attack with appropriate vocalization would be expected to show the mobilization of those energy resources associated with sympathetic activation.

The hypothalamus is implicated in integrating a number of specific changes, which lead to greater expenditure of energy on the one hand and to a conservation or recouping of energies on the other hand. Thus, the hypothalamus plays a role in the regulation of heat output and loss, cardiovascular responses and pituitary secretions. The hypothalamus, in turn, is regulated by the primitive systems described, by the limbic system and the neocortex.

In a general way the anterolateral hypothalamus is associated with energy-conserving functions and the posteromedial with energy-dissipating functions. Anatomically, the hypothalamus is divided into a *lateral* and a *medial* portion by a somewhat vertical plane defined by the position of the descending *columna fornicis* which penetrates the hypothalamic substance (Figs. 112–115). The posterior hypothalamus is defined as the area immediately surrounding and including the *corpora mamillaria* (Fig. 111). Observe the area as well as the region of the *tuber cinerum*. Locate the approximate position of the *supraoptic* and *paraventricular* nuclei at the rostral end of the hypothalamus. The former is dorsal to the *tractus opticus* while the latter is laterally adjacent to the rostral end of the ventriculus tertius.

1. Hypothalamic afferents

The major afferent supply to the hypothalamus enters by way of the *fornix*, *medial forebrain bundle*, *stria terminalis*, the *mamillary peduncle* and fibers associated with the *ansa peduncularis*. The fornix distributes fibers from the *hippocampus* and nuclei of the *septum pellucidum* to the *medial hypothalamus*, including the *corpora mamillaria*. The stria terminalis distributes fibers from the *amygdala* and possibly from the *olfactory cortex* of the lobus temporalis to the medial hypothalamus. Other fibers from the amygdala pass rostrally and dorsally over the tractus opticus to enter the lateral hypothalamus. These fibers first enter the ansa peduncularis and then turn caudally into the medial forebrain bundle. The fibers in the ansa also provide for an inpact from the dorsal thalamus. The medial forebrain bundle collects fibers also from the nuclei of the septum, from the tertiary olfactory territories, and from the orbital cortex and distributes them in a caudal direction to the lateral hypothalamus. It also collects fibers from the griseum centrale mesencephali and tegmentum of the mesencephalon, and distributes them in a rostral direction to the lateral hypothalamus. Short fibers arising in the lateral hypothalamus connect with the medial hypothalamic groups. The fornix, stria terminalis, ansa peduncularis, and medial forebrain bundle may be observed in Pal–Weigert preparations. The medial forebrain bundle runs through the dorsal aspect of the *substantia perforata anterior* (and is not well defined in man), the lateral preoptic area, the lateral hypothalamus and through the hypothalamic–mesencephalic transition. Fibers entering via the mamillary peduncle arise from the dorsal and ventral mesencephalic tegmental nuclei.

2. Hypothalamic efferents

The hypothalamus is likely to make its connections with the *nucleus dorsalis nervi vagi* and with the *salivatory nuclei* by way of the *fasciculus longitudinalis dorsalis*, a fascicle of fibers which travels through the *griseum centrale mesencephali* and can be clearly seen dorsal to the *nucleus hypoglossi*. The connections of the hypothalamus with the *cornu lateralis* of the spinal cord (Fig. 91) are probably accomplished through a multisynaptic system of fibers penetrating the reticular core. The outflow of the cells of the cornu lateralis is through the ventral roots. A well defined hypothalamic outflow arises from the *nuclei supraopticus et paraventricularis* to terminate in the neurohypophysis.

K. Some important visceral afferents

Any discussion of the nerve supply of the viscera would be incomplete without mentioning some important visceral afferent fibers. Those afferents particularly worthy of mention are those implicated in such specific activities as breathing, eating, vomiting and elimination. Other afferents of importance are those implicated in cardiovascular changes. The *nervus vagus* carries afferents leading to inhibition of inspiration, triggering of vomiting, and to the individual's appreciation of 'hunger pangs'. The *nervus glossopharyngeus* carries afferents of taste receptors, pressor receptors, and throat 'tickle' receptors. Activation of the latter results in coughing. Many of the afferents represented in the ninth nerve are also carried by the vagus. The *nervus facialis* carries afferents of taste. The *nervus trigeminus* carries afferents for the sneezing reflex although the fifth nerve is not ordinarily regarded as a visceral afferent nerve. The afferent limbs for elimination reflexes exist in the sacral nerves.

The *seventh*, *ninth* and *tenth nerves* contribute to the formation of the *tractus solitarius* which is visible in the brain stem series (Figs. 139–143). It is surrounded by the *nucleus of the tractus solitarius*. Fibers from the latter nucleus and tract make connections with the *area postrema* (vomiting center), the *medullary reticular core* (a breathing and cardiovascular reflex area), and the *nucleus dorsalis vagi*. Connections with the reticular core provide for upstream conduction in the pathways of the primitive sensory system. The diencephalic areas reached are the *hypothalamus*, *midline nuclei* and the *nucleus medialis thalami* (dorsomedial nucleus). Taste is thought to connect with *gustatory nuclei* at the upper end of the tractus solitarius and probably reaches the *nucleus ventralis posterior medialis* of the thalamus. Cortical projections exist in accordance with the outline of projections of the diencephalic areas involved.

The sacral visceral afferents also reach the diencephalic area, but through pathways which are uncertain. These are, of course, the sacral afferents related to bladder and bowel control. Knowledge obtained in gross anatomy should suggest that the final control of these functions is mediated through both somatic and visceral motor systems.

L. Limbic system

Some components of the limbic system may be observed in the Pal–Weigert preparations. Identify the *septum pellucidum* (Figs. 17–19, 119), an important landmark. The *septal area* (Fig. 19) is considered as having a rather central role in the function of this system. Two components of the *fornix* run through the system. The *post-commissural fornix* descends caudal to the commissura anterior as a compact, paired bundle which enters the hypothalamus. It can be followed as far as the *corpora mamillaria*. The *pre-commissural fornix* gives collaterals to the *septal nuclei* (Fig. 118), then contributes to the gyrus paraterminalis (Figs. 18, 19, 116,

117) and descends anterior to the commissura anterior to end on cells which lie among its fibers. The diagonal band of Broca, which runs through the gyrus para-terminalis, can be traced as far as the lateral preoptic area. Finally, fibers from the septal nuclei enter the fornix and travel to the hippocampus (Figs. 62, 69, 70, 129–131).

From the corpus mamillare a compact bundle, the *fasciculus mamillo-thalamicus* (Figs. 112–116, 122–125) may be traced to the *nucleus anterior thalami*. Fibers arising directly from the fornix also terminate in the nucleus anterior but cannot be as easily seen in Pal–Weigert sections. This input is relayed to the rostral portion of the gyrus cinguli. The nuclei of the septum pellucidum connect with the hypo-thalamus both by fibers running with those of the post-commissural fornical fibers and via the *medial forebrain bundle*. Septal fibers enter the medial forebrain bundle through the diagonal band. The septal nuclei contribute a large contingent of fibers which reach the *habenular nuclei* via the *stria medullaris thalami*. The haben-ular nuclei in turn connect with the *nucleus interpeduncularis*, a part of the mesen-cephalic tegmentum, via the *fasciculus retroflexus* (Fig. 111). The stria medullaris and the fasciculus retroflexus may be followed in the sections.

Other components of the limbic system exist, but they cannot be easily demon-strated in Pal–Weigert preparations.

Acknowledgement

The authors wish to express their appreciation to Drs. Walter Riss and Frank Scalia for their contributions to the material contained in the text for this atlas.

SECTION II

Gross Anatomy

The following series of photographs of the gross brain commence with the brain at autopsy, prior to removal and fixation. Thus, in Fig. 1, the brain is still covered over by the dura in which the ramifications of the meningeal vessels can be seen. The series progresses through a dissection of the brain while it is still in the skull (Figs. 2–8), ending when the brain has been completely removed. In the succeeding figures, the formalin-fixed brain has been used. First the major larger subdivisions are indicated, followed by the small gyral and sulcal units (Figs. 9–22). This series deals primarily with telencephalic and diencephalic structures. These are followed by a separate group depicting brain stem structures (Figs. 23–32). More than one brain has been used in this section of the gross brain so that the student may better appreciate the variation between brains. Figures 33–38 are devoted to a dissection of the spinal cord in situ.

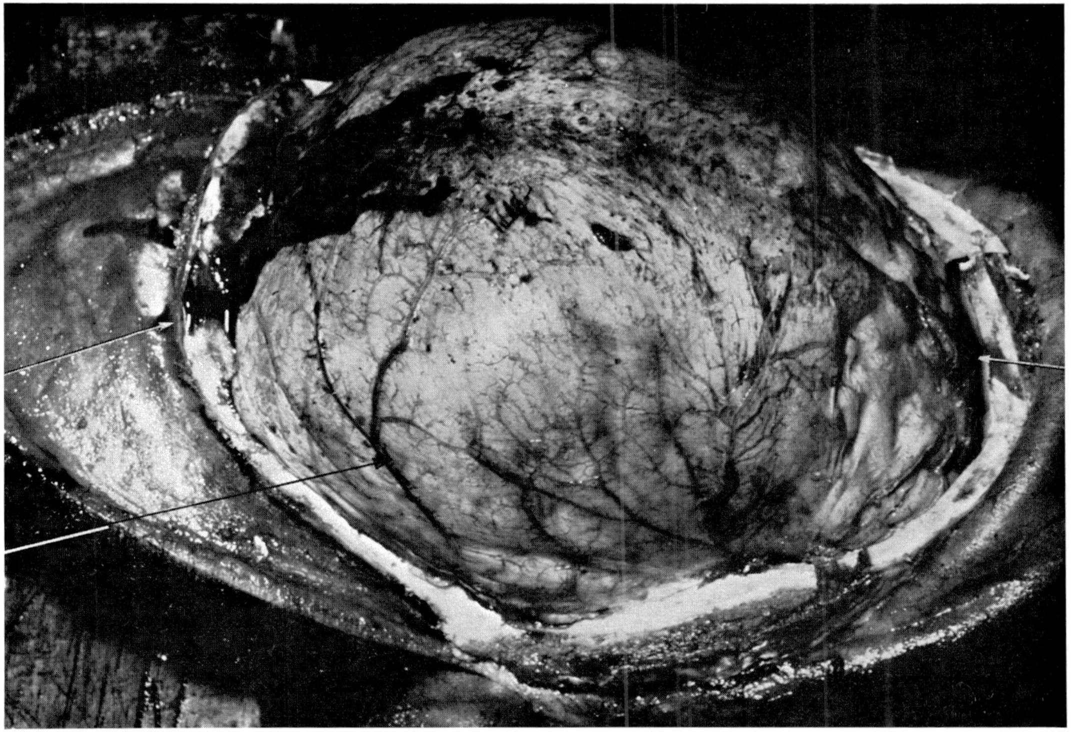

Polus frontalis

Polus occipitalis

Meningeal vessels

Fig. 1. Outer surface of dura mater after reflection of skin and bone. Note the prominent meningeal arteries.

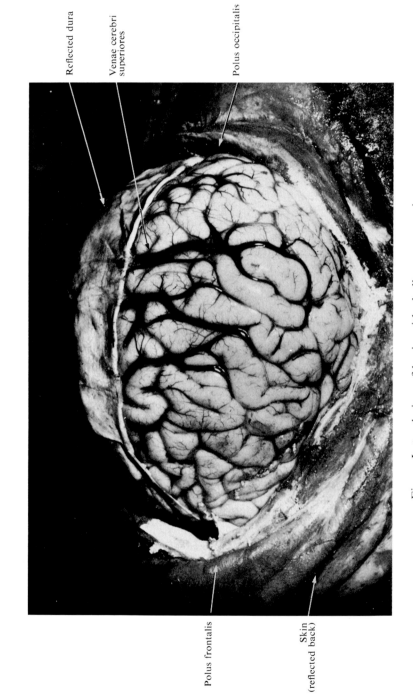

Reflected dura

Venae cerebri
superiores

Polus occipitalis

Polus frontalis

Skin
(reflected back)

Fig. 2. Lateral view of brain with skull cap removed.

62

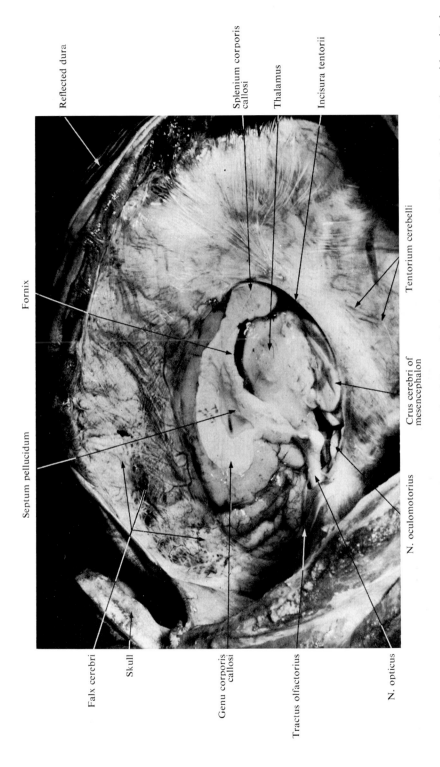

Reflected dura

Splenium corporis callosi

Thalamus

Incisura tentorii

Tentorium cerebelli

Fornix

Crus cerebri of mesencephalon

Septum pellucidum

N. oculomotorius

Falx cerebri

Skull

Genu corporis callosi

Tractus olfactorius

N. opticus

Fig. 3. Left cerebral hemisphere removed to demonstrate the falx cerebri and tentorium cerebelli in relation to the mid-sagittal structures of the forebrain.

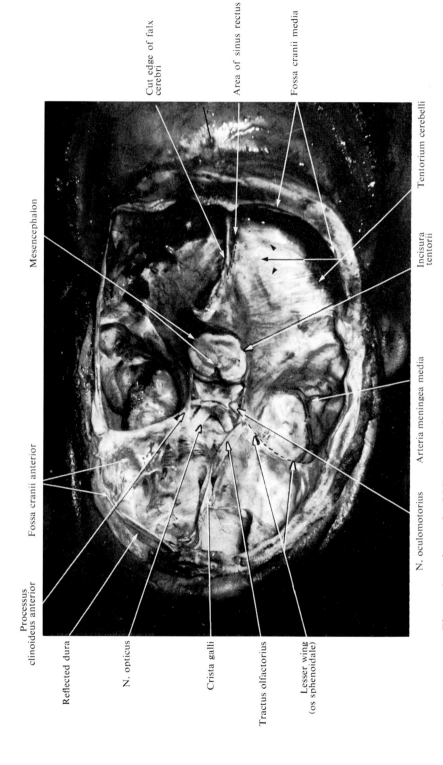

Fig. 4. Anterior and middle cranial fossae after removal of telencephalon and diencephalon.

Cut edge of falx cerebri

Area of sinus rectus

Fossa cranii media

Tentorium cerebelli

Incisura tentorii

Mesencephalon

Fossa cranii anterior

Processus clinoideus anterior

Reflected dura

N. opticus

Crista galli

Tractus olfactorius

Lesser wing (os sphenoidale)

N. oculomotorius

Arteria meningea media

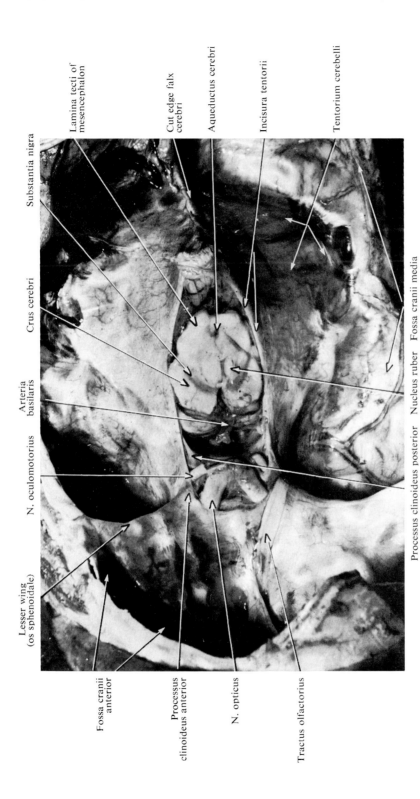

Lesser wing
(os sphenoidale)

N. oculomotorius

Arteria
basilaris

Crus cerebri

Substantia nigra

Lamina tecti of
mesencephalon

Cut edge falx
cerebri

Aqueductus cerebri

Incisura tentorii

Tentorium cerebelli

Fossa cranii
anterior

Processus
clinoideus anterior

N. opticus

Tractus olfactorius

Processus clinoideus posterior   Nucleus ruber   Fossa cranii media

Fig. 5. Enlarged view of Fig. 4, illustrating the relationship of the mesencephalon to the incisura tentorii.

65

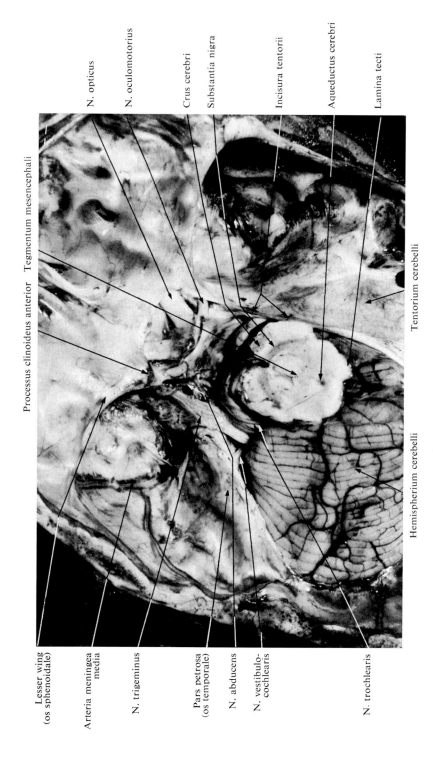

Fig. 6. Partial removal of tentorium cerebelli.

N. opticus

N. oculomotorius

Crus cerebri

Substantia nigra

Incisura tentorii

Aqueductus cerebri

Lamina tecti

Processus clinoideus anterior   Tegmentum mesencephali

Tentorium cerebelli

Hemispherium cerebelli

Lesser wing
(os sphenoidale)

Arteria meningea
media

N. trigeminus

Pars petrosa
(os temporale)

N. abducens

N. vestibulo-
cochlearis

N. trochlearis

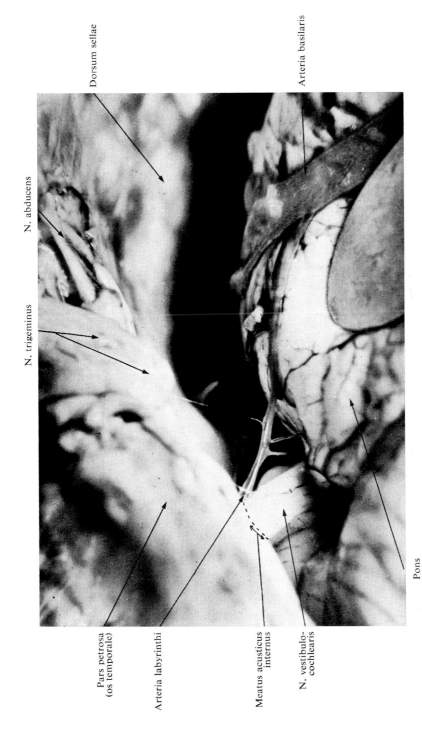

N. abducens

Dorsum sellae

N. trigeminus

Arteria basilaris

Pars petrosa
(os temporale)

Arteria labyrinthi

Meatus acusticus
internus

N. vestibulo-
cochlearis

Pons

Fig. 7. View of ventral aspect of the pons in relation to the dorsum sellae demonstrating the arteria labyrinthi.

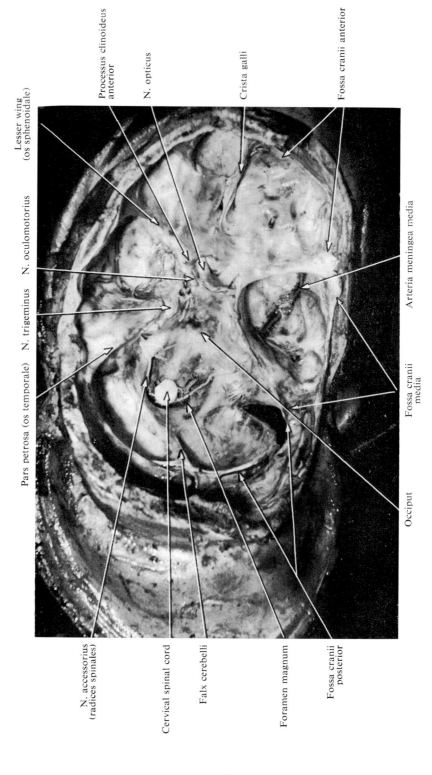

Lesser wing
(os sphenoidale)

Processus clinoideus
anterior

N. opticus

Crista galli

Fossa cranii anterior

Pars petrosa (os temporale) N. trigeminus N. oculomotorius

Arteria meningea media

Fossa cranii
media

Occiput

N. accessorius
(radices spinales)

Cervical spinal cord

Falx cerebelli

Foramen magnum

Fossa cranii
posterior

Fig. 8. Floor of skull with brain removed.

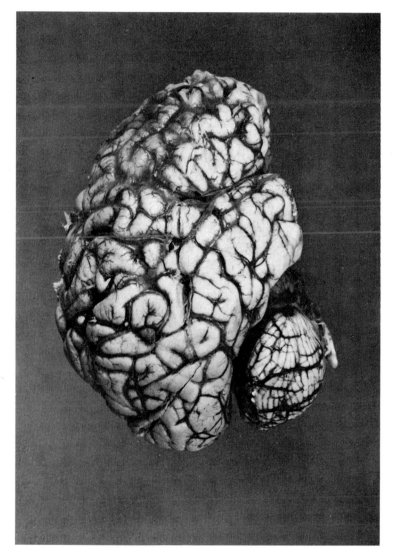

Fig. 9. Lateral view of brain with vessels and leptomeninges intact.

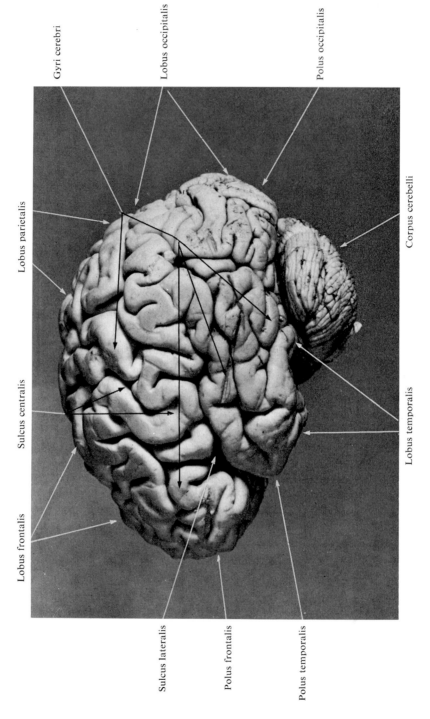

Gyri cerebri

Lobus occipitalis

Polus occipitalis

Corpus cerebelli

Lobus parietalis

Sulcus centralis

Lobus temporalis

Lobus frontalis

Sulcus lateralis

Polus frontalis

Polus temporalis

Fig. 10. Lateral view of the brain illustrating major gross subdivisions.

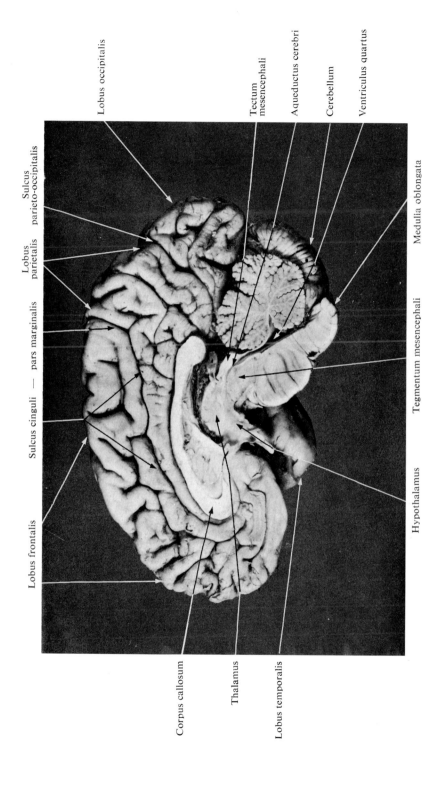

Lobus occipitalis

Sulcus parieto-occipitalis

Lobus parietalis

Sulcus cinguli — pars marginalis

Lobus frontalis

Tectum mesencephali

Aqueductus cerebri

Cerebellum

Ventriculus quartus

Medulla oblongata

Tegmentum mesencephali

Hypothalamus

Corpus callosum

Thalamus

Lobus temporalis

Fig. 11. Midsagittal surface of the brain illustrating the major gross subdivisions.

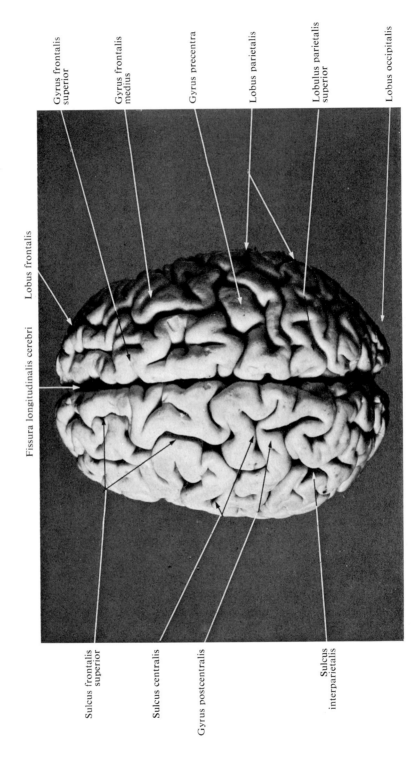

Gyrus frontalis superior

Gyrus frontalis medius

Gyrus precentra

Lobus parietalis

Lobulus parietalis superior

Lobus occipitalis

Lobus frontalis

Fissura longitudinalis cerebri

Sulcus frontalis superior

Sulcus centralis

Gyrus postcentralis

Sulcus interparietalis

Fig. 12. Dorsal aspect of cerebral hemispheres.

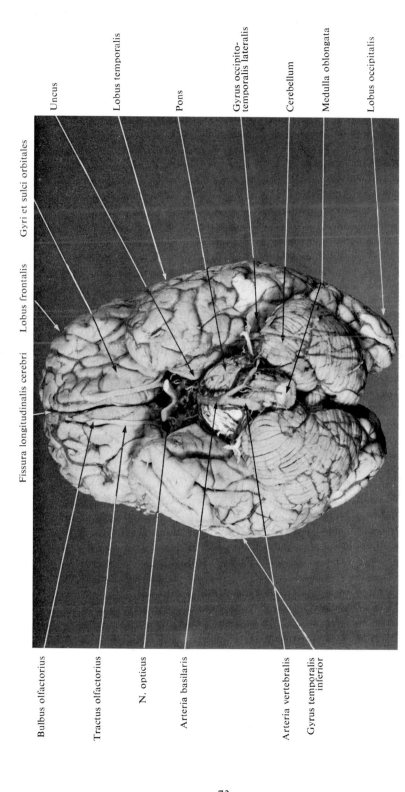

Fissura longitudinalis cerebri   Lobus frontalis   Gyri et sulci orbitales

Bulbus olfactorius

Tractus olfactorius

N. opticus

Arteria basilaris

Arteria vertebralis

Gyrus temporalis inferior

Uncus

Lobus temporalis

Pons

Gyrus occipito-temporalis lateralis

Cerebellum

Medulla oblongata

Lobus occipitalis

Fig. 13. Ventral aspect of the brain illustrating major subdivisions.

73

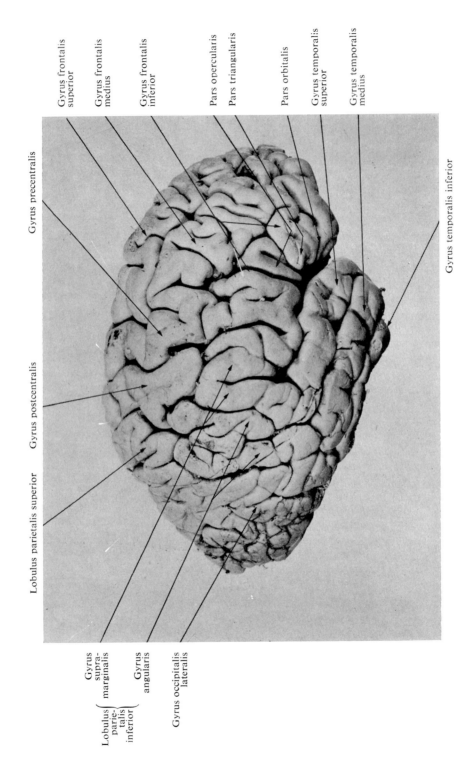

Gyrus frontalis superior

Gyrus frontalis medius

Gyrus frontalis inferior

Pars opercularis

Pars triangularis

Pars orbitalis

Gyrus temporalis superior

Gyrus temporalis medius

Gyrus precentralis

Gyrus temporalis inferior

Lobulus parietalis superior

Gyrus postcentralis

Gyrus supra-marginalis

Lobulus parie-talis inferior

Gyrus angularis

Gyrus occipitalis lateralis

Fig. 14. Cerebral gyri from lateral aspect.

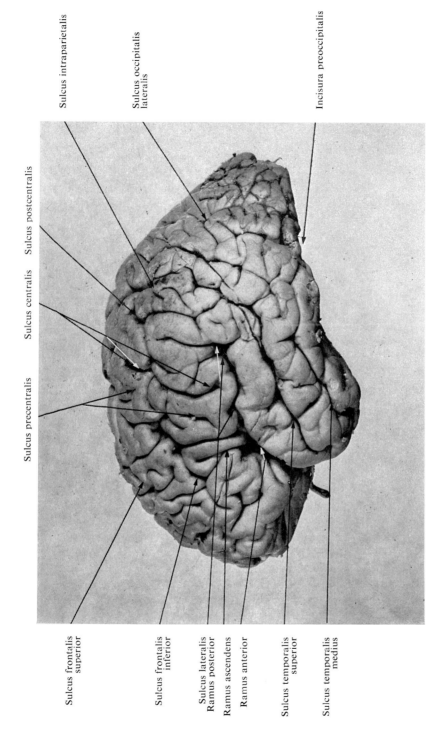

Sulcus intraparietalis

Sulcus occipitalis lateralis

Incisura preoccipitalis

Sulcus postcentralis

Sulcus centralis

Sulcus precentralis

Sulcus frontalis superior

Sulcus frontalis inferior

Sulcus lateralis
Ramus posterior

Ramus ascendens

Ramus anterior

Sulcus temporalis superior

Sulcus temporalis medius

Fig. 15. Cerebral sulci from lateral aspect.

75

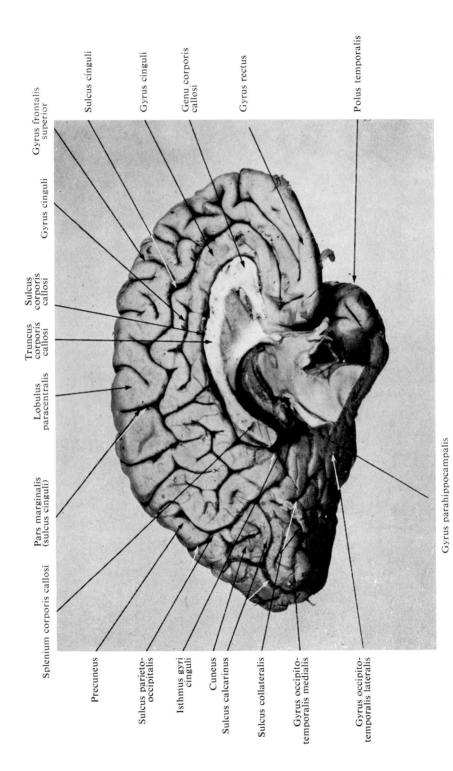

Gyrus frontalis
superior

Sulcus cinguli

Gyrus cinguli

Genu corporis
callosi

Gyrus rectus

Polus temporalis

Gyrus cinguli

Sulcus
corporis
callosi

Truncus
corporis
callosi

Lobulus
paracentralis

Pars marginalis
(sulcus cinguli)

Splenium corporis callosi

Gyrus parahippocampalis

Precuneus

Sulcus parieto-
occipitalis

Isthmus gyri
cinguli

Cuneus

Sulcus calcarinus

Sulcus collateralis

Gyrus occipito-
temporalis medialis

Gyrus occipito-
temporalis lateralis

Fig. 16. Cerebral gyri and sulci, medial aspect.

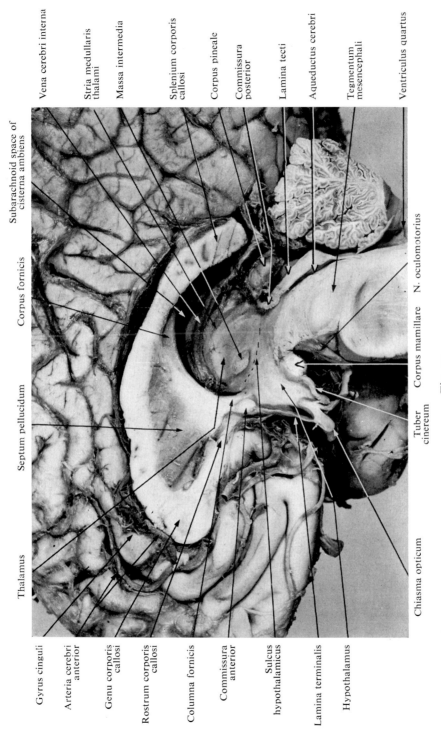

Vena cerebri interna

Stria medullaris thalami

Massa intermedia

Splenium corporis callosi

Corpus pineale

Commissura posterior

Lamina tecti

Aqueductus cerebri

Tegmentum mesencephali

Ventriculus quartus

Subarachnoid space of cisterna ambiens

Corpus fornicis

Septum pellucidum

Thalamus

Gyrus cinguli

Arteria cerebri anterior

Genu corporis callosi

Rostrum corporis callosi

Columna fornicis

Commissura anterior

Sulcus hypothalamicus

Lamina terminalis

Hypothalamus

Chiasma opticum

Tuber cinereum

Corpus mamillare

N. oculomotorius

Fig. 17.

77

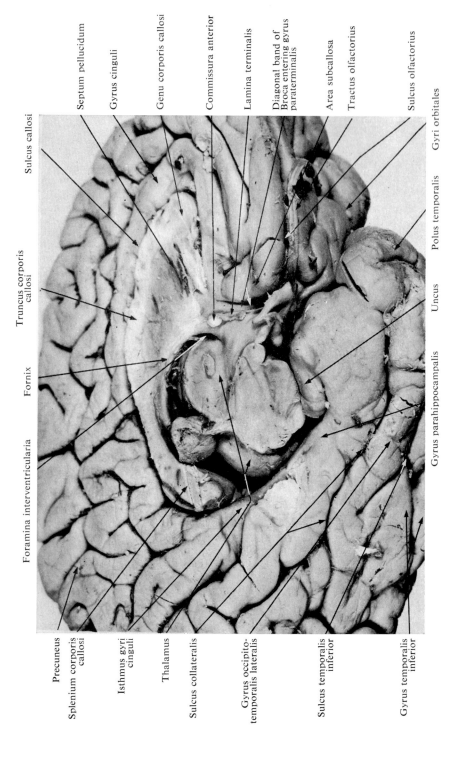

Septum pellucidum

Gyrus cinguli

Genu corporis callosi

Commissura anterior

Lamina terminalis

Diagonal band of
Broca entering gyrus
paraterminalis

Area subcallosa

Tractus olfactorius

Sulcus olfactorius

Sulcus callosi

Truncus corporis
callosi

Fornix

Foramina interventricularia

Gyri orbitales

Polus temporalis

Uncus

Gyrus parahippocampalis

Precuneus

Splenium corporis
callosi

Isthmus gyri
cinguli

Thalamus

Sulcus collateralis

Gyrus occipito-
temporalis lateralis

Sulcus temporalis
inferior

Gyrus temporalis
inferior

Fig. 18. Ventro-medial aspect of the brain.

78

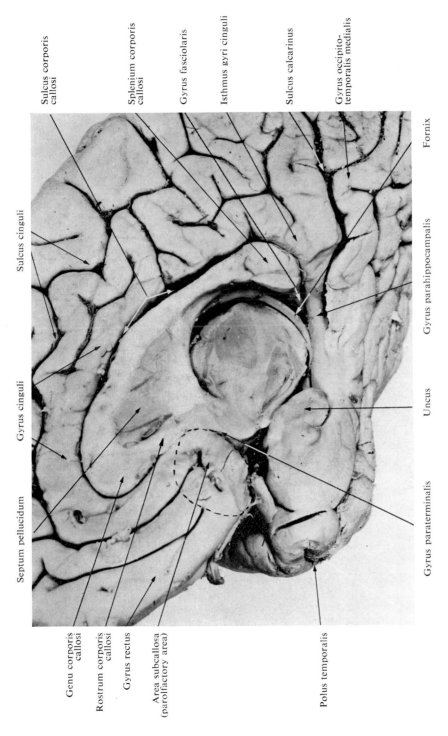

Sulcus corporis callosi

Splenium corporis callosi

Gyrus fasciolaris

Isthmus gyri cinguli

Sulcus calcarinus

Gyrus occipito-temporalis medialis

Sulcus cinguli

Gyrus cinguli

Septum pellucidum

Fornix

Gyrus parahippocampalis

Uncus

Gyrus paraterminalis

Genu corporis callosi

Rostrum corporis callosi

Gyrus rectus

Area subcallosa (parolfactory area)

Polus temporalis

Fig. 19. Superficial components of the limbic system.

79

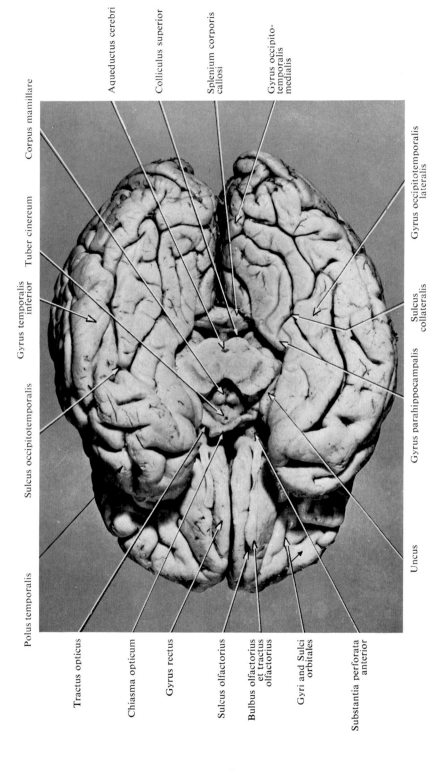

Aqueductus cerebri

Colliculus superior

Splenium corporis callosi

Gyrus occipito-temporalis medialis

Corpus mamillare

Tuber cinereum

Gyrus temporalis inferior

Sulcus occipitotemporalis

Polus temporalis

Gyrus occipitotemporalis lateralis

Sulcus collateralis

Gyrus parahippocampalis

Uncus

Tractus opticus

Chiasma opticum

Gyrus rectus

Sulcus olfactorius

Bulbus olfactorius et tractus olfactorius

Gyri and Sulci orbitales

Substantia perforata anterior

Fig. 20. Inferior aspect of the brain.

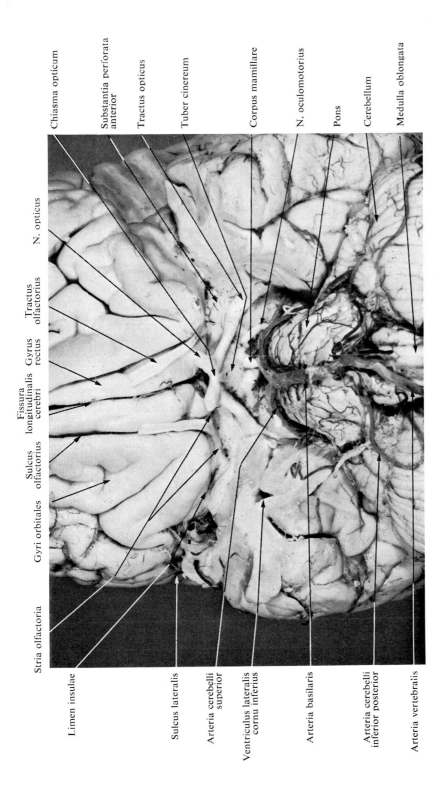

Chiasma opticum
Substantia perforata anterior
Tractus opticus
Tuber cinereum
Corpus mamillare
N. oculomotorius
Pons
Cerebellum
Medulla oblongata

N. opticus
Tractus olfactorius
Gyrus rectus
Fissura longitudinalis cerebri
Sulcus olfactorius
Gyri orbitales
Stria olfactoria

Limen insulae
Sulcus lateralis
Arteria cerebelli superior
Ventriculus lateralis cornu inferius
Arteria basilaris
Arteria cerebelli inferior posterior
Arteria vertebralis

Fig. 21. Ventral aspect of the brain, with the polus temporalis removed bilaterally.

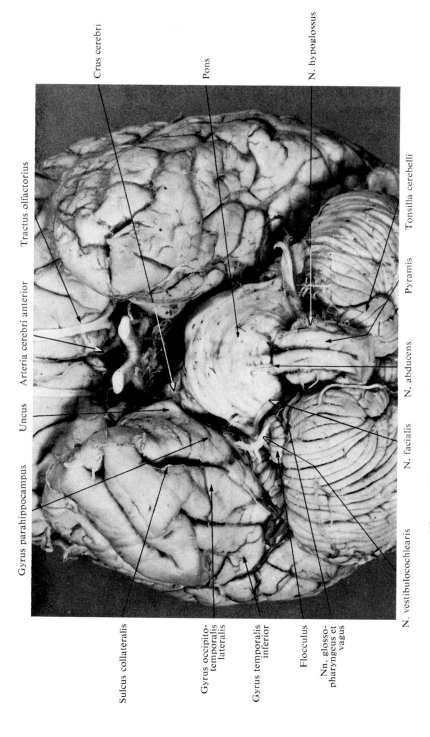

Crus cerebri

Pons

N. hypoglossus

Tractus olfactorius

Arteria cerebri anterior

Uncus

Tonsilla cerebelli

Gyrus parahippocampus

Pyramis

N. abducens

N. facialis

N. vestibulocochlearis

Sulcus collateralis

Gyrus occipito-
temporalis
lateralis

Gyrus temporalis
inferior

Flocculus

Nn. glosso-
pharyngeus et
vagus

Fig. 22. Ventral aspect of the brain stem and related structures.

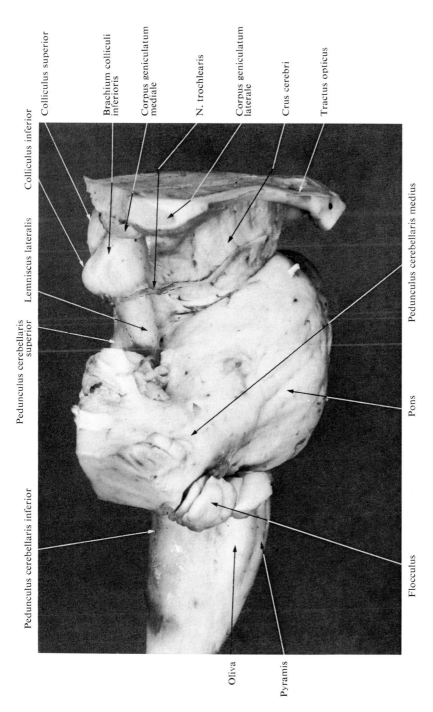

Colliculus superior

Brachium colliculi inferioris

Corpus geniculatum mediale

N. trochlearis

Corpus geniculatum laterale

Crus cerebri

Tractus opticus

Colliculus inferior

Lemniscus lateralis

Pedunculus cerebellaris superior

Pedunculus cerebellaris inferior

Pedunculus cerebellaris medius

Pons

Flocculus

Oliva

Pyramis

Fig. 23. Lateral view of the brain stem stripped of meninges and cerebellar hemisphere.

83

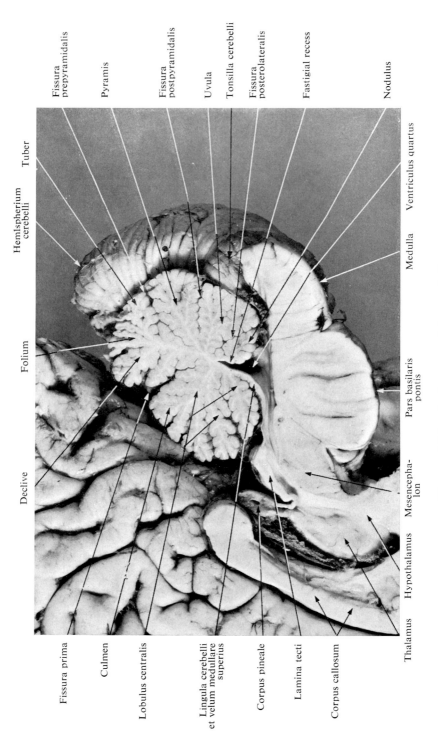

Fissura
prepyramidalis

Pyramis

Fissura
postpyramidalis

Uvula

Tonsilla cerebelli

Fissura
posterolateralis

Fastigial recess

Nodulus

Tuber

Hemlspherium
cerebelli

Ventriculus quartus

Folium

Medulla

Declive

Pars basilaris
pontis

Mesencepha-
lon

Fissura prima

Culmen

Lobulus centralis

Lingula cerebelli
et velum medullare
superius

Corpus pineale

Lamina tecti

Corpus callosum

Thalamus

Hypothalamus

Fig. 24. Midsagittal aspect of the cerebellum.

84

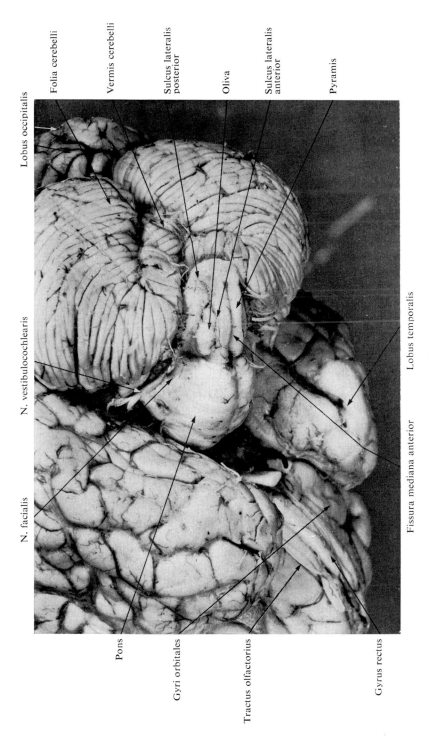

Lobus occipitalis

Folia cerebelli

Vermis cerebelli

Sulcus lateralis
posterior

Oliva

Sulcus lateralis
anterior

Pyramis

N. vestibulocochlearis

N. facialis

Pons

Gyri orbitales

Tractus olfactorius

Gyrus rectus

Fissura mediana anterior

Lobus temporalis

Fig. 25. Ventral aspect of the brain stem.

N. trigeminus

N. vestibulocochlearis

Pons

Sulcus basilaris

Oliva inferior

Fissura mediana anterior

Pyramis

Decussatio pyramidum

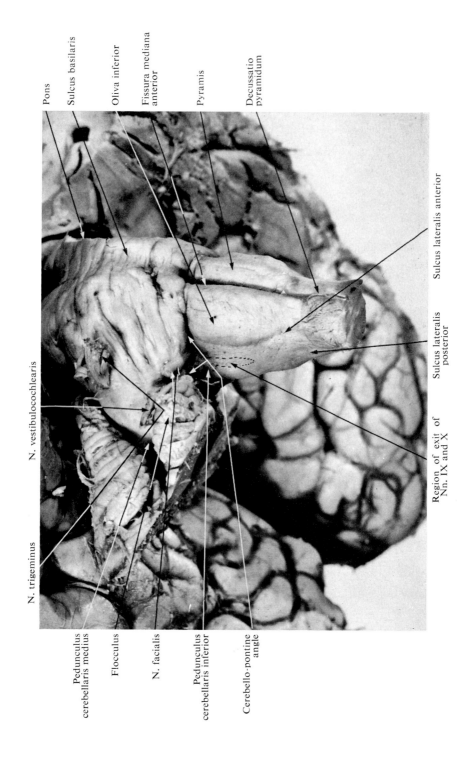

Pedunculus cerebellaris medius

Flocculus

N. facialis

Pedunculus cerebellaris inferior

Cerebello-pontine angle

Region of exit of Nn. IX and X

Sulcus lateralis posterior

Sulcus lateralis anterior

Fig. 26. Ventro-lateral aspect of the medulla oblongata and pons.

86

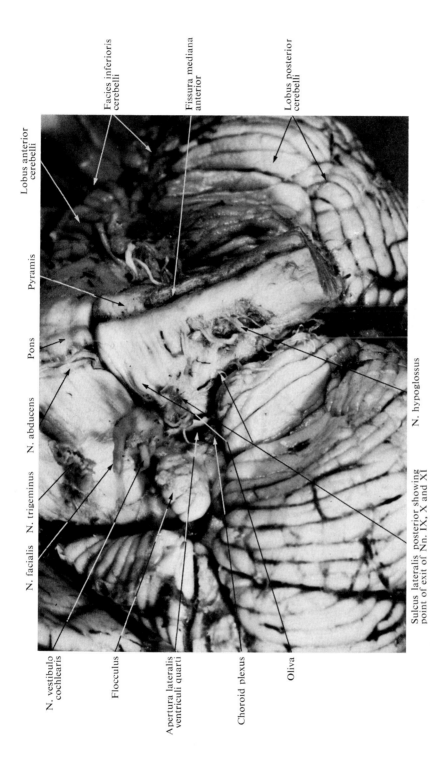

Lobus anterior cerebelli

Facies inferioris cerebelli

Fissura mediana anterior

Lobus posterior cerebelli

N. facialis   N. trigeminus   N. abducens   Pons   Pyramis

N. vestibulo cochlearis

Flocculus

Apertura lateralis ventriculi quarti

Choroid plexus

Oliva

Sulcus lateralis posterior showing point of exit of Nn. IX, X and XI

N. hypoglossus

Fig. 27. Ventro-lateral aspect of the medulla.

87

N. hypoglossus

Fissura mediana anterior

Pyramis

Oliva

Fibrae arcuatae externae

Flocculus

Apertura
lateralis ventriculi
quarti

N. glosso-
pharyngeus

N. vagus

Pedunculus cerebellaris inferior

N. accessorius

Fig. 28. Ventro-lateral aspect of the medulla.

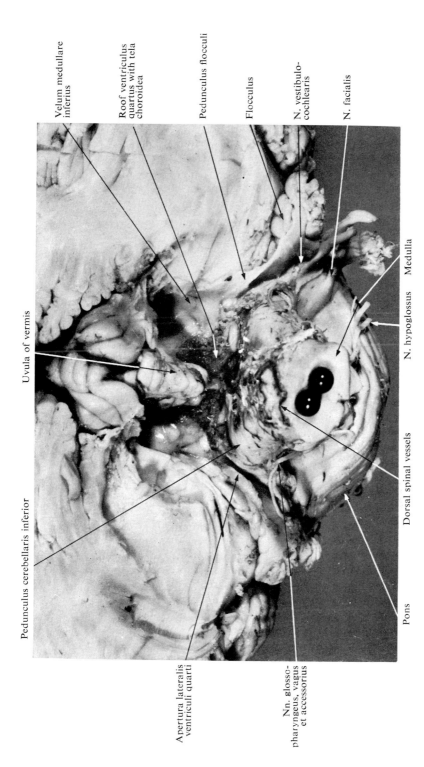

Velum medullare inferius

Roof ventriculus quartus with tela choroidea

Pedunculus flocculi

Flocculus

N. vestibulo-cochlearis

N. facialis

Uvula of vermis

Pedunculus cerebellaris inferior

Apertura lateralis ventriculi quarti

Nn. glosso-pharyngeus, vagus et accessorius

Medulla

N. hypoglossus

Dorsal spinal vessels

Pons

Fig. 29. Postero-caudal aspect of the medulla.

89

Sulcus medianus

Colliculus facialis

Area vestibularis

Tuberculum nuclei gracilis

Sulcus intermedius posterior

Fasciculus gracilis

Fasciculus cuneatus

Sulcus limitans

Velum medullare anterior

Fovea superior

Stria medullaris

Fovea inferior

Tuberculum nuclei cuneati

Obex

Trigeminal eminence

Sulcus medianus posterior

Fig. 30. Posterior aspect of the medulla oblongata.

90

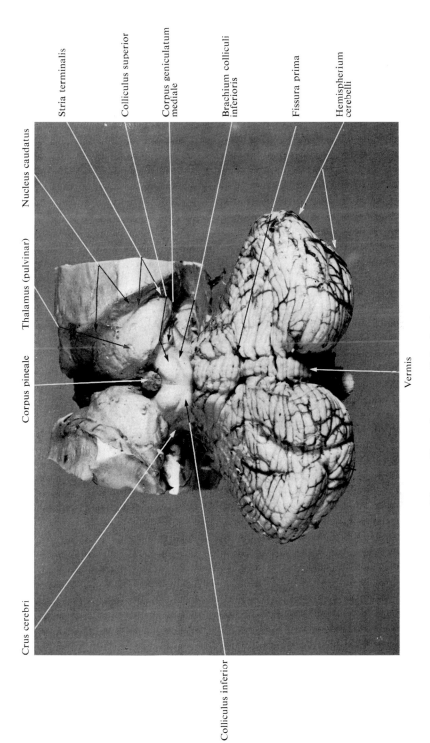

Stria terminalis

Colliculus superior

Corpus geniculatum mediale

Brachium colliculi inferioris

Fissura prima

Hemispherium cerebelli

Nucleus caudatus

Thalamus (pulvinar)

Corpus pineale

Crus cerebri

Colliculus inferior

Vermis

Fig. 31. Dorsal aspect of the brain stem.

91

Colliculus inferior   Thalamus (pulvinar)   Trigonum habenulae   Corpus pineale   ' Colliculus superior

Corpus geniculatum mediale

Crus cerebri

Pedunculus cerebellaris superior

Nucleus dentatus

Laminae albae

Cortex cerebelli

Velum medullare superius

Fossa rhomboidea

Velum medullare inferius

Vermis

Tonsilla cerebelli

Fig. 32. Dorsal aspect of the brain stem with exposing ventriculus quartus.

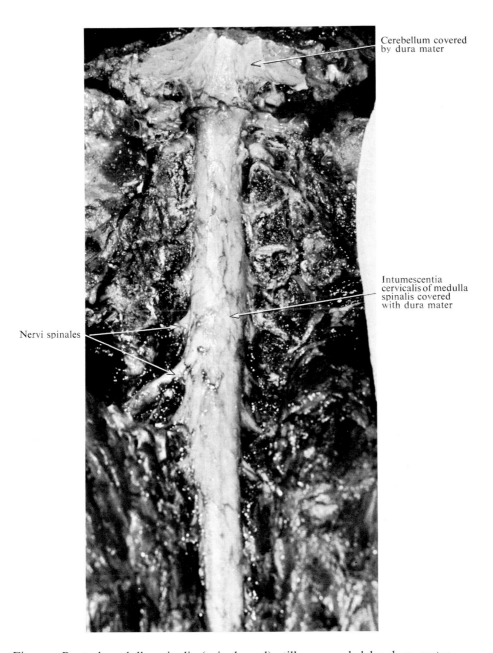

Cerebellum covered
by dura mater

Intumescentia
cervicalis of medulla
spinalis covered
with dura mater

Nervi spinales

Fig. 33. Rostral medulla spinalis (spinal cord) still surrounded by dura mater.
Note that the dorsal vessels of the cord may be seen through the dura.

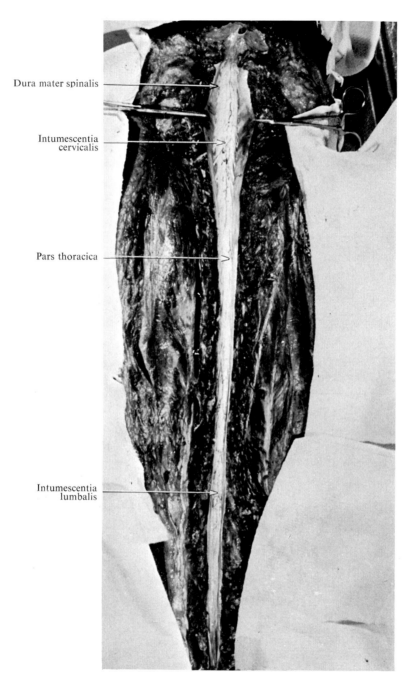

Dura mater spinalis

Intumescentia
cervicalis

Pars thoracica

Intumescentia
lumbalis

Fig. 34. Complete exposure of the medulla spinalis with the dura mater reflected.

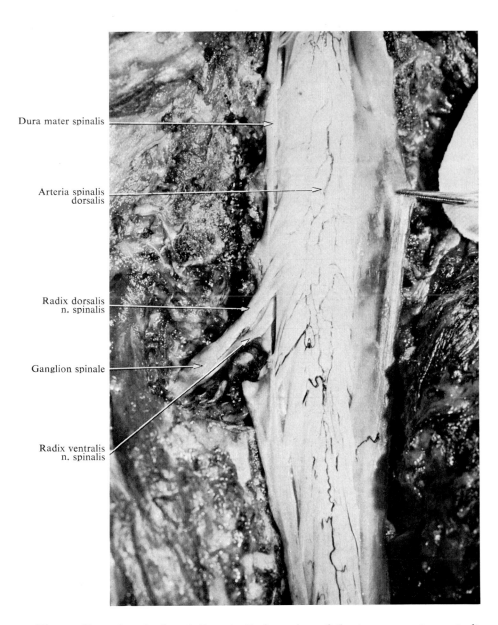

Dura mater spinalis

Arteria spinalis
dorsalis

Radix dorsalis
n. spinalis

Ganglion spinale

Radix ventralis
n. spinalis

Fig. 35. Rostral end of medulla spinalis in region of the *intumescentia cervicalis* with one pair of spinal radices dissected out to the ganglion spinale.

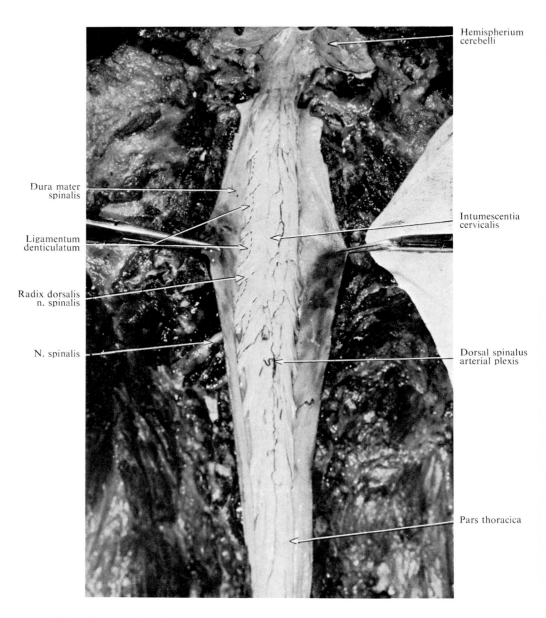

Fig. 36. Rostral end of medulla spinalis with dissection to demonstrate the *liga-mentum denticulatum*.

96

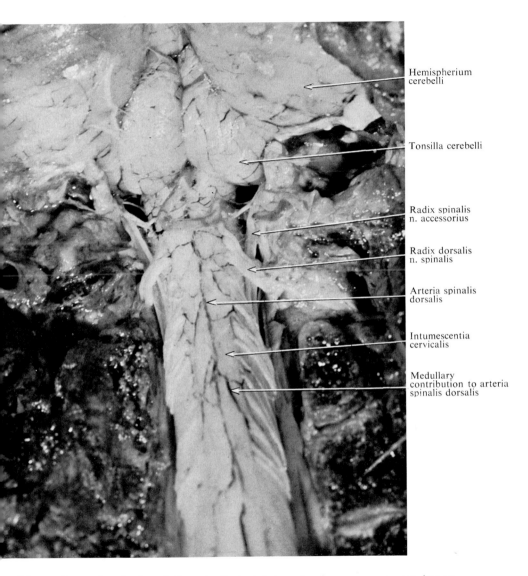

Hemispherium
cerebelli

Tonsilla cerebelli

Radix spinalis
n. accessorius

Radix dorsalis
n. spinalis

Arteria spinalis
dorsalis

Intumescentia
cervicalis

Medullary
contribution to arteria
spinalis dorsalis

Fig. 37. Rostral end of medulla spinalis just below the foramen magnum demonstrating the course of the *radix spinalis n. accessorius.*

Conus medullaris

Filum terminale

Intumescentia
lumbalis

Cauda equina

SECTION III

Vessels

This group of photographs (Figs. 39–51) depicts the major arteries and veins of the brain. Additional views of most of these structures may be seen in Section I and IV. In some cases the vessels are presented as they would be seen on the fixed brain, while in others the structures around the vessels have been dissected away to provide for a more unobstructed view. In some instances, this has been done on the unfixed brain, immediately after removal at autopsy.

Arteria cerebri media

Arteria choroidea anterior

Crus cerebri

Arteria cerebri posterior

Arteria cerebelli superior

Tractus opticus

Arteria cerebri anterior

Arteria communicans anterior

Arteria carotis interna

Tuber cinereum

Arteria communicans posterior

Distal mesencephalic arteries

Pons

Arteria basilaris

Fig. 39. The circle of Willis.

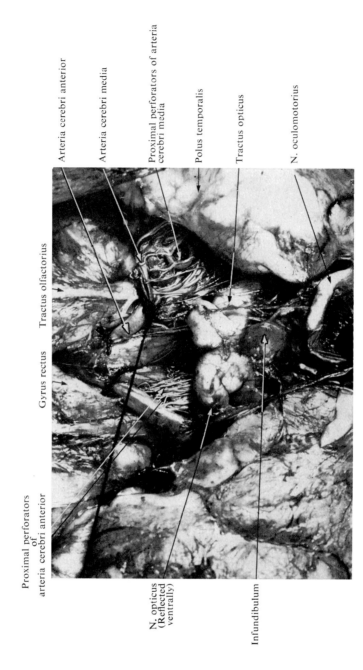

Proximal perforators
of
arteria cerebri anterior

Gyrus rectus

Tractus olfactorius

Arteria cerebri anterior

Arteria cerebri media

Proximal perforators of arteria
cerebri media

Polus temporalis

Tractus opticus

N. oculomotorius

N. opticus
(Reflected
ventrally)

Infundibulum

Fig. 40. Ventral aspect of the diencephalon.

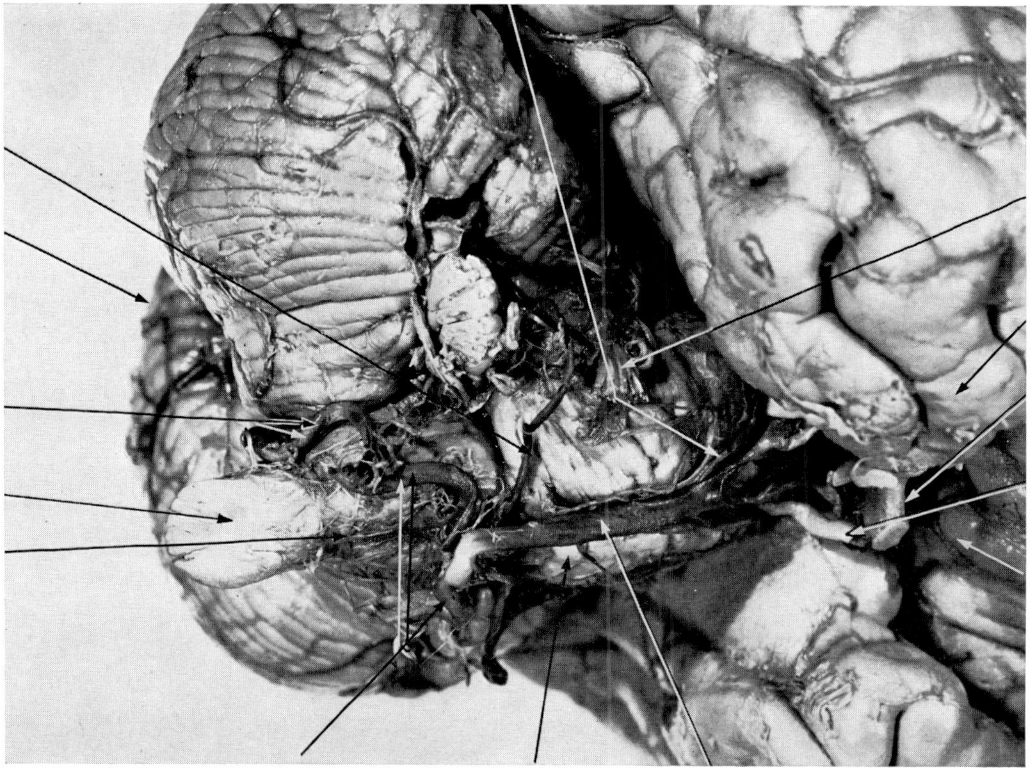

N. trigeminus

Polus temporalis

N. opticus

N. oculomotorius

Orbital surface lobus
frontalis

Arteria cerebelli superior

Arteria basilaris

Pons

Arteria cerebelli
inferior anterior

Cerebellum

Arteria cerebelli
inferior posterior

Medulla oblongata

Arteria spinalis
anterior

Arteriae vertebrales

Fig. 41. Ventral aspect of the brain.

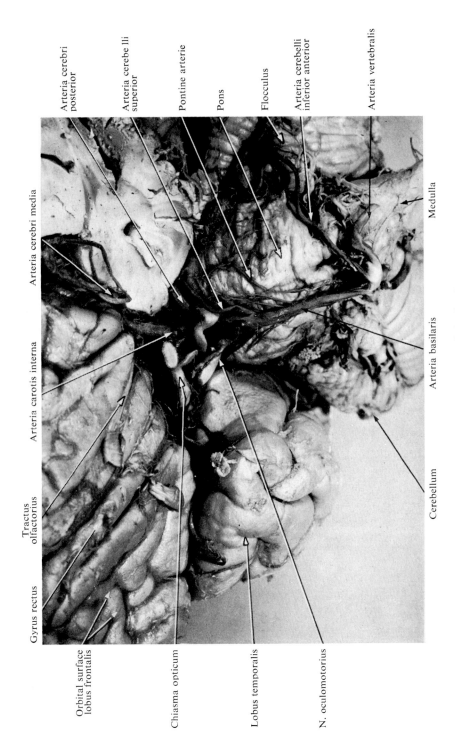

Arteria cerebri posterior

Arteria cerebe lli superior

Pontine arterie

Pons

Flocculus

Arteria cerebelli inferior anterior

Arteria vertebralis

Arteria cerebri media

Medulla

Arteria carotis interna

Tractus olfactorius

Gyrus rectus

Arteria basilaris

Cerebellum

Orbital surface lobus frontalis

Chiasma opticum

Lobus temporalis

N. oculomotorius

Fig. 42. Ventral aspect of the brain.

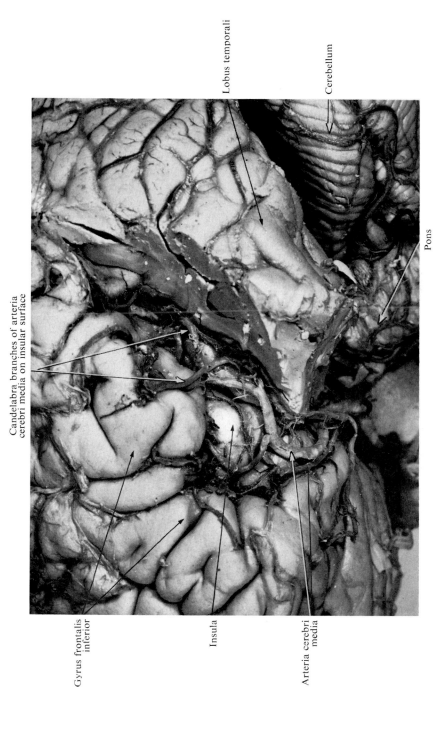

Candelabra branches of arteria
cerebri media on insular surface

Lobus temporali

Cerebellum

Pons

Gyrus frontalis
inferior

Insula

Arteria cerebri
media

Fig. 43. Lateral aspect showing candelabra branches of arteria cerebri media on the insular cortex following removal of much of the operculum.

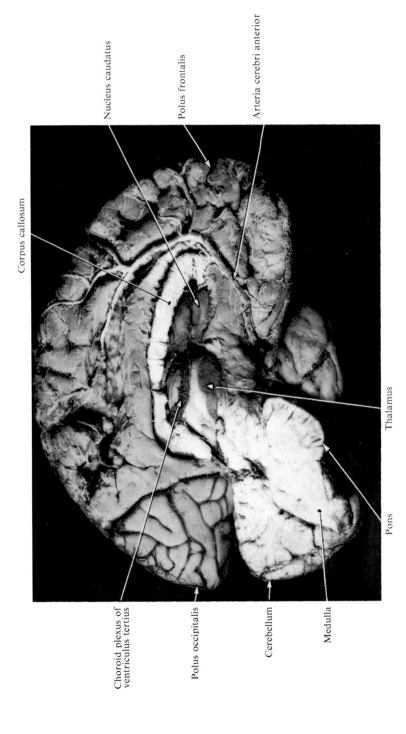

Nucleus caudatus

Polus frontalis

Arteria cerebri anterior

Corpus callosum

Choroid plexus of
ventriculus tertius

Polus occipitalis

Cerebellum

Medulla

Pons

Thalamus

Fig. 44. Midsagittal surface illustrating the branches of arteria cerebri anterior.

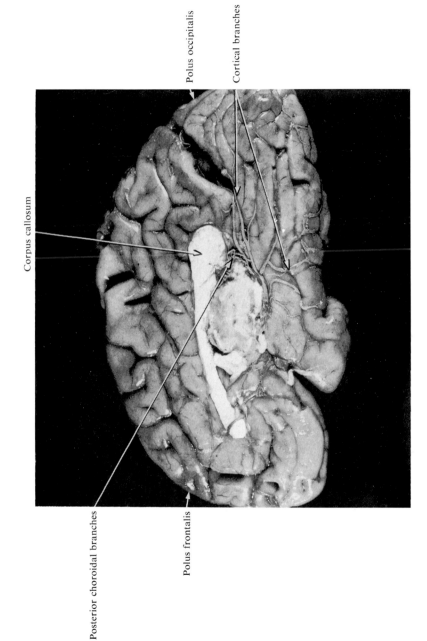

Corpus callosum

Polus occipitalis

Cortical branches

Posterior choroidal branches

Polus frontalis

Fig. 45. Midsagittal surface illustrating the branches of arteria cerebri posterior.

107

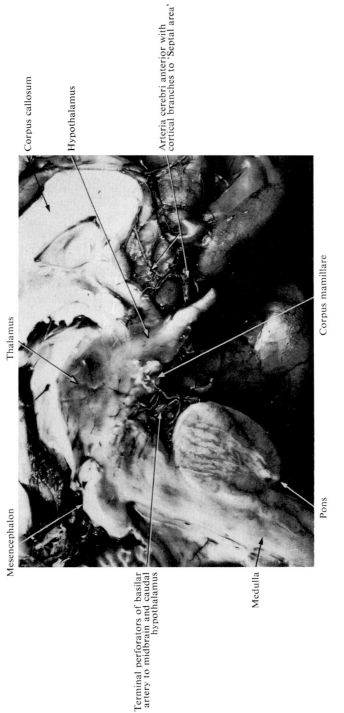

Corpus callosum

Hypothalamus

Arteria cerebri anterior with
cortical branches to 'Septal area'

Thalamus

Corpus mamillare

Mesencephalon

Pons

Terminal perforators of basilar
artery to midbrain and caudal
hypothalamus

Medulla

Fig. 46. Basilar and anterior cerebral arteries.

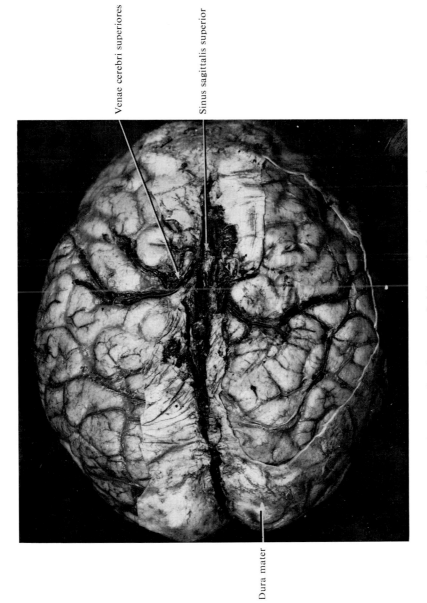

Venae cerebri superiores

Sinus sagittalis superior

Dura mater

Fig. 47. Dorsal aspect showing superficial cortical venous drainage.

Nucleus caudatus

Vena subependymalis

Thalamus

Vena choroidea

Vena cerebri magna (Galen)

Vena septi pellucidi

Vena thalamostriata

Vena cerebri interna

Vena basalis

Vena occipitalis

Cerebellum

Fig. 48. Dissection of deep venous system.

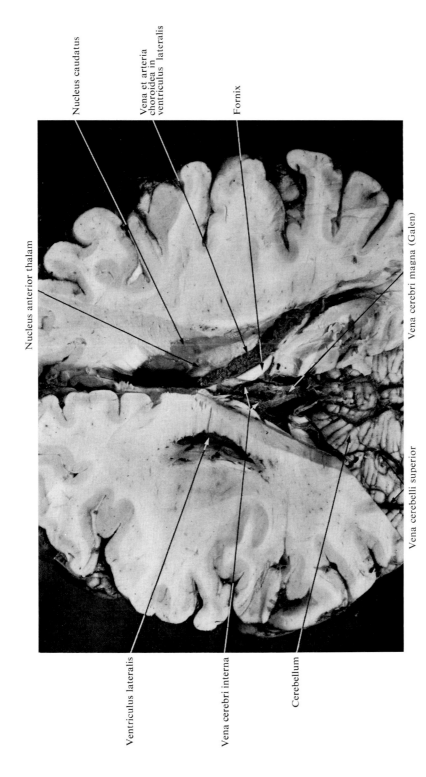

Nucleus caudatus

Vena et arteria
choroidea in
ventriculus lateralis

Fornix

Nucleus anterior thalam

Vena cerebri magna (Galen)

Vena cerebelli superior

Ventriculus lateralis

Vena cerebri interna

Cerebellum

Fig. 49. Dorsal aspect of deep venous system I.

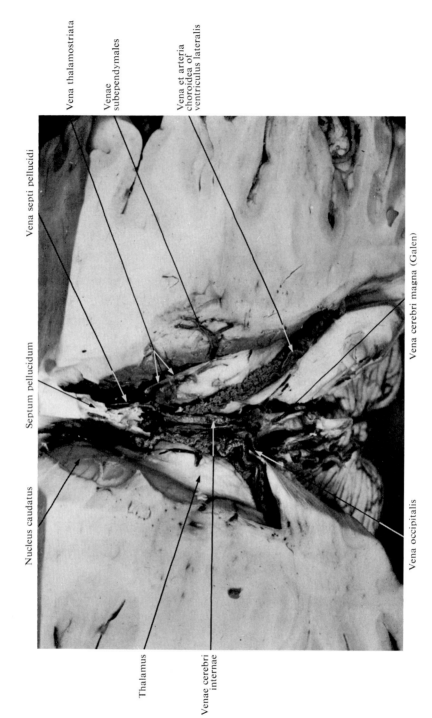

Vena thalamostriata

Venae subependymales

Vena et arteria choroidea of ventriculus lateralis

Vena septi pellucidi

Septum pellucidum

Nucleus caudatus

Thalamus

Venae cerebri internae

Vena cerebri magna (Galen)

Vena occipitalis

Fig. 50. Dorsal aspect of deep venous system II.

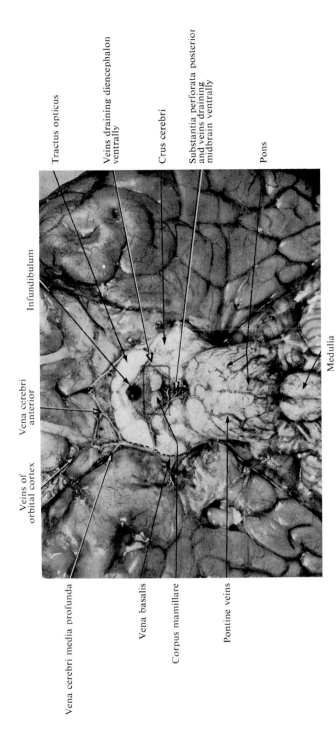

Tractus opticus

Veins draining diencephalon ventrally

Crus cerebri

Substantia perforata posterior and veins draining midbrain ventrally

Pons

Infundibulum

Vena cerebri anterior

Veins of orbital cortex

Medulla

Vena cerebri media profunda

Vena basalis

Corpus mamillare

Pontine veins

Fig. 51. Basal venous system.

SECTION IV

Dissection

Several rather informative dissections may be done on the formalin-fixed brain. This is due, in part certainly, to the rather elastic quality given to the nerve fibers by such fixation. Furthermore, when fiber bundles run at different angles to each other, there is some tendency to form cleavage planes at these points. In addition, the grey matter, or other nuclear regions may be scraped away from the white matter due to the rather different textures of cellular and fibrous areas. Thus, one can start at the lateral surface (Fig. 52) and dissect away the operculum covering the insula, remove the insular cortex and claustrum to view the external capsule (Fig. 56) and so on, and demonstrate the long and short association bundles of the cerebral hemispheres, the commissural bundles and projection fiber systems. After removing all the cortex and superficial fiber groups of the telencephalon, the ventricular cavities may be opened up and examined as a final step in this dissection (Figs. 60–62). Similar dissections may also be done on the brain stem to demonstrate particular tract fiber systems.

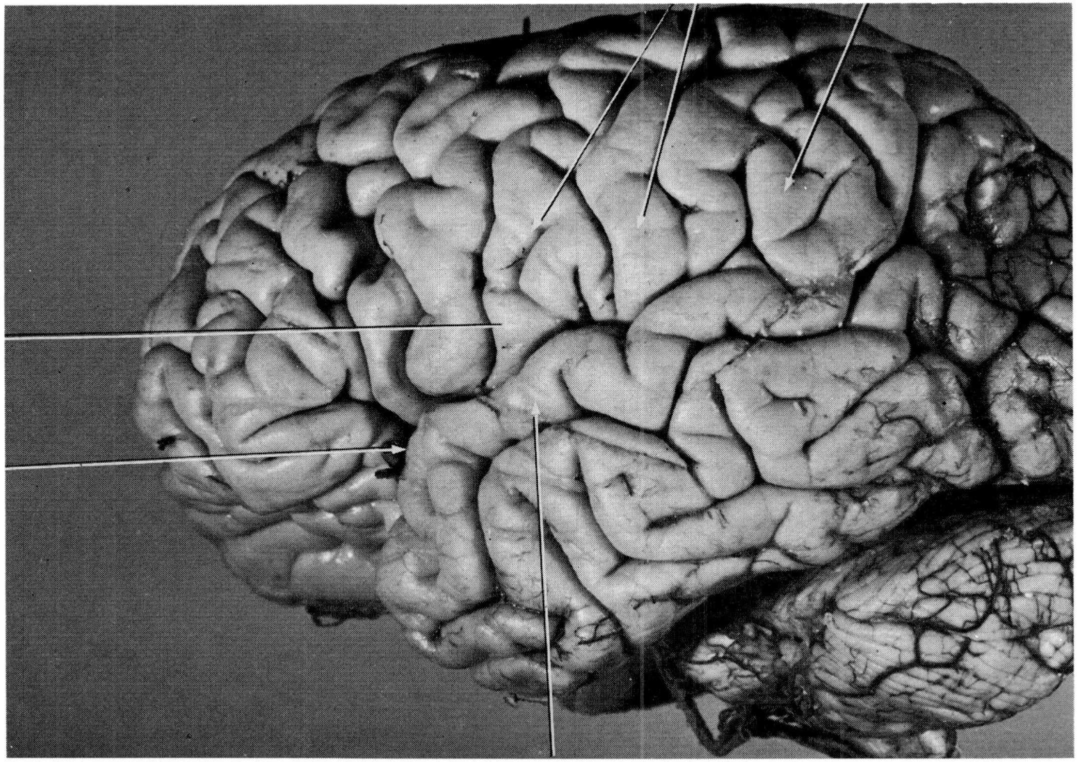

Operculum fronto-parietale (gyrus precentralis, postcentralis et supramarginalis)

Operculum temporale (gyrus temporalis superior)

Operculum frontale (Gyrus frontalis inferior)

Sulcus lateralis

Fig. 52. Frontal-parietal-temporal operculum.

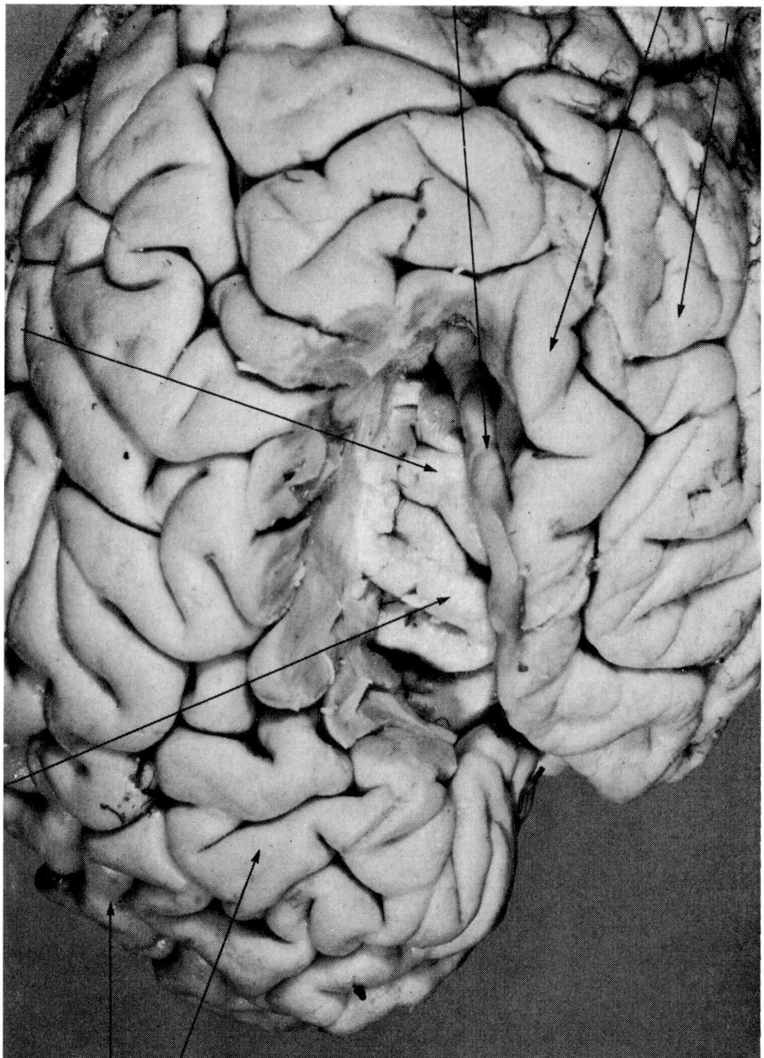

Gyri temporales transversi

Gyrus temporalis superior et medius

Gyrus longus insulae

Gyri breves insulae

Gyrus frontalis superior et medius

Fig. 53. Lateral exposure of insula I.

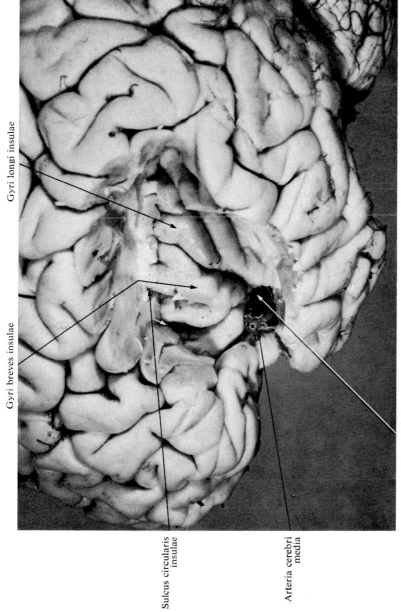

Gyri longi insulae

Gyri breves insulae

Sulcus circularis
insulae

Arteria cerebri
media

Limen insulae

Fig. 54. Lateral exposure of insula II.

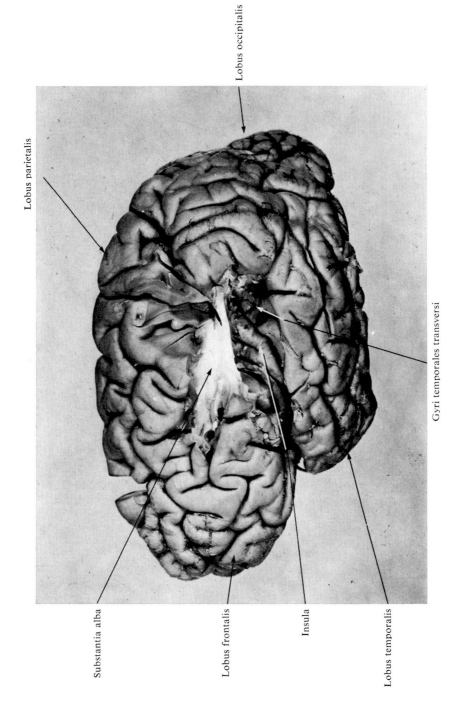

Lobus occipitalis

Lobus parietalis

Gyri temporales transversi

Substantia alba

Lobus frontalis

Insula

Lobus temporalis

Fig. 55. Lateral aspect showing first step in dissection of the deep association bundles of the forebrain.

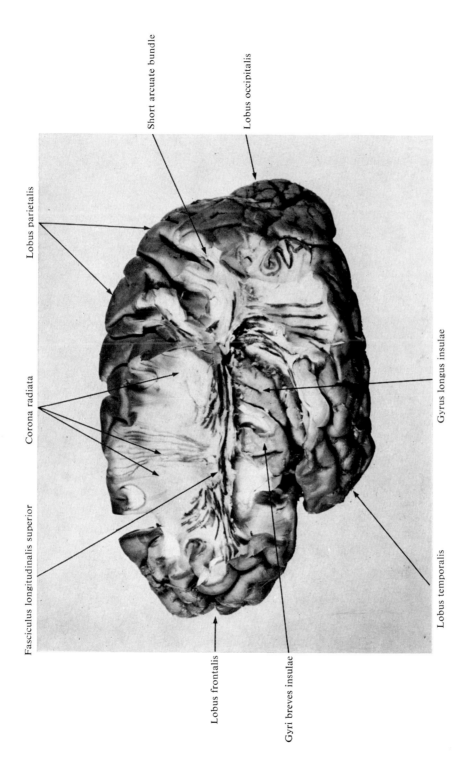

Short arcuate bundle

Lobus occipitalis

Lobus parietalis

Corona radiata

Fasciculus longitudinalis superior

Gyrus longus insulae

Lobus temporalis

Lobus frontalis

Gyri breves insulae

Fig. 56. Lateral aspect of the dissected hemisphere illustrating some of the long and short association bundles.

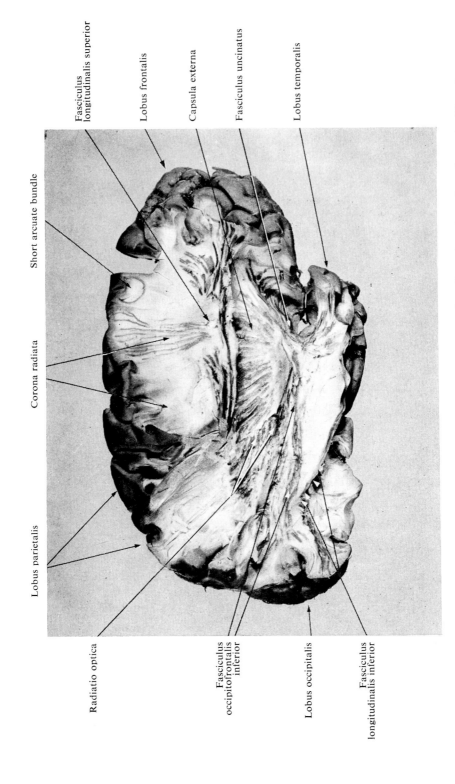

Fasciculus longitudinalis superior

Lobus frontalis

Capsula externa

Fasciculus uncinatus

Lobus temporalis

Short arcuate bundle

Corona radiata

Lobus parietalis

Radiatio optica

Fasciculus occipitofrontalis inferior

Lobus occipitalis

Fasciculus longitudinalis inferior

Fig. 57. Lateral aspect of the hemisphere illustrating a more extensive dissection than that shown in Fig. 56.

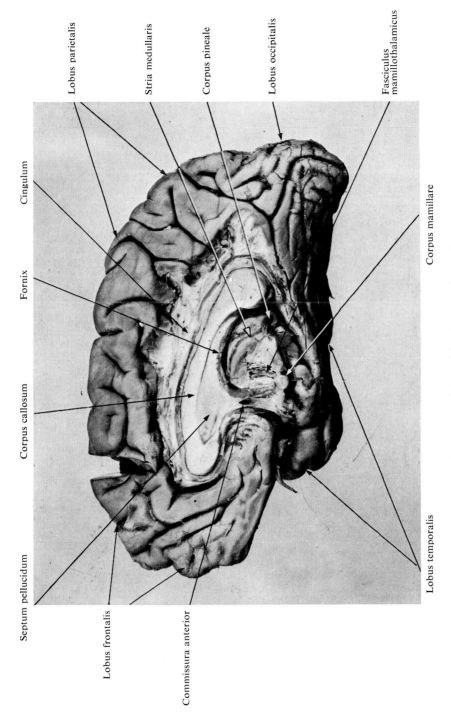

Lobus parietalis

Stria medullaris

Corpus pineale

Lobus occipitalis

Fasciculus
mamillothalamicus

Cingulum

Corpus mamillare

Fornix

Corpus callosum

Septum pellucidum

Lobus frontalis

Commissura anterior

Lobus temporalis

Fig. 58. Dissection of the midsagittal surface of the brain.

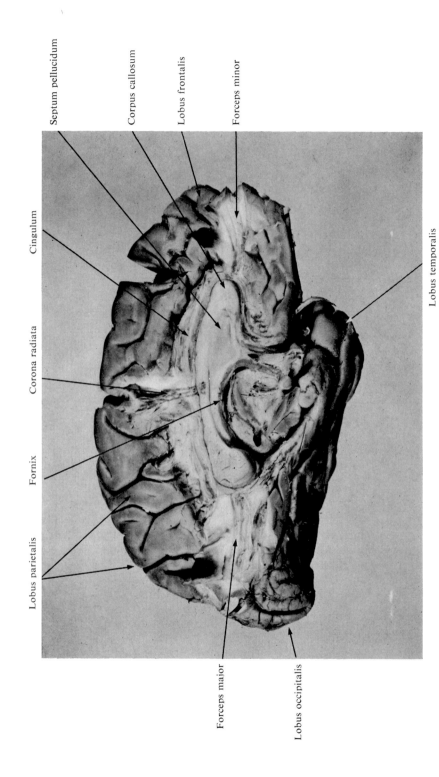

Septum pellucidum

Corpus callosum

Lobus frontalis

Forceps minor

Cingulum

Corona radiata

Fornix

Lobus parietalis

Lobus temporalis

Forceps major

Lobus occipitalis

Fig. 59. Second phase of dissection of the midsagittal surface of the brain illustrating the forceps major and minor.

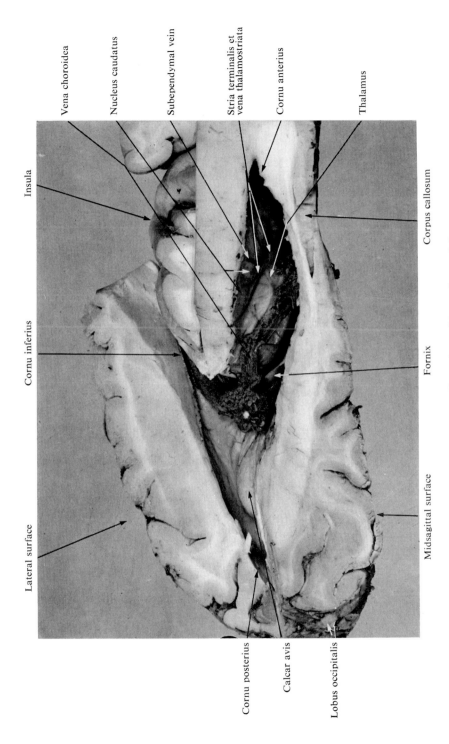

Vena choroidea

Nucleus caudatus

Subependymal vein

Stria terminalis et
vena thalamostriata

Cornu anterius

Thalamus

Insula

Corpus callosum

Cornu inferius

Fornix

Lateral surface

Midsagittal surface

Cornu posterius

Calcar avis

Lobus occipitalis

Fig. 60. Dorsal aspect, dissection of lateral ventricle.

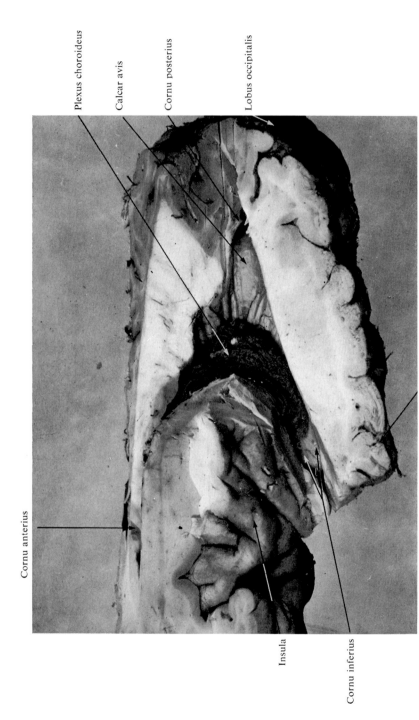

Plexus choroideus

Calcar avis

Cornu posterius

Lobus occipitalis

Cornu anterius

Lobus temporalis

Insula

Cornu inferius

Fig. 61. Dissection of lateral ventricle, lateral aspect.

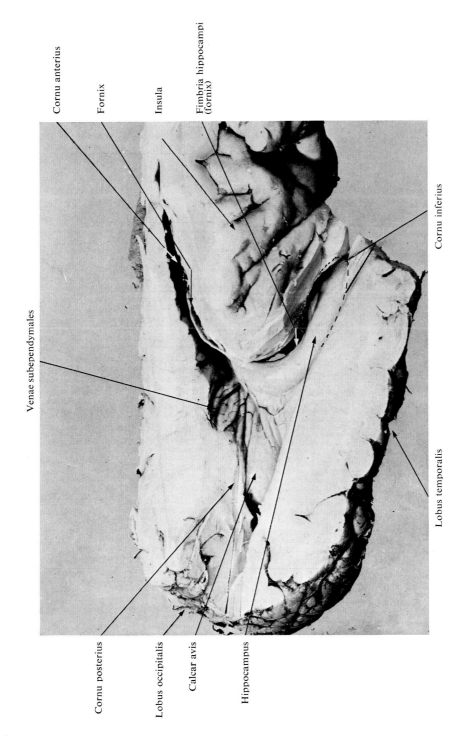

Cornu anterius

Fornix

Insula

Fimbria hippocampi (fornix)

Venae subependymales

Cornu inferius

Lobus temporalis

Cornu posterius

Lobus occipitalis

Calcar avis

Hippocampus

Fig. 62. Dissection of lateral ventricle, lateral aspect. The choroid plexus has been removed.

SECTION V

The Sectional Anatomy of the Gross Brain

Two different brains have been sectioned in the coronal plane and arranged in a mixed series starting at the rostral end (Figs. 63–72). This group is followed by a series cut in a plane parallel to the optic tracts (Figs. 73–76). This series is particularly good for appreciating the relationships of the lateral and third ventricles. The next six sections in the series constitute a parasagittal study, commencing laterally and progressing medially (Figs. 77–82). The last sections represent a series cut in the coronal plane through the brain stem (Figs. 83–88). A thorough knowledge of the structures seen in the three planes of section should facilitate the subsequent identification of structures seen in a standard series of brain-stem sections stained for myelin (Pal–Weigert series). An understanding of structures of the brain and their relation to each other in these three planes of section, learned in conjunction with the study of the gross surface morphology, should aid the student in developing a three dimensional concept of the brain.

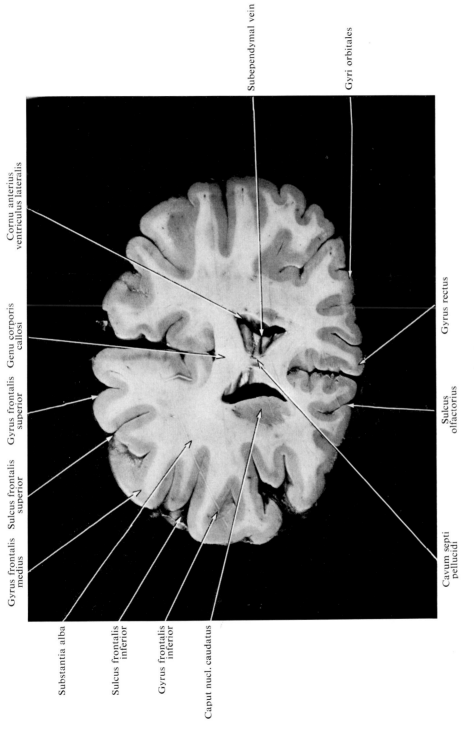

Cornu anterius
ventriculus lateralis

Genu corporis
callosi

Gyrus frontalis
superior

Sulcus frontalis
superior

Gyrus frontalis
medius

Substantia alba

Sulcus frontalis
inferior

Gyrus frontalis
inferior

Caput nucl. caudatus

Subependymal vein

Gyri orbitales

Gyrus rectus

Sulcus
olfactorius

Cavum septi
pellucidi

Fig. 63.

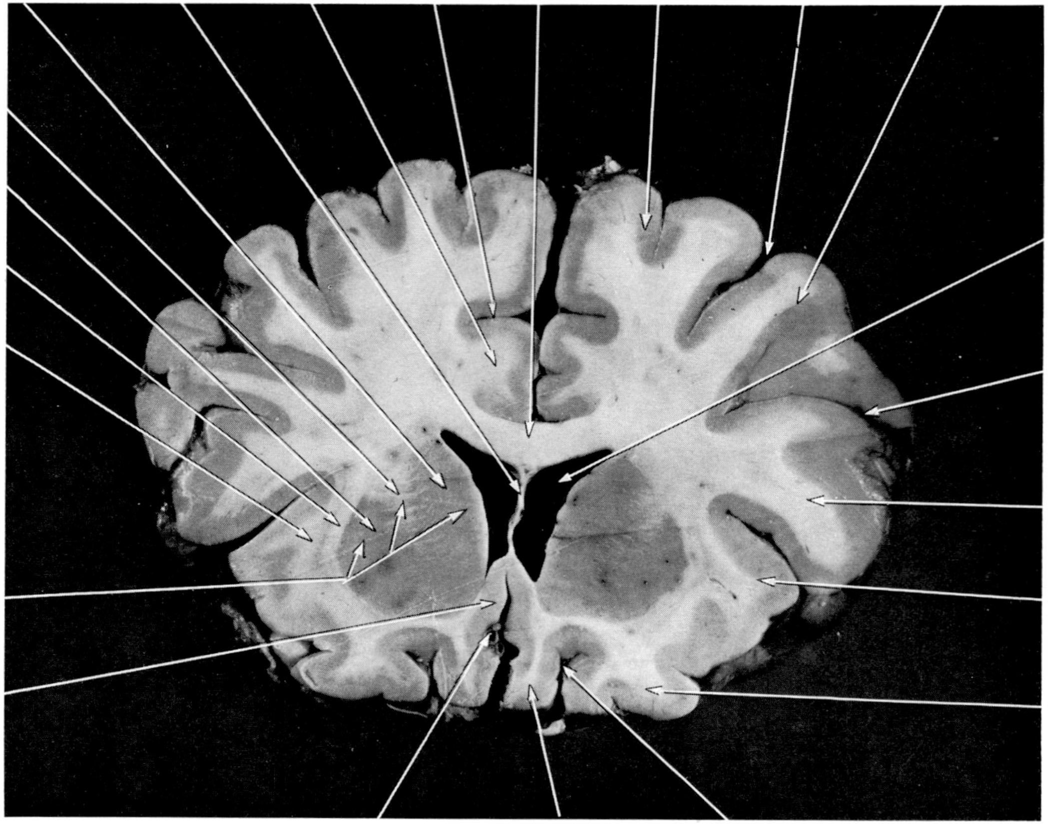

Fig. 64.

Gyrus frontalis medius

Sulcus frontalis superior

Gyrus frontalis superior

Genu corporis callosi

Sulcus cinguli

Gyrus cinguli

Septum pelluci-dum

Caput nucl. caudatus

Cornu anterius ventr. lat.

Sulcus frontalis inferior

Gyrus frontalis inferior

Insula, gyri breves

Gyri orbitales

Sulcus olfactorius

Gyrus rectus

Arteria cerebri anterior

Capsula interna

Putamen

Capsula externa

Capsula extrema

Corpus striatum

Area subcallosa

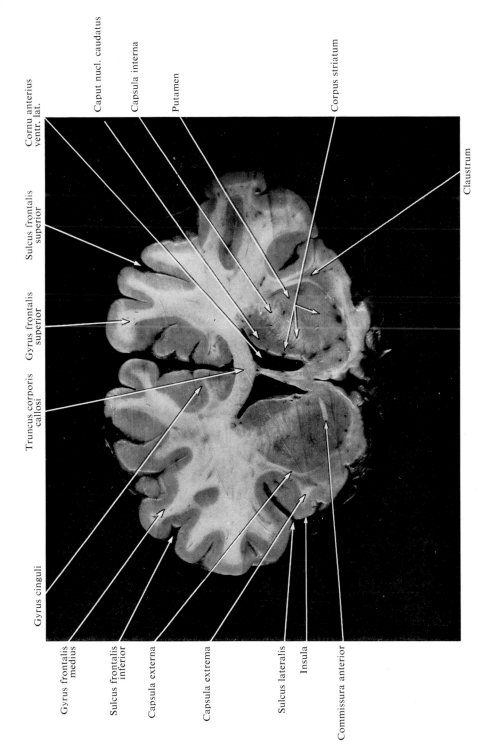

Cornu anterius
ventr. lat.

Caput nucl. caudatus

Capsula interna

Putamen

Corpus striatum

Claustrum

Sulcus frontalis
superior

Gyrus frontalis
superior

Truncus corporis
callosi

Gyrus cinguli

Gyrus frontalis
medius

Sulcus frontalis
inferior

Capsula externa

Capsula extrema

Sulcus lateralis

Insula

Commissura anterior

Fig. 65.

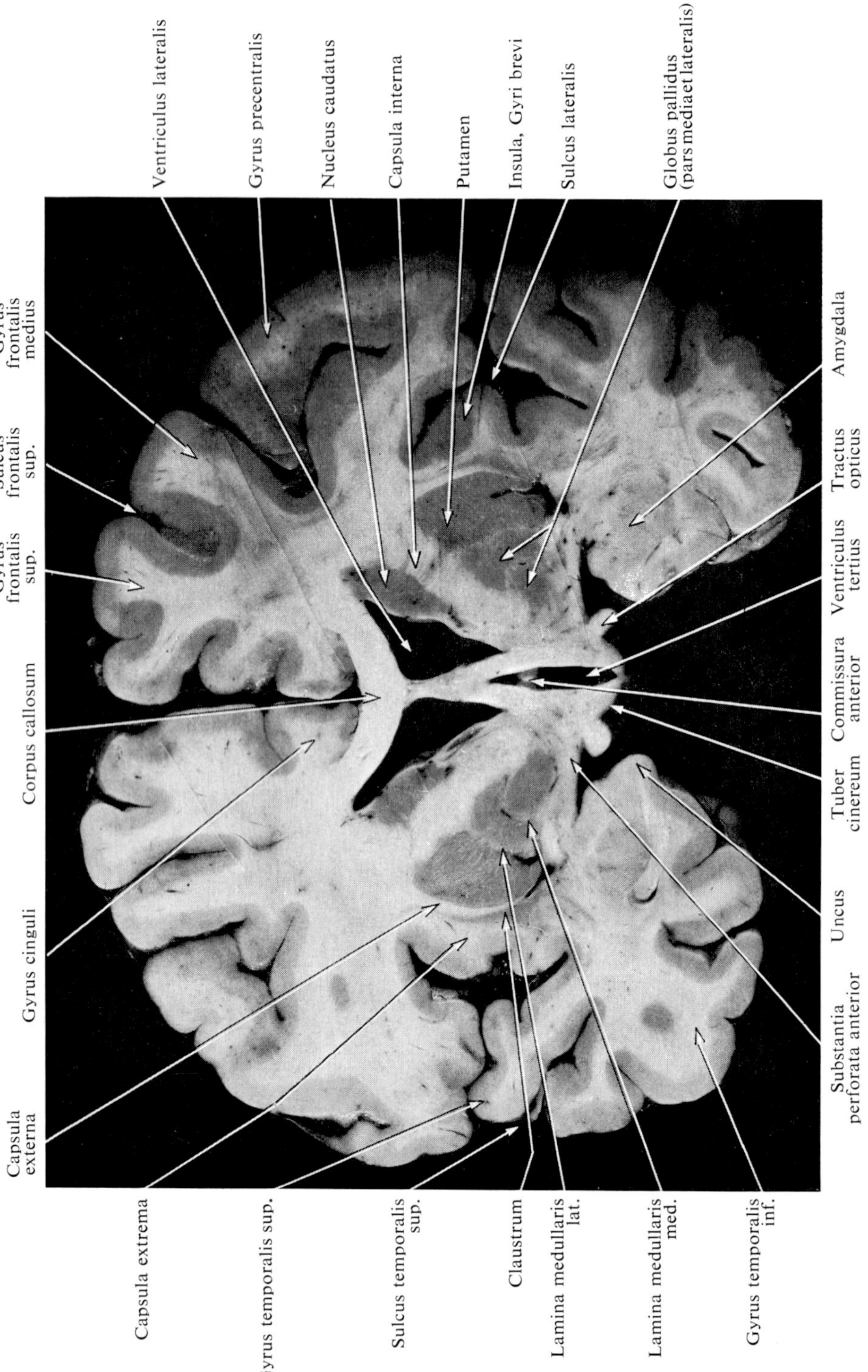

Ventriculus lateralis

Gyrus precentralis

Nucleus caudatus

Capsula interna

Putamen

Insula, Gyri brevi

Sulcus lateralis

Globus pallidus
(pars mediae et lateralis)

Gyrus
frontalis
medius

Sulcus
frontalis
sup.

Gyrus
frontalis
sup.

Corpus callosum

Gyrus cinguli

Capsula
externa

Capsula extrema

Gyrus temporalis sup.

Sulcus temporalis sup.

Claustrum

Lamina medullaris
lat.

Lamina medullaris
med.

Gyrus temporalis
inf.

Substantia
perforata anterior

Uncus

Tuber
cinereum

Commissura
anterior

Ventriculus
tertius

Tractus
opticus

Amygdala

Fig. 66.

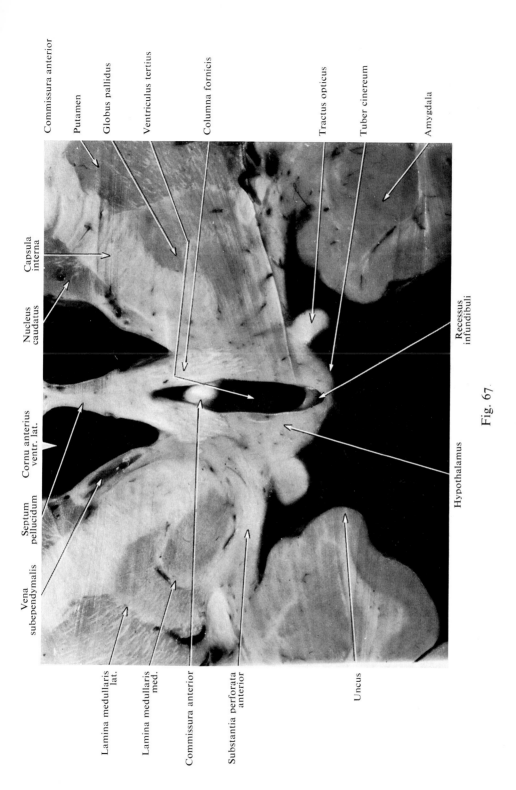

Commissura anterior

Putamen

Globus pallidus

Ventriculus tertius

Columna fornicis

Tractus opticus

Tuber cinereum

Amygdala

Capsula interna

Nucleus caudatus

Cornu anterius ventr. lat.

Septum pellucidum

Vena subependymalis

Recessus infundibuli

Hypothalamus

Lamina medullaris lat.

Lamina medullaris med.

Commissura anterior

Substantia perforata anterior

Uncus

Fig. 67

135

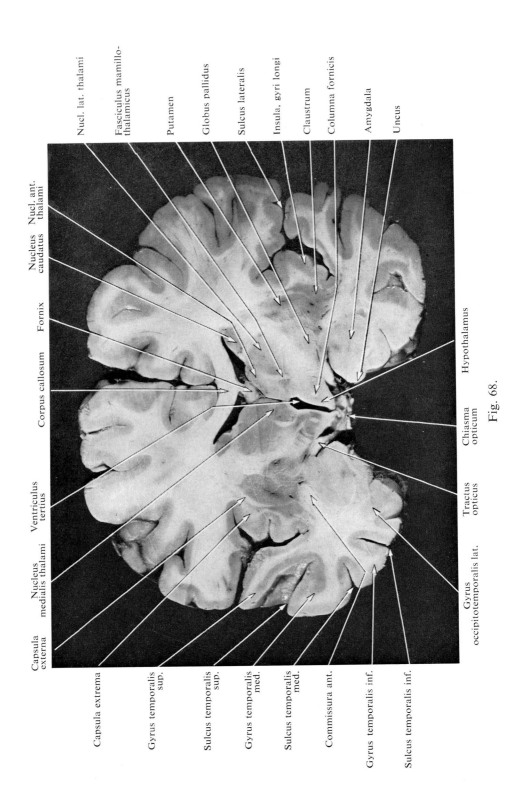

Nucl. lat. thalami

Fasciculus mamillo-thalamicus

Putamen

Globus pallidus

Sulcus lateralis

Insula, gyri longi

Claustrum

Columna fornicis

Amygdala

Uncus

Nucl. ant. thalami

Nucleus caudatus

Fornix

Corpus callosum

Ventriculus tertius

Nucleus medialis thalami

Capsula externa

Capsula extrema

Gyrus temporalis sup.

Sulcus temporalis sup.

Gyrus temporalis med.

Sulcus temporalis med.

Commissura ant.

Gyrus temporalis inf.

Sulcus temporalis inf.

Gyrus occipitotemporalis lat.

Tractus opticus

Chiasma opticum

Hypothalamus

Fig. 68.

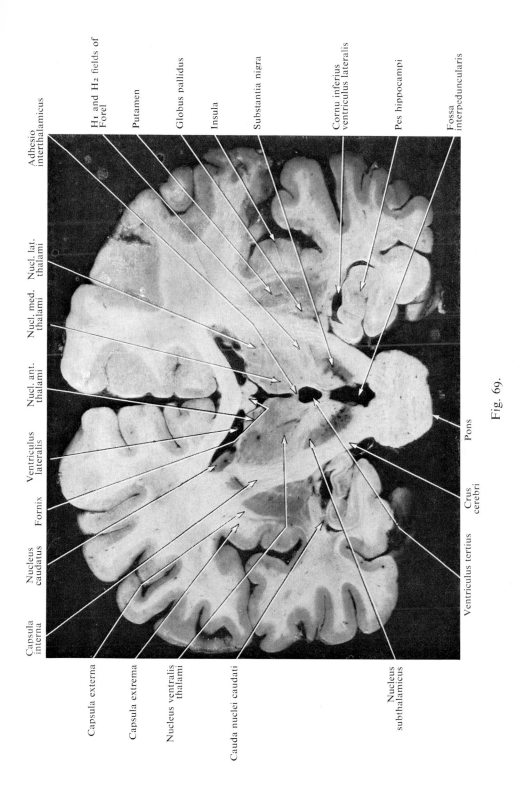

Adhesio interthalamicus

H1 and H2 fields of Forel

Putamen

Globus pallidus

Insula

Substantia nigra

Cornu inferius ventriculus lateralis

Pes hippocampi

Fossa interpeduncularis

Nucl. lat. thalami

Nucl. med. thalami

Nucl. ant. thalami

Ventriculus lateralis

Fornix

Nucleus caudatus

Capsula interna

Capsula externa

Capsula extrema

Nucleus ventralis thalami

Cauda nuclei caudati

Nucleus subthalamicus

Ventriculus tertius

Crus cerebri

Pons

Fig. 69.

137

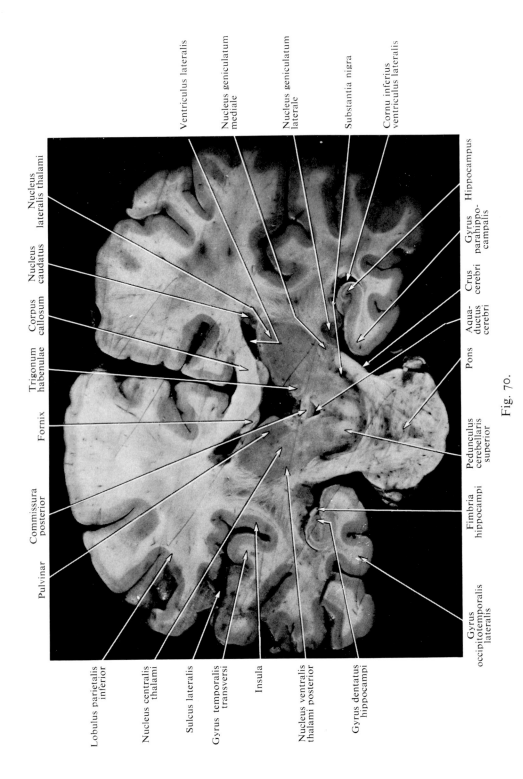

Ventriculus lateralis

Nucleus geniculatum mediale

Nucleus geniculatum laterale

Substantia nigra

Cornu inferius ventriculus lateralis

Nucleus lateralis thalami

Nucleus caudatus

Corpus callosum

Trigonum habenulae

Fornix

Commissura posterior

Pulvinar

Hippocampus

Gyrus parahippo-campalis

Crus cerebri

Aqua-ductus cerebri

Pons

Pedunculus cerebellaris superior

Fimbria hippocampi

Gyrus occipitotemporalis lateralis

Lobulus parietalis inferior

Nucleus centralis thalami

Sulcus lateralis

Gyrus temporalis transversi

Insula

Nucleus ventralis thalami posterior

Gyrus dentatus hippocampi

Fig. 70.

138

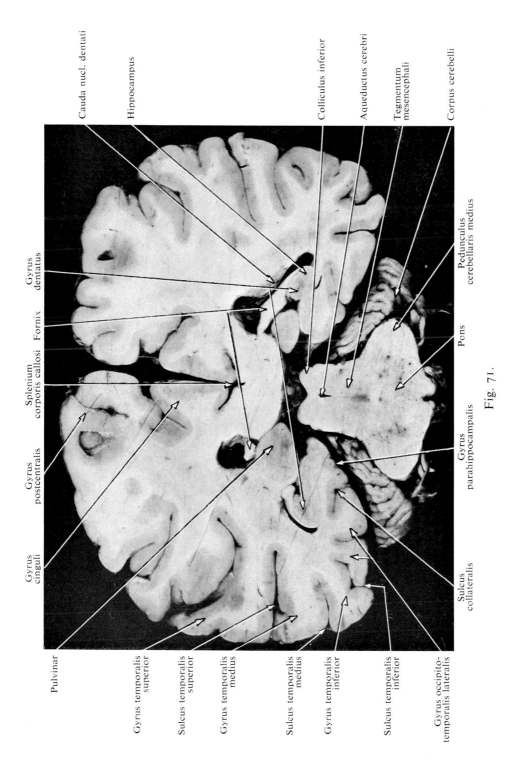

Cauda nucl. dentati

Hippocampus

Colliculus inferior

Aqueductus cerebri

Tegmentum mesencephali

Corpus cerebelli

Gyrus dentatus

Fornix

Splenium corporis callosi

Gyrus postcentralis

Gyrus cinguli

Pulvinar

Gyrus temporalis superior

Sulcus temporalis superior

Gyrus temporalis medius

Sulcus temporalis medius

Gyrus temporalis inferior

Sulcus temporalis inferior

Gyrus occipito-temporalis lateralis

Sulcus collateralis

Gyrus parahippocampalis

Pons

Pedunculus cerebellaris medius

Fig. 71.

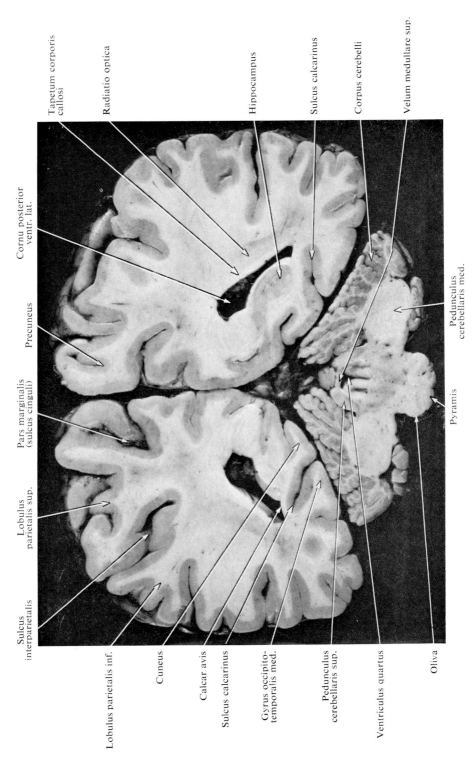

Tapetum corporis callosi

Radiatio optica

Hippocampus

Sulcus calcarinus

Corpus cerebelli

Velum medullare sup.

Cornu posterior ventr. lat.

Precuneus

Pedunculus cerebellaris med.

Pars marginalis (sulcus cinguli)

Pyramis

Lobulus parietalis sup.

Sulcus occipitotemporalis.

Sulcus interparietalis

Lobulus parietalis inf.

Cuneus

Calcar avis

Sulcus calcarinus

Gyrus occipito-temporalis med.

Pedunculus cerebellaris sup.

Ventriculus quartus

Oliva

Fig. 72. Sulcus occipitotemporalis.

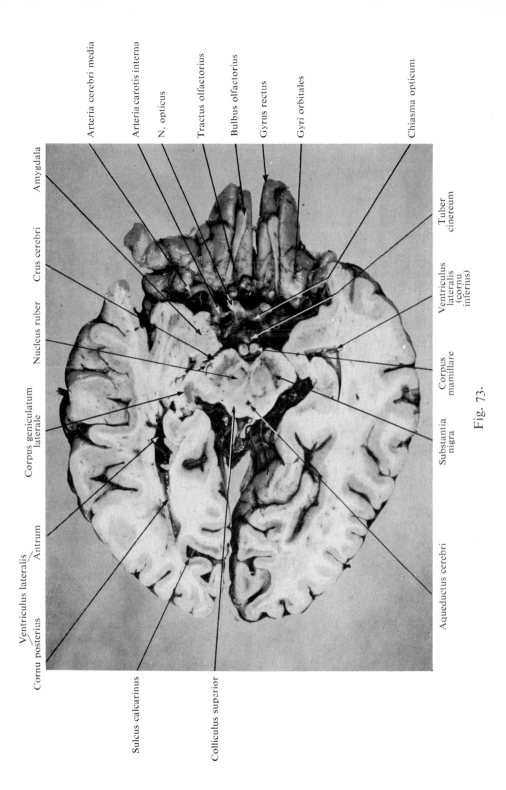

Arteria cerebri media
Arteria carotis interna
N. opticus
Tractus olfactorius
Bulbus olfactorius
Gyrus rectus
Gyri orbitales
Chiasma opticum

Amygdala
Crus cerebri
Nucleus ruber
Corpus geniculatum laterale

Ventriculus lateralis
Cornu posterius
Antrum

Sulcus calcarinus
Colliculus superior

Aqueductus cerebri

Substantia nigra
Corpus mamillare
Ventriculus lateralis (cornu inferius)
Tuber cinereum

Fig. 73.

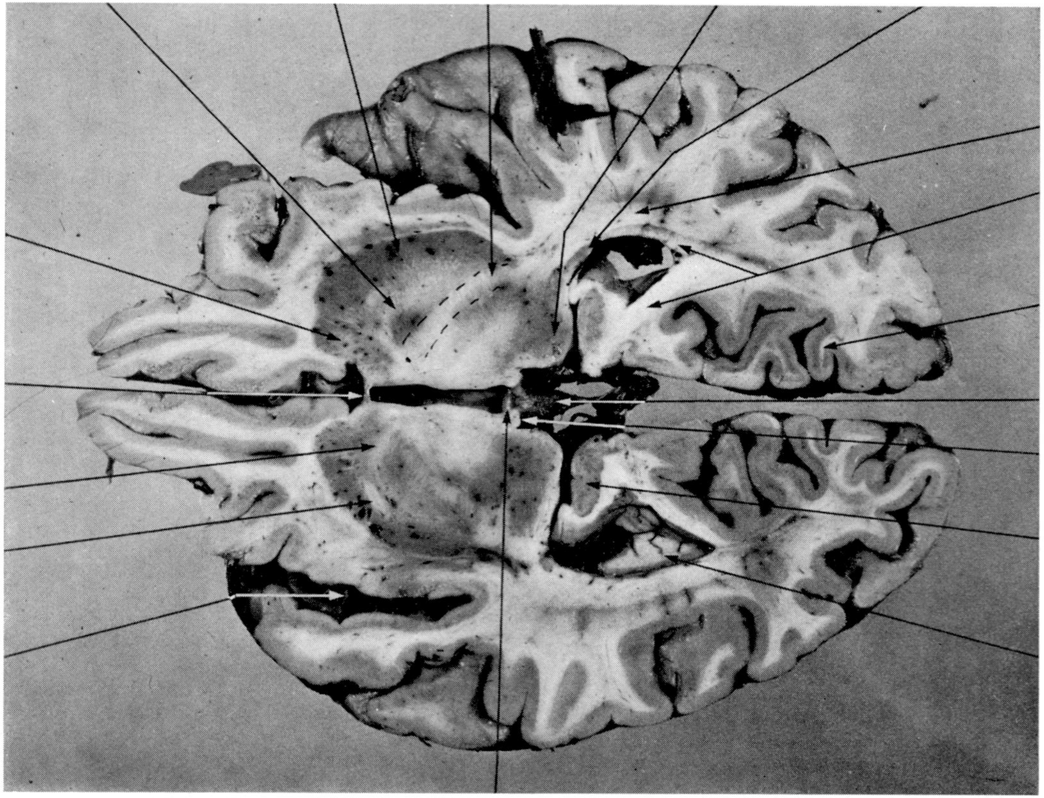

Radiatio optica

Corpus callosum

Area striata

Corpus pineale

Habenula

Gyrus fasciolaris

Ventriculus lateralis
(antrum et cornu
posterius)

Nucleus caudatus
(cauda)

Pulvinar

Capsula interna
(crus posterius)

Putamen

Globus pallidus

Nucleus caudatus
(caput)

Lamina terminalis

Ansa peduncularis

Commissura anterior

Sulcus lateralis

Commissura posterior

Fig. 74.

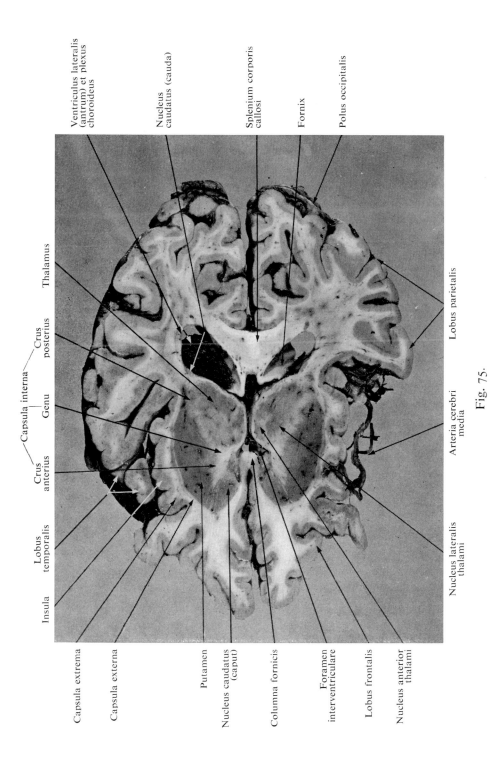

Ventriculus lateralis (antrum) et plexus choroideus

Nucleus caudatus (cauda)

Splenium corporis callosi

Fornix

Polus occipitalis

Thalamus

Capsula interna

Crus posterius

Genu

Crus anterius

Lobus temporalis

Insula

Capsula extrema

Capsula externa

Putamen

Nucleus caudatus (caput)

Columna fornicis

Foramen interventriculare

Lobus frontalis

Nucleus anterior thalami

Nucleus lateralis thalami

Arteria cerebri media

Lobus parietalis

Fig. 75.

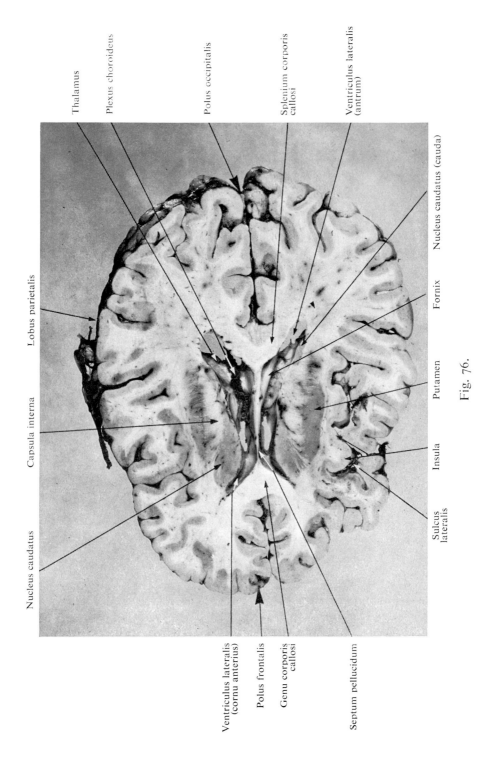

Thalamus

Plexus choroideus

Polus occipitalis

Splenium corporis callosi

Ventriculus lateralis (antrum)

Lobus parietalis

Capsula interna

Nucleus caudatus

Nucleus caudatus (cauda)

Fornix

Putamen

Insula

Sulcus lateralis

Ventriculus lateralis (cornu anterius)

Polus frontalis

Genu corporis callosi

Septum pellucidum

Fig. 76.

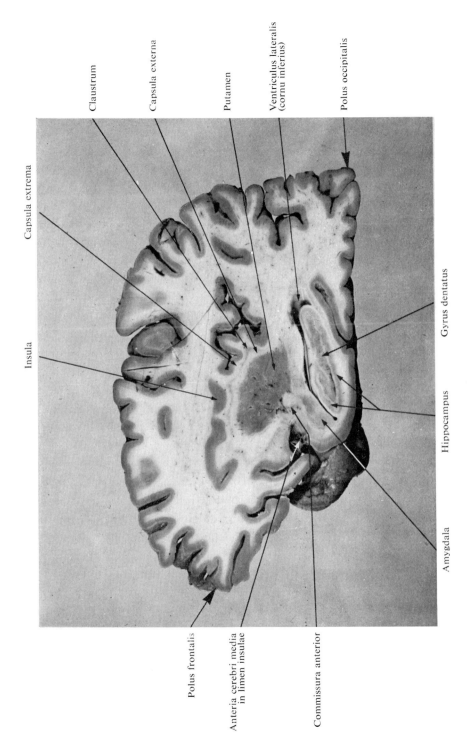

Claustrum

Capsula externa

Putamen

Ventriculus lateralis
(cornu inferius)

Polus occipitalis

Capsula extrema

Insula

Gyrus dentatus

Polus frontalis

Anteria cerebri media
in limen insulae

Commissura anterior

Hippocampus

Amygdala

Fig. 77.

145

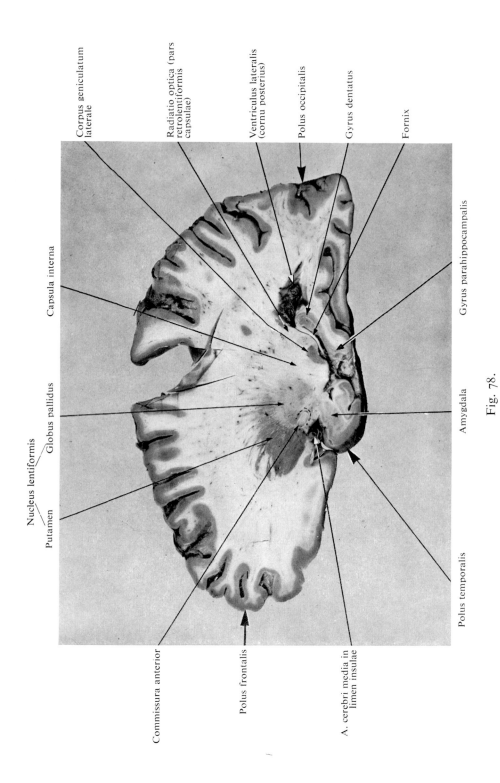

Corpus geniculatum laterale

Radiatio optica (pars retrolentiformis capsulae)

Ventriculus lateralis (cornu posterius)

Polus occipitalis

Gyrus dentatus

Fornix

Capsula interna

Nucleus lentiformis

Globus pallidus

Putamen

Gyrus parahippocampalis

Amygdala

Fig. 78.

Polus temporalis

Commissura anterior

Polus frontalis

A. cerebri media in limen insulae

146

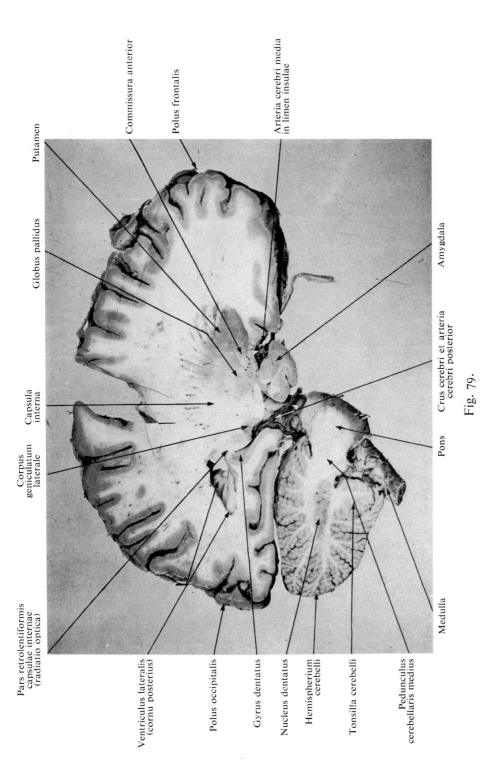

Commissura anterior

Polus frontalis

Arteria cerebri media
in limen insulae

Putamen

Globus pallidus

Amygdala

Capsula
interna

Corpus
geniculatum
laterale

Crus cerebri et arteria
cerebri posterior

Pons

Fig. 79.

Pars retrolentiformis
capsulae internae
(radiatio optica)

Ventriculus lateralis
(cornu posterius)

Polus occipitalis

Gyrus dentatus

Nucleus dentatus

Hemispherium
cerebelli

Tonsilla cerebelli

Pedunculus
cerebellaris medius

Medulla

147

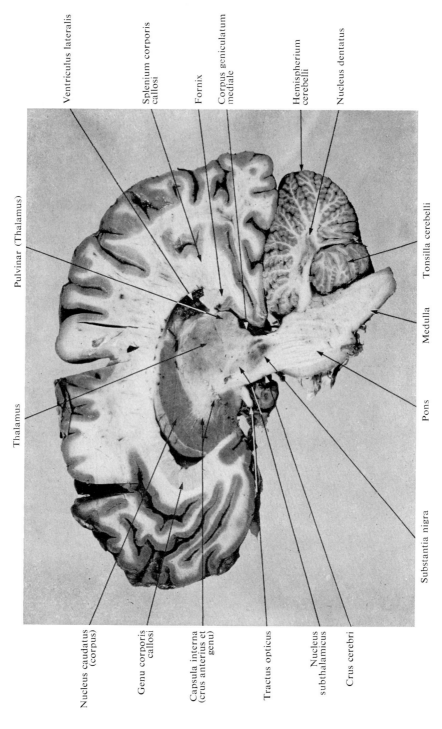

Ventriculus lateralis

Splenium corporis
callosi

Fornix

Corpus geniculatum
mediale

Hemispherium
cerebelli

Nucleus dentatus

Pulvinar (Thalamus)

Thalamus

Tonsilla cerebelli

Medulla

Pons

Fig. 80.

Substantia nigra

Nucleus caudatus
(corpus)

Genu corporis
callosi

Capsula interna
(crus anterius et
genu)

Tractus opticus

Nucleus
subthalamicus

Crus cerebri

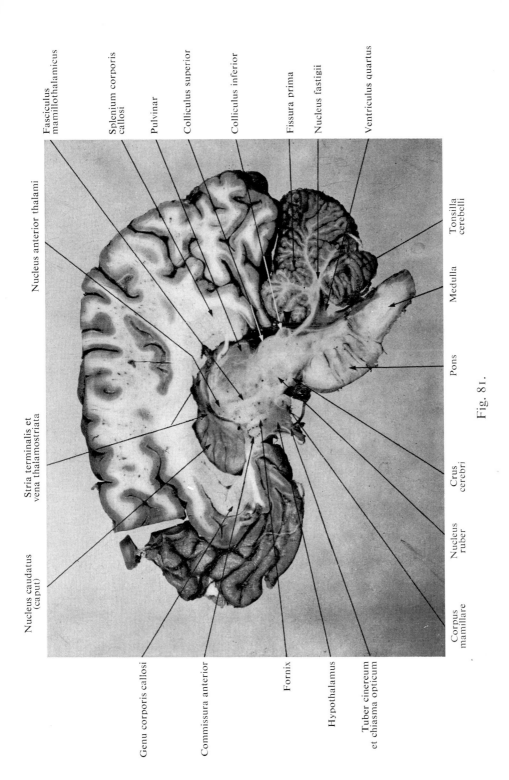

Fasciculus mamillothalamicus

Splenium corporis callosi

Pulvinar

Colliculus superior

Colliculus inferior

Fissura prima

Nucleus fastigii

Ventriculus quartus

Nucleus anterior thalami

Stria terminalis et vena thalamostriata

Nucleus caudatus (caput)

Tonsilla cerebelli

Medulla

Pons

Crus cerebri

Nucleus ruber

Corpus mamillare

Genu corporis callosi

Commissura anterior

Fornix

Hypothalamus

Tuber cinereum et chiasma opticum

Fig. 81.

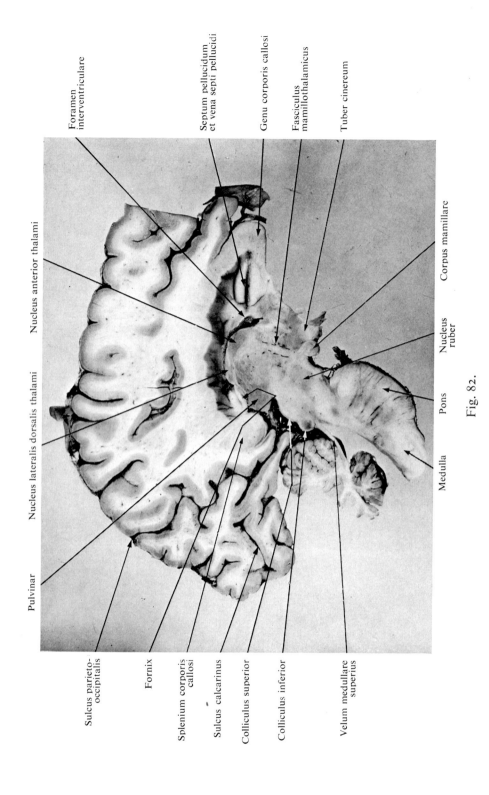

Foramen
interventriculare

Nucleus anterior thalami

Nucleus lateralis dorsalis thalami

Pulvinar

Septum pellucidum
et vena septi pellucidi

Genu corporis callosi

Fasciculus
mamillothalamicus

Tuber cinereum

Corpus mamillare

Nucleus
ruber

Pons

Medulla

Sulcus parieto-
occipitalis

Fornix

Splenium corporis
callosi

Sulcus calcarinus

Colliculus superior

Colliculus inferior

Velum medullare
superius

Fig. 82.

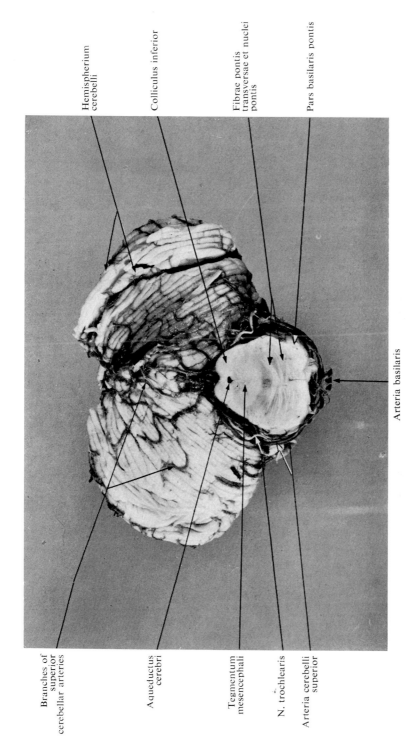

Hemispherium cerebelli

Colliculus inferior

Fibrae pontis transversae et nuclei pontis

Pars basilaris pontis

Branches of superior cerebellar arteries

Aqueductus cerebri

Tegmentum mesencephali

N. trochlearis

Arteria cerebelli superior

Arteria basilaris

Fig. 83.

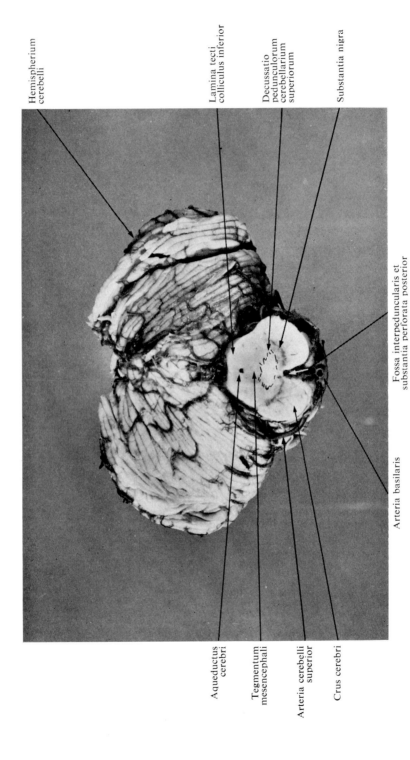

Hemispherium
cerebelli

Lamina tecti
colliculus inferior

Decussatio
pedunculorum
cerebellarium
superiorum

Substantia nigra

Aqueductus
cerebri

Tegmentum
mesencephali

Arteria cerebelli
superior

Crus cerebri

Arteria basilaris

Fossa interpeduncularis et
substantia perforata posterior

Fig. 84.

Hemispherium cerebelli

Vermis

Tegmentum at junction of pons and mesencephalon

Fibrae pontis transversae et nuclei pontis

Pars basilaris pontis

Aqueductus cerebri

Region of isthmus rhombencephali

N. trigeminus

A. basilaris

Fig. 85.

153

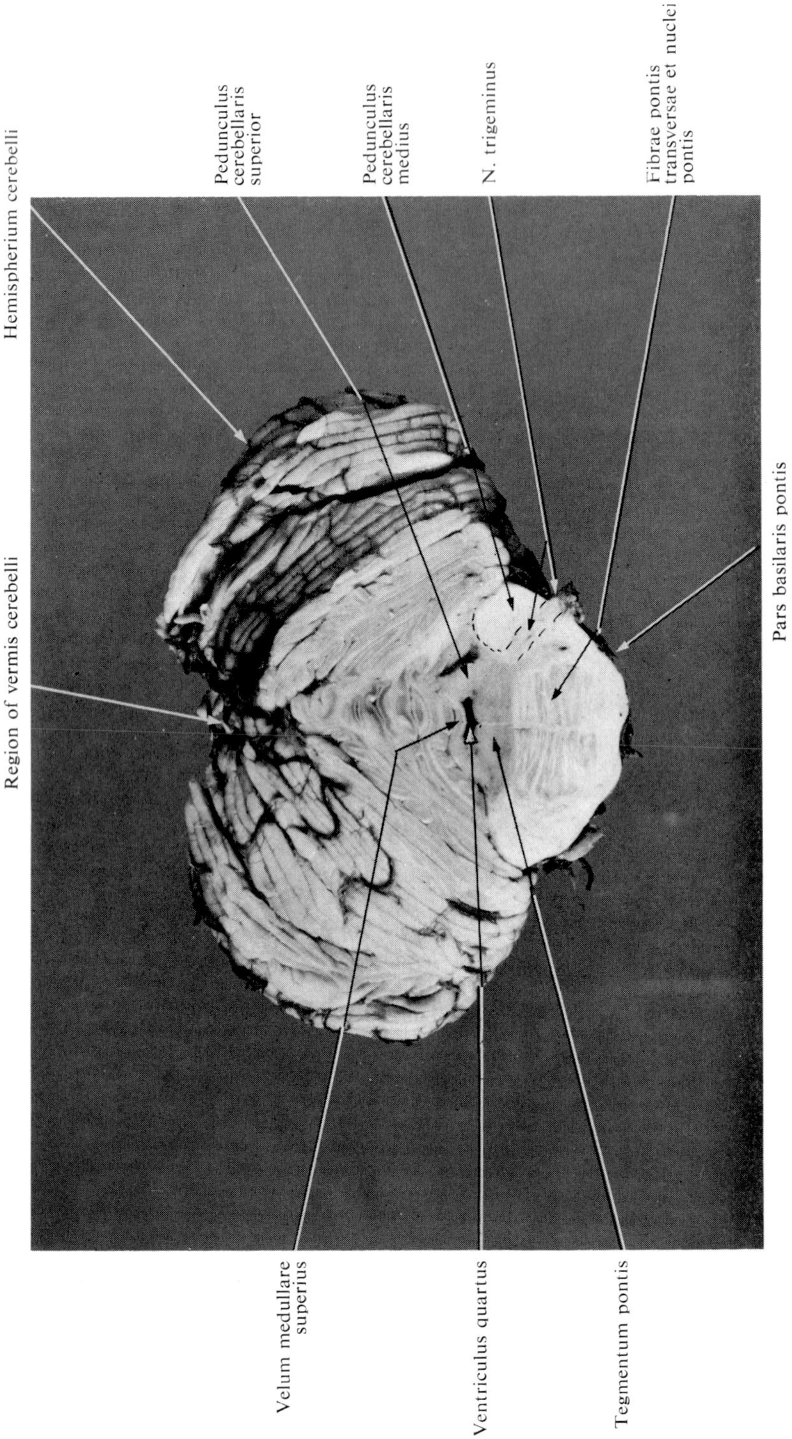

Pedunculus
cerebellaris
superior

Pedunculus
cerebellaris
medius

N. trigeminus

Fibrae pontis
transversae et nuclei
pontis

Hemispherium cerebelli

Region of vermis cerebelli

Pars basilaris pontis

Velum medullare
superius

Ventriculus quartus

Tegmentum pontis

Fig. 86.

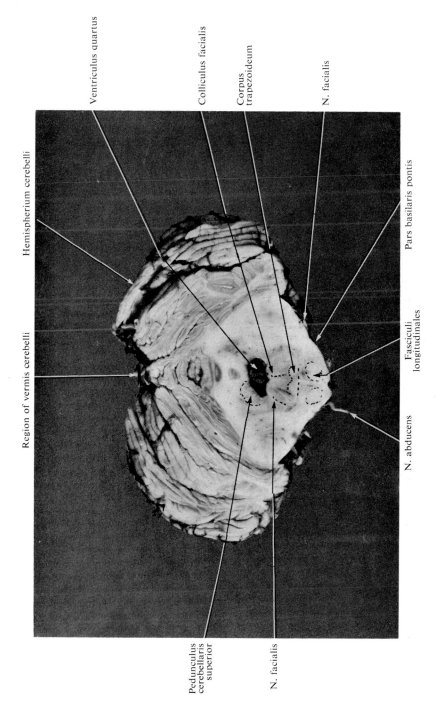

Ventriculus quartus

Colliculus facialis

Corpus
trapezoideum

N. facialis

Hemispherium cerebelli

Pars basilaris pontis

Region of vermis cerebelli

Fasciculi
longitudinales

Fig. 87.

N. abducens

Pedunculus
cerebellaris
superior

N. facialis

Nodulus (vermis)

Ventriculus quartus

N. vestibulo-
cochlearis

N. facialis

Pyramis

Region of vermis cerebelli

N. abducens

Nucleus dentatus

Pedunculus
cerebellaris
inferior

Junction pons
and medulla

Fig. 88.

156

SECTION VI

Pal–Weigert Atlas

This section of the atlas is devoted to a series of sections stained for myelin (Pal–Weigert Method). In Fig. 89A the brain is represented in the mid-sagittal plane, while the isolated brain stem is viewed from the lateral aspect in Fig. 89B. Seven of the planes of section for the Pal–Weigert series are indicated. All planes of section caudal to and including plane 103 are parallel to each other. All planes rostral to and including plane 104 are parallel to plane 104 which also parallels the course of the optic tract. In the hind brain area, starting at the ponto-medullary junction (Fig. 94), certain of the figures are followed by enlarged views of the tegmentum. Thus, Fig. 95 is an enlargement of the tegmentum for Fig. 94. This then applies to the following pairs of figures: 96–97, 98–99, 100–101, 102–103, and 104–105.

A series of Pal-Weigert sections cut in the sagittal plane is represented by Fig. 121–131. Fig. 120 is a dorsal view of the brain stem, illustrating the planes of sections and approximate position of some of the numbered planes. Note that the dorso-ventral plane of the section is not quite perpendicular to the true horizontal plane. Thus, all the sections are on a slightly oblique angle.

The final part of this section consists of a special series of sections (figures 132–145) through the medulla oblongata. On facing pages the left and the right part of the section are represented. The labeling of the structures was made in such a way as to facilitate reviewing and checking of the brain structures in an easy way.

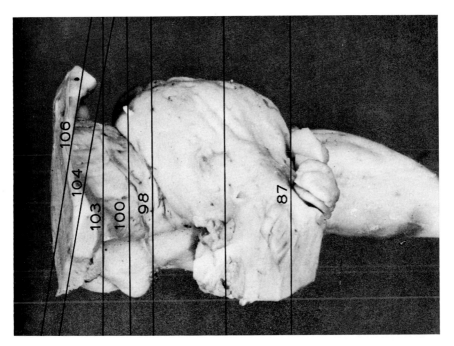

Fig. 89B.

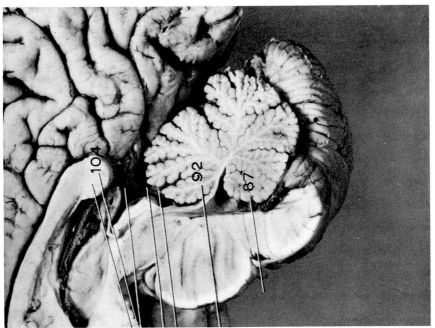

Fig. 89A.

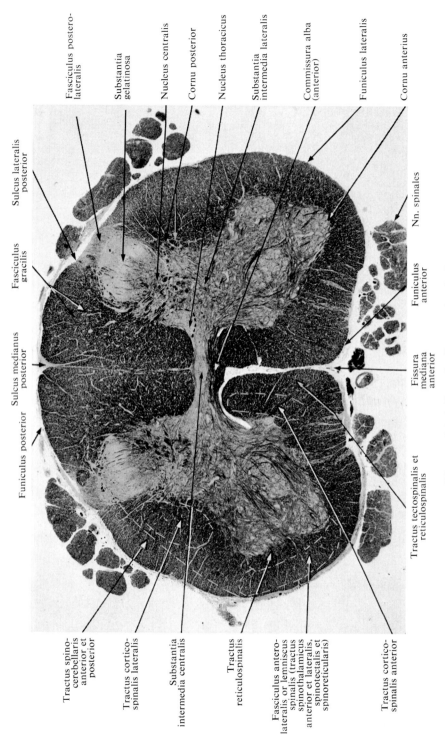

Fasciculus postero-
lateralis

Substantia
gelatinosa

Nucleus centralis

Cornu posterior

Nucleus thoracicus

Substantia
intermedia lateralis

Commissura alba
(anterior)

Funiculus lateralis

Cornu anterius

Sulcus lateralis
posterior

Fasciculus
gracilis

Funiculus posterior

Sulcus medianus
posterior

Nn. spinales

Funiculus
anterior

Fissura
mediana
anterior

Tractus tectospinalis et
reticulospinalis

Tractus spino-
cerebellaris
anterior et
posterior

Tractus cortico-
spinalis lateralis

Substantia
intermedia centralis

Tractus
reticulospinalis

Fasciculus antero-
lateralis or lemniscus
spinalis (tractus
spinothalamicus
anterior et lateralis,
spinotectalis et
spinoreticularis)

Tractus cortico-
spinalis anterior

Fig. 90. Medulla spinalis, pars lumbalis.

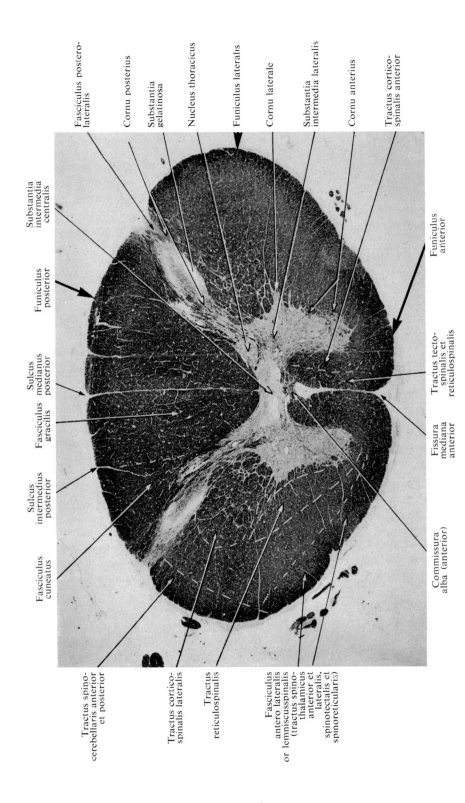

Fasciculus postero-lateralis

Cornu posterius

Substantia gelatinosa

Nucleus thoracicus

Funiculus lateralis

Cornu laterale

Substantia intermedia lateralis

Cornu anterius

Tractus cortico-spinalis anterior

Substantia intermedia centralis

Funiculus posterior

Sulcus medianus posterior

Fasciculus gracilis

Sulcus intermedius posterior

Fasciculus cuneatus

Funiculus anterior

Tractus tecto-spinalis et reticulospinalis

Fissura mediana anterior

Commissura alba (anterior)

Tractus spino-cerebellaris anterior et posterior

Tractus cortico-spinalis lateralis

Tractus reticulospinalis

Fasciculus antero lateralis or lemniscusspinalis (tractus spino-thalamicus anterior et lateralis, spinotectalis et spinoreticularis)

Fig. 91. Medulla spinalis, pars thoracica.

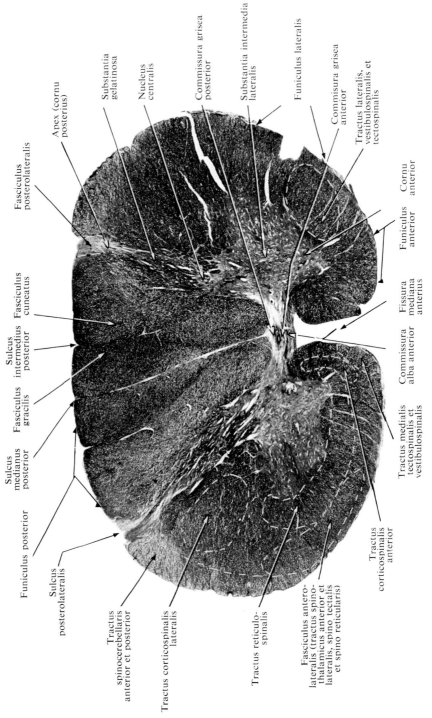

Fasciculus posterolateralis

Apex (cornu posterius)

Substantia gelatinosa

Nucleus centralis

Commissura grisea posterior

Substantia intermedia lateralis

Funiculus lateralis

Commissura grisea anterior

Tractus lateralis, vestibulospinalis et tectospinalis

Cornu anterior

Funiculus anterior

Fissura mediana anterius

Commissura alba anterior

Tractus medialis tectospinalis et vestibulospinalis

Tractus corticospinalis anterior

Fasciculus cuneatus

Sulcus intermedius posterior

Fasciculus gracilis

Sulcus medianus posterior

Funiculus posterior

Sulcus posterolateralis

Tractus spinocerebellaris anterior et posterior

Tractus corticospinalis lateralis

Tractus reticulospinalis

Fasciculus antero-lateralis (tractus spino-thalamicus anterior et lateralis, spino. tectalis et spino reticularis)

Fig. 92. Medulla spinalis, pars cervicalis.

162

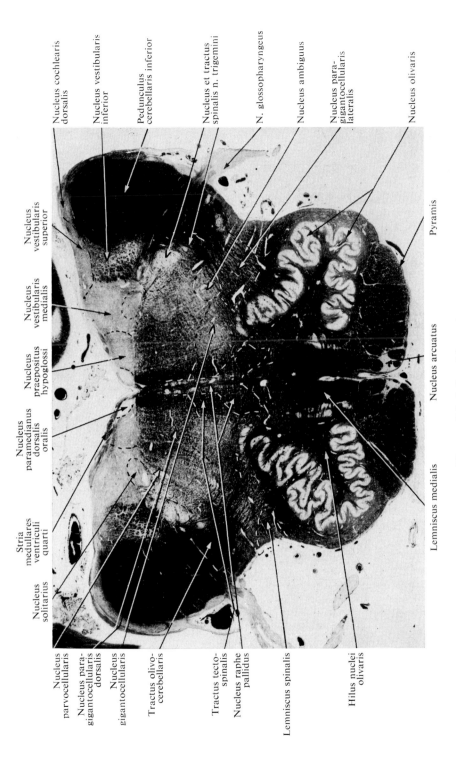

Nucleus cochlearis dorsalis

Nucleus vestibularis inferior

Pedunculus cerebellaris inferior

Nucleus et tractus spinalis n. trigemini

N. glossopharyngeus

Nucleus ambiguus

Nucleus para-gigantocellularis lateralis

Nucleus olivaris

Nucleus vestibularis superior

Nucleus vestibularis medialis

Nucleus praepositus hypoglossi

Nucleus paramedianus dorsalis oralis

Stria medullares ventriculi quarti

Nucleus solitarius

Pyramis

Nucleus arcuatus

Lemniscus medialis

Nucleus parvocellularis

Nucleus para-gigantocellularis dorsalis

Nucleus gigantocellularis

Tractus olivo-cerebellaris

Tractus tecto-spinalis

Nucleus raphe pallidus

Lemniscus spinalis

Hilus nuclei olivaris

Fig. 93. Medulla oblongata.

163

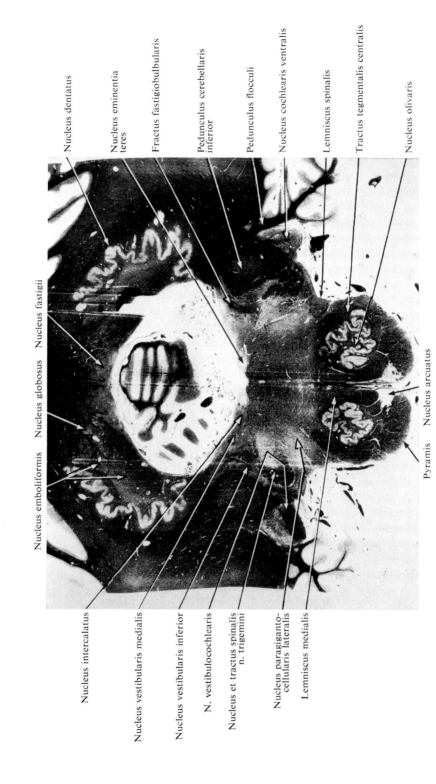

Nucleus dentatus

Nucleus eminentia teres

Fractus fastigiobulbularis

Pedunculus cerebellaris inferior

Pedunculus flocculi

Nucleus cochlearis ventralis

Lemniscus spinalis

Tractus tegmentalis centralis

Nucleus olivaris

Nucleus emboliformis   Nucleus globosus   Nucleus fastigii

Nucleus intercalatus

Nucleus vestibularis medialis

Nucleus vestibularis inferior

N. vestibulocochlearis

Nucleus et tractus spinalis n. trigemini

Nucleus paragiganto-cellularis lateralis

Lemniscus medialis

Pyramis   Nucleus arcuatus

Fig. 94. Pontomedullary junction.

164

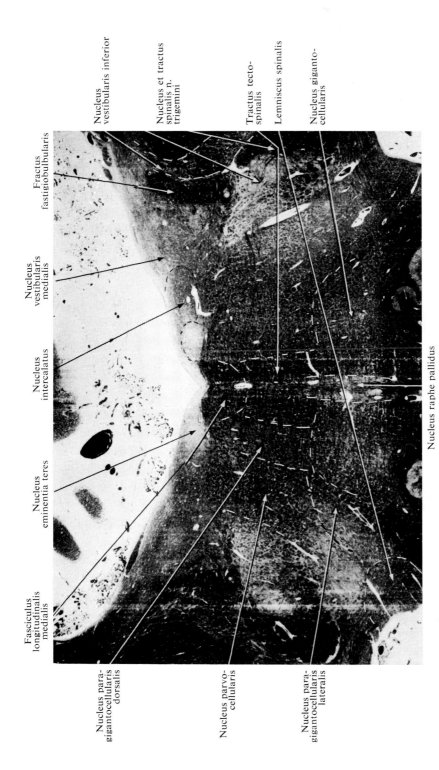

Nucleus vestibularis inferior

Nucleus et tractus spinalis n. trigemini

Tractus tecto-spinalis

Lemniscus spinalis

Nucleus giganto-cellularis

Fractus fastigiobulbularis

Nucleus vestibularis medialis

Nucleus intercalatus

Nucleus eminentia teres

Fasciculus longitudinalis medialis

Nucleus para-gigantocellularis dorsalis

Nucleus parvo-cellularis

Nucleus para-gigantocellularis lateralis

Nucleus raphe pallidus

Fig. 95. Pontomedullary junction.

165

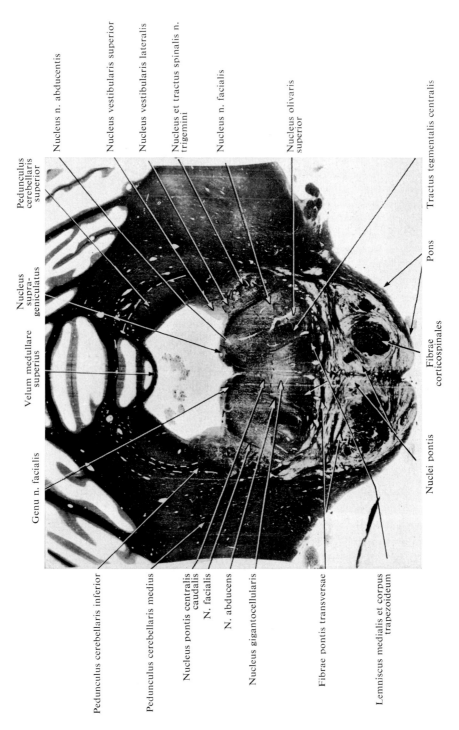

Nucleus n. abducentis

Nucleus vestibularis superior

Nucleus vestibularis lateralis

Nucleus et tractus spinalis n. trigemini

Nucleus n. facialis

Nucleus olivaris superior

Pedunculus cerebellaris superior

Nucleus supra-geniculatus

Velum medullare superius

Genu n. facialis

Pedunculus cerebellaris inferior

Pedunculus cerebellaris medius

Nucleus pontis centralis caudalis

N. facialis

N. abducens

Nucleus gigantocellularis

Fibrae pontis transversae

Lemniscus medialis et corpus trapezoideum

Nuclei pontis

Pons

Fibrae corticospinales

Tractus tegmentalis centralis

Fig. 96. Pons.

166

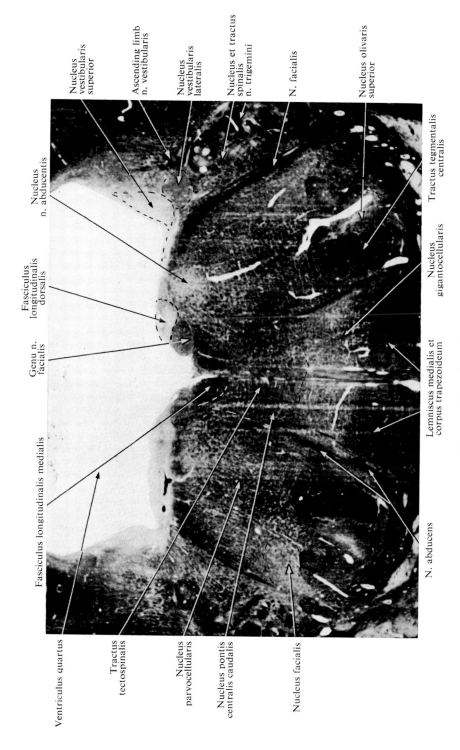

Fig. 97. Pars dorsalis pontis.

167

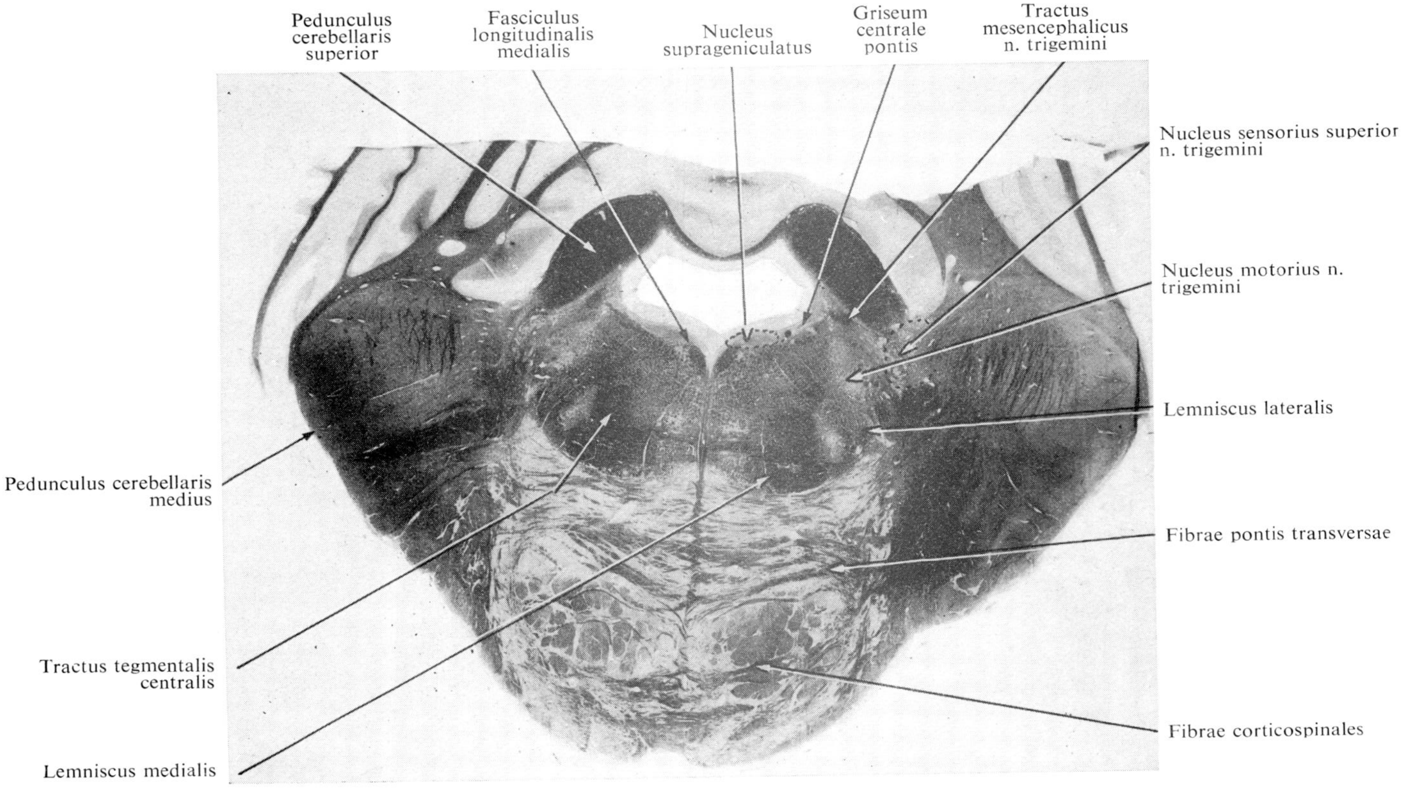

Nucleus sensorius superior n. trigemini

Nucleus motorius n. trigemini

Lemniscus lateralis

Fibrae pontis transversae

Fibrae corticospinales

Tractus mesencephalicus n. trigemini

Griseum centrale pontis

Nucleus suprageniculatus

Fasciculus longitudinalis medialis

Pedunculus cerebellaris superior

Pedunculus cerebellaris medius

Tractus tegmentalis centralis

Lemniscus medialis

Fig. 98. Pons

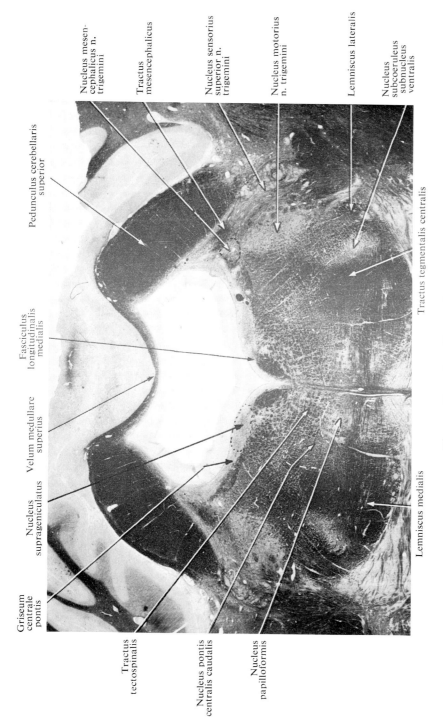

Griseum
centrale
pontis

Nucleus
suprageniculatus

Velum medullare
superius

Fasciculus
longitudinalis
medialis

Pedunculus cerebellaris
superior

Nucleus mesen-
cephalicus n.
trigemini

Tractus
mesencephalicus

Nucleus sensorius
superior n.
trigemini

Nucleus motorius
n. trigemini

Lemniscus lateralis

Nucleus
subcoeruleus
subnucleus
ventralis

Tractus tegmentalis centralis

Lemniscus medialis

Tractus
tectospinalis

Nucleus pontis
centralis caudalis

Nucleus
papilloformis

Fig. 99. Pars dorsalis pontis.

169

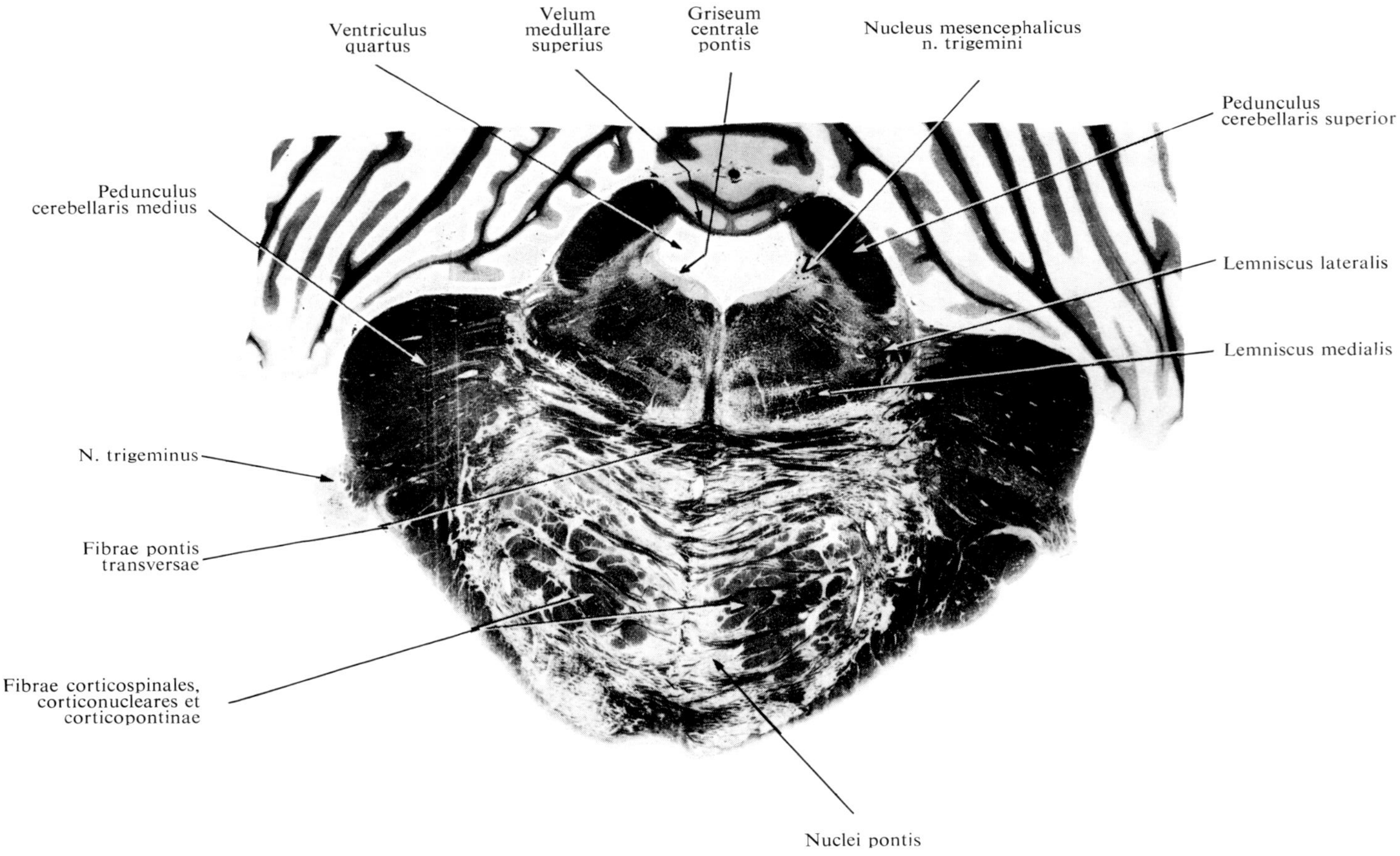

Pedunculus cerebellaris superior

Lemniscus lateralis

Lemniscus medialis

Nucleus mesencephalicus n. trigemini

Griseum centrale pontis

Velum medullare superius

Ventriculus quartus

Pedunculus cerebellaris medius

N. trigeminus

Fibrae pontis transversae

Fibrae corticospinales, corticonucleares et corticopontinae

Nuclei pontis

Fig. 100. Pons.

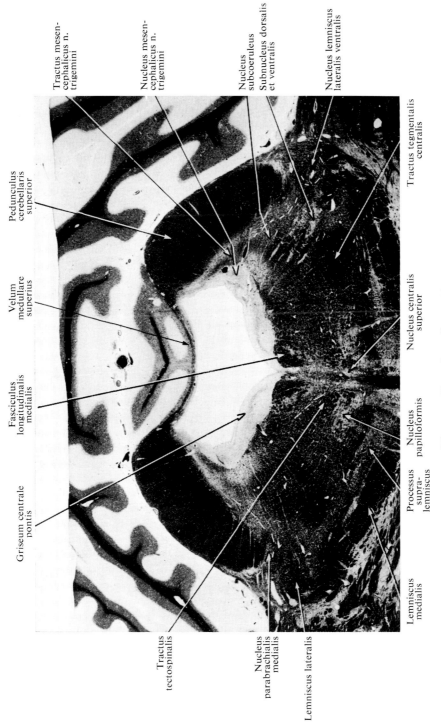

Tractus mesen-
cephalicus n.
trigemini

Nucleus mesen-
cephalicus n.
trigemini

Nucleus
subcoeruleus

Subnucleus dorsalis
et ventralis

Nucleus lemniscus
lateralis ventralis

Pedunculus
cerebellaris
superior

Tractus tegmentalis
centralis

Velum
medullare
superius

Nucleus centralis
superior

Fasciculus
longitudinalis
medialis

Nucleus
papilloformis

Griseum centrale
pontis

Processus
supra-
lemniscus

Lemniscus
medialis

Tractus
tectospinalis

Nucleus
parabrachialis
medialis

Lemniscus lateralis

Fig. 101. Pars dorsalis pontis.

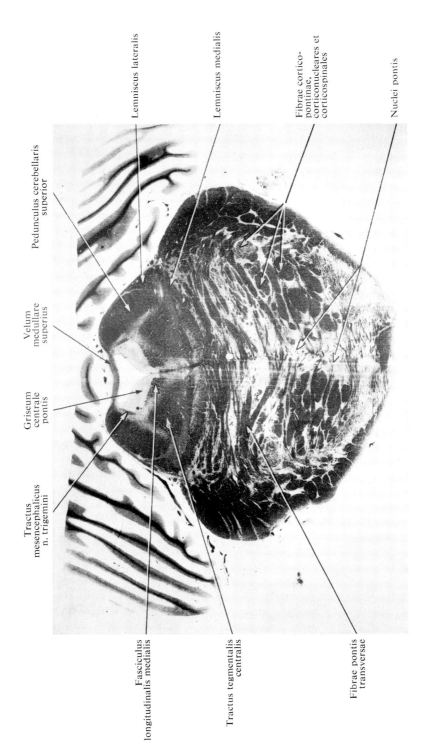

Lemniscus lateralis

Lemniscus medialis

Fibrae cortico-
pontinae,
corticonucleares et
corticospinales

Nuclei pontis

Pedunculus cerebellaris
superior

Velum
medullare
superius

Griseum
centrale
pontis

Tractus
mesencephalicus
n. trigemini

Fasciculus
longitudinalis medialis

Tractus tegmentalis
centralis

Fibrae pontis
transversae

Fig. 102. Pons.

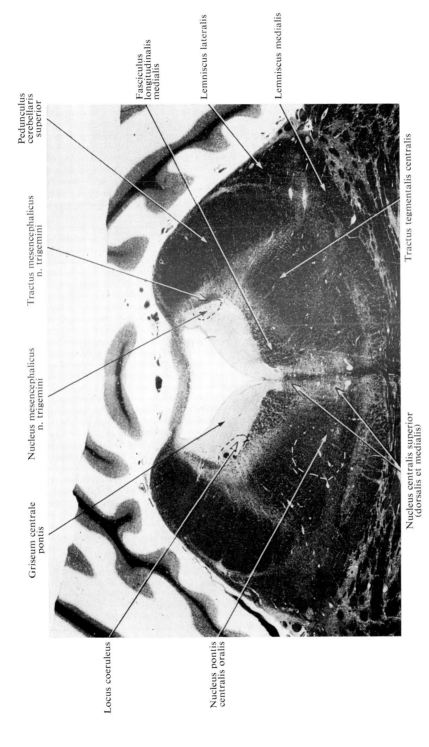

Pedunculus
cerebellaris
superior

Fasciculus
longitudinalis
medialis

Lemniscus lateralis

Lemniscus medialis

Tractus mesencephalicus
n. trigemini

Tractus tegmentalis centralis

Nucleus mesencephalicus
n. trigemini

Griseum centrale
pontis

Nucleus centralis superior
(dorsalis et medialis)

Locus coeruleus

Nucleus pontis
centralis oralis

Fig. 103. Pars dorsalis pontis.

Tractus tegmentalis centralis

Fasciculus longitudinalis medialis

Fibrae pontis transversae

Fibrae corticopontinae, corticonucleares et corticospinales

Tractus mesen-cephalicus n. trigemini

Decussatio N. trochlearis

Lemniscus lateralis

Lemniscus spinalis

Lemniscus medialis

Nucleus centralis superior

Nuclei pontis

Fig. 104. Pons and isthmus rhombencephali.

174

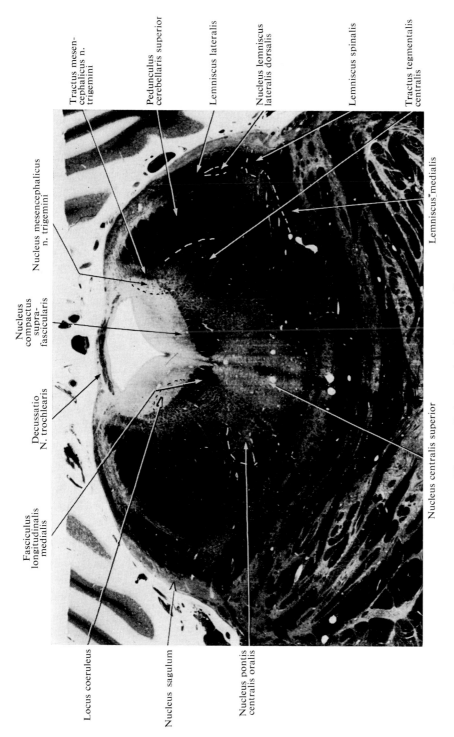

Tractus mesen-
cephalicus n.
trigemini

Pedunculus
cerebellaris superior

Lemniscus lateralis

Nucleus lemniscus
lateralis dorsalis

Lemniscus spinalis

Tractus tegmentalis
centralis

Nucleus mesencephalicus
n. trigemini

Nucleus
compactus
supra-
fascicularis

Decussatio
N. trochlearis

Fasciculus
longitudinalis
medialis

Locus coeruleus

Nucleus sagulum

Nucleus pontis
centralis oralis

Nucleus centralis superior

Lemniscus medialis

Fig. 105. Isthmus rhombencephali.

175

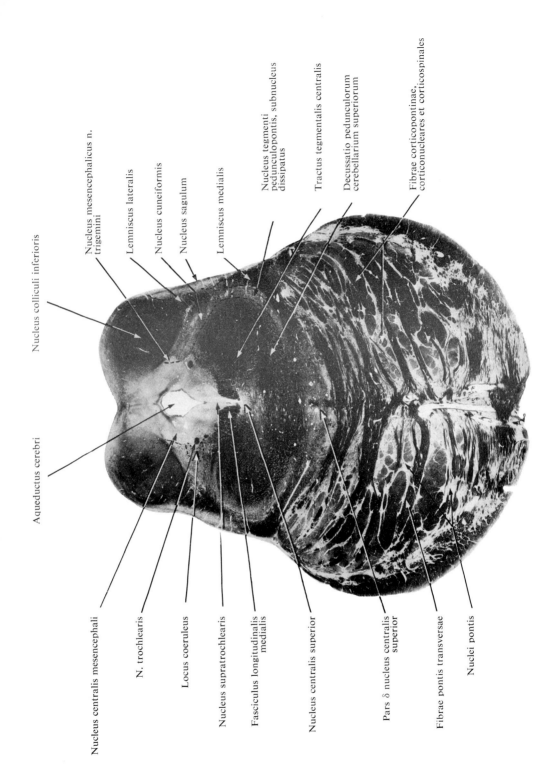

Nucleus colliculi inferioris

Aqueductus cerebri

Nucleus mesencephalicus n. trigemini

Lemniscus lateralis

Nucleus cuneiformis

Nucleus sagulum

Lemniscus medialis

Nucleus tegmenti pedunculopontis, subnucleus dissipatus

Tractus tegmentalis centralis

Decussatio pedunculorum cerebellarium superiorum

Fibrae corticopontinae, corticonucleares et corticospinales

Nucleus centralis mesencephali

N. trochlearis

Locus coeruleus

Nucleus supratrochlearis

Fasciculus longitudinalis medialis

Nucleus centralis superior

Pars δ nucleus centralis superior

Fibrae pontis transversae

Nuclei pontis

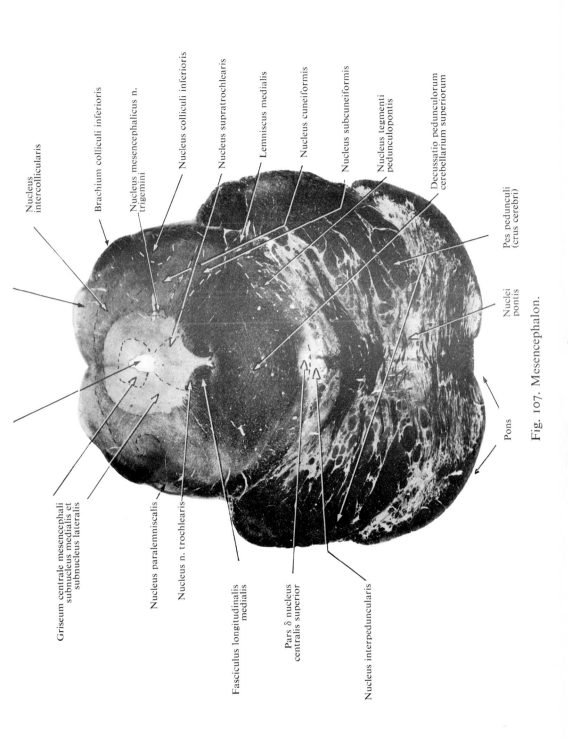

Nucleus intercollicularis

Brachium colliculi inferioris

Nucleus mesencephalicus n. trigemini

Nucleus colliculi inferioris

Nucleus supratrochlearis

Lemniscus medialis

Nucleus cuneiformis

Nucleus subcuneiformis

Nucleus tegmenti pedunculopontis

Decussatio pedunculorum cerebellarium superiorum

Pes pedunculi (crus cerebri)

Nuclei pontis

Pons

Fig. 107. Mesencephalon.

Griseum centrale mesencephali subnucleus medialis et subnucleus lateralis

Nucleus paralemniscalis

Nucleus n. trochlearis

Fasciculus longitudinalis medialis

Pars δ nucleus centralis superior

Nucleus interpeduncularis

177

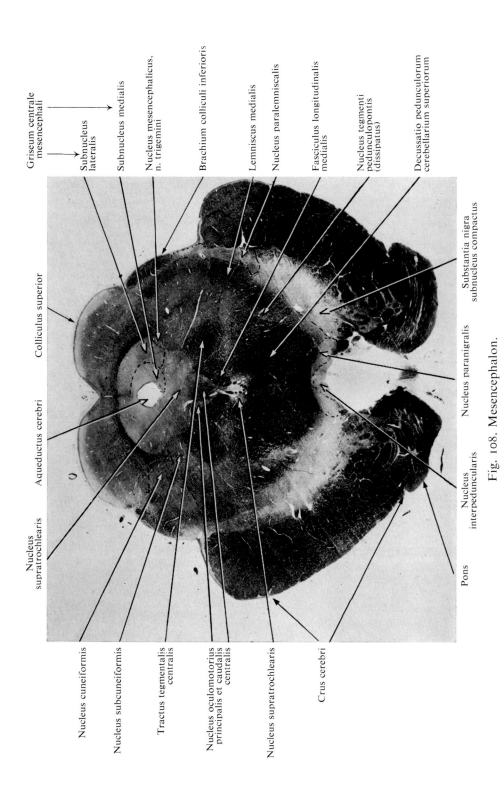

Griseum centrale
mesencephali

Subnucleus
lateralis

Subnucleus medialis

Nucleus mesencephalicus,
n. trigemini

Brachium colliculi inferioris

Lemniscus medialis

Nucleus paralemniscalis

Fasciculus longitudinalis
medialis

Nucleus tegmenti
pedunculopontis
(dissipatus)

Decussatio pedunculorum
cerebellarium superiorum

Nucleus
supratrochlearis

Aqueductus cerebri

Colliculus superior

Substantia nigra
subnucleus compactus

Nucleus cuneiformis

Nucleus subcuneiformis

Tractus tegmentalis
centralis

Nucleus oculomotorius
principalis et caudalis
centralis

Nucleus supratrochlearis

Crus cerebri

Nucleus paranigralis

Nucleus
interpeduncularis

Pons

Fig. 108. Mesencephalon.

178

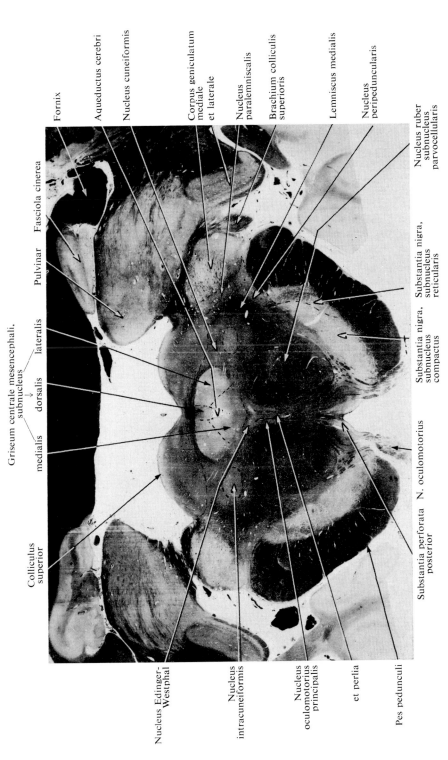

Griseum centrale mesencephali,
subnucleus

Fornix

Aqueductus cerebri

Nucleus cuneiformis

Corpus geniculatum
mediale
et laterale

Nucleus
paralemniscalis

Brachium colliculis
superioris

Lemniscus medialis

Nucleus
peripeduncularis

Nucleus ruber
subnucleus
parvocellularis

Fasciola cinerea

Pulvinar

lateralis

dorsalis

medialis

Colliculus
superior

Nucleus Edinger-
Westphal

Nucleus
intracuneiformis

Nucleus
oculomotorius
principalis

et perlia

Pes pedunculi

Substantia perforata
posterior

N. oculomotorius

Substantia nigra,
subnucleus
compactus

Substantia nigra,
subnucleus
reticularis

Fig. 109. Mesencephalon-diencephalon.

179

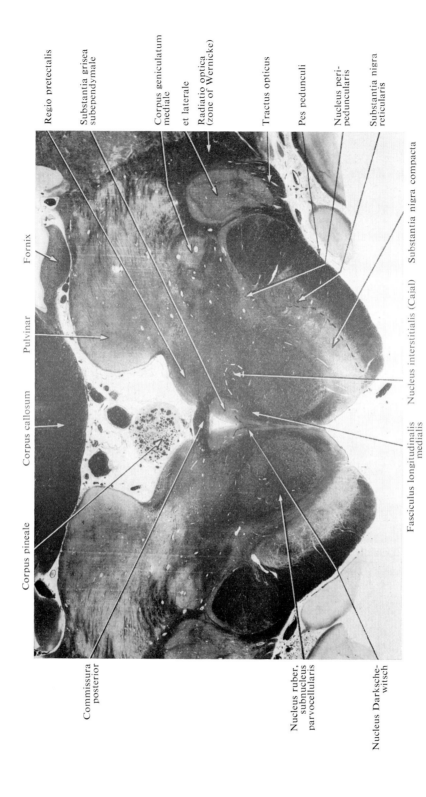

Corpus pineale Corpus callosum Pulvinar Fornix

Regio pretectalis

Substantia grisea
subependymale

Corpus geniculatum
mediale

et laterale

Radiatio optica
(zone of Wernicke)

Tractus opticus

Pes pedunculi

Nucleus peri-
peduncularis

Substantia nigra
reticularis

Commissura
posterior

Nucleus ruber,
subnucleus
parvocellularis

Nucleus Darksche-
witsch

Fasciculus longitudinalis   Nucleus interstitialis (Cajal)   Substantia nigra compacta
medialis

110. Mesencephalon-diencephalon.

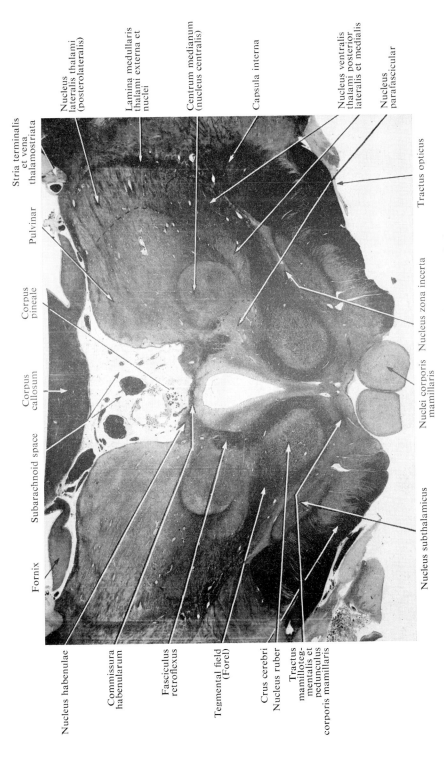

Nucleus
laterialis thalami
(posterolateralis)

Lamina medullaris
thalami externa et
nuclei

Centrum medianum
(nucleus centralis)

Capsula interna

Nucleus ventralis
thalami posterior
lateralis et medialis

Nucleus
parafascicular

Stria terminalis
et vena
thalamostriata

Pulvinar

Corpus
pineale

Corpus
callosum

Subarachnoid space

Fornix

Tractus opticus

Nucleus zona incerta

Nuclei corporis
mamillaris

Nucleus subthalamicus

Nucleus habenulae

Commissura
habenularum

Fasciculus
retroflexus

Tegmental field
(Forel)

Crus cerebri

Nucleus ruber

Tractus
mamillotegmentalis et
pedunculus
corporis mamillaris

Fig. 111. Diencephalon and most rostral mesencephalon.

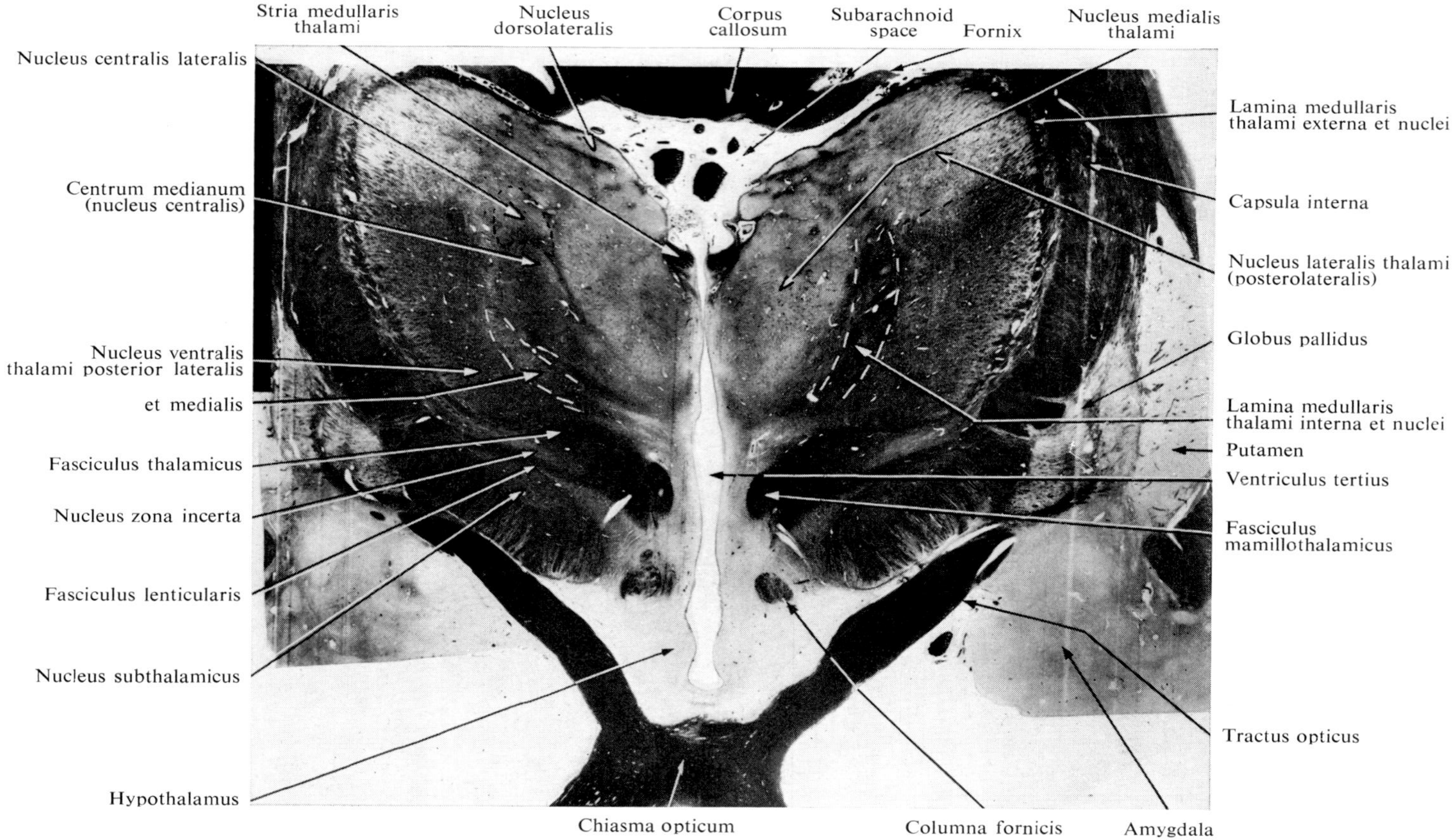

Fig. 112. Diencephalon.

182

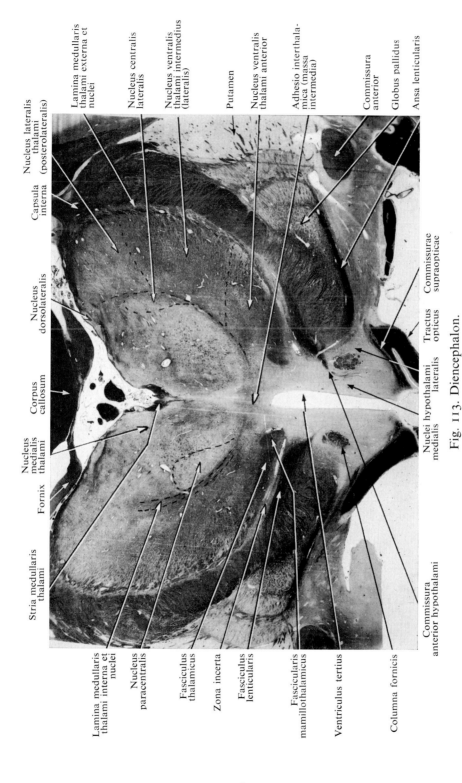

Nucleus lateralis thalami (posterolateralis)

Capsula interna

Nucleus dorsolateralis

Corpus callosum

Nucleus medialis thalami

Fornix

Stria medullaris thalami

Lamina medullaris thalami externa et nuclei

Nucleus centralis lateralis

Nucleus ventralis thalami intermedius (lateralis)

Putamen

Nucleus ventralis thalami anterior

Adhesio interthalamica (massa intermedia)

Commissura anterior

Globus pallidus

Ansa lenticularis

Commissurae supraopticae

Tractus opticus

Nuclei hypothalami lateralis medialis

Commissura anterior hypothalami

Columna fornicis

Ventriculus tertius

Fasciculus mamillothalamicus

Fasciculus lenticularis

Zona incerta

Fasciculus thalamicus

Nucleus paracentralis

Lamina medullaris thalami interna et nuclei

Fig. 113. Diencephalon.

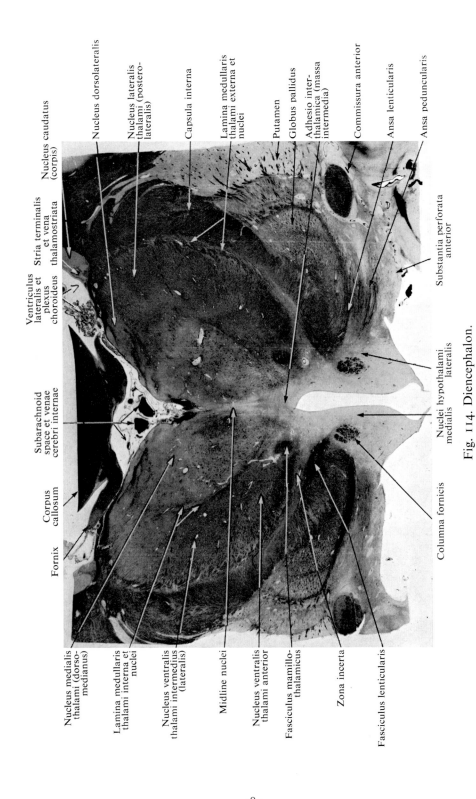

Nucleus caudatus (corpis)

Nucleus dorsolateralis

Nucleus lateralis thalami (postero-lateralis)

Capsula interna

Lamina medullaris thalami externa et nuclei

Putamen

Globus pallidus

Adhesio inter-thalamica (massa intermedia)

Commissura anterior

Ansa lenticularis

Ansa peduncularis

Stria terminalis et vena thalamostriata

Ventriculus lateralis et plexus choroideus

Subarachnoid space et venae cerebri internae

Corpus callosum

Fornix

Substantia perforata anterior

Nuclei hypothalami lateralis

Nuclei hypothalami medialis

Columna fornicis

Nucleus medialis thalami (dorso-medianus)

Lamina medullaris thalami interna et nuclei

Nucleus ventralis thalami intermedius (lateralis)

Midline nuclei

Nucleus ventralis thalami anterior

Fasciculus mamillo-thalamicus

Zona incerta

Fasciculus lenticularis

Fig. 114. Diencephalon.

184

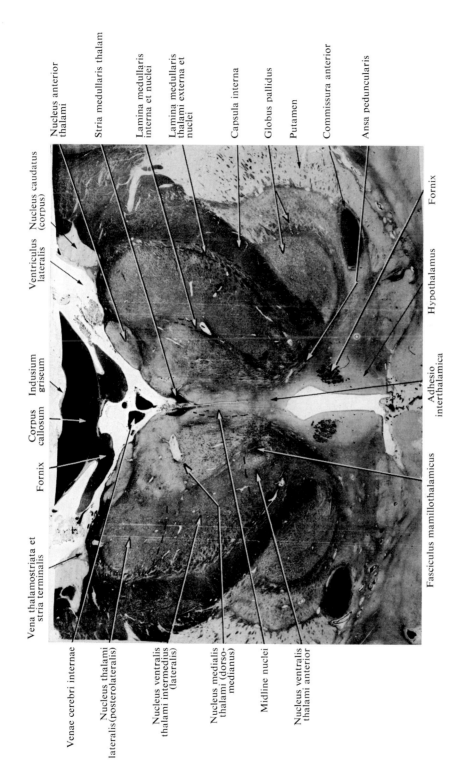

Nucleus anterior thalami

Stria medullaris thalam

Lamina medullaris interna et nuclei

Lamina medullaris thalami externa et nuclei

Capsula interna

Globus pallidus

Putamen

Commissura anterior

Ansa peduncularis

Nucleus caudatus (corpus)

Ventriculus lateralis

Indusium griseum

Corpus callosum

Fornix

Vena thalamostriata et stria terminalis

Venae cerebri internae

Nucleus thalami lateralis(posterolateralis)

Nucleus ventralis thalami intermedius (lateralis)

Nucleus medialis thalami (dorso-medianus)

Midline nuclei

Nucleus ventralis thalami anterior

Fasciculus mamillothalamicus

Adhesio interthalamica

Hypothalamus

Fornix

Fig. 115. Diencephalon.

185

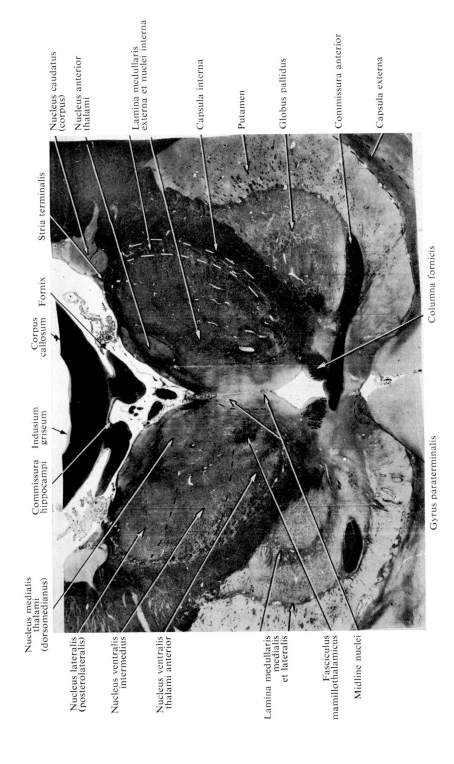

Nucleus caudatus (corpus)

Nucleus anterior thalami

Lamina medullaris externa et nuclei interna

Capsula interna

Putamen

Globus pallidus

Commissura anterior

Capsula externa

Stria terminalis

Fornix

Corpus callosum

Indusium griseum

Commissura hippocampi

Nucleus medialis thalami (dorsomedianus)

Nucleus lateralis (posterolateralis)

Nucleus ventralis intermedius

Nucleus ventralis thalami anterior

Lamina medullaris medialis et lateralis

Fasciculus mamillothalamicus

Midline nuclei

Columna fornicis

Gyrus paraterminalis

Fig. 116. Diencephalon.

186

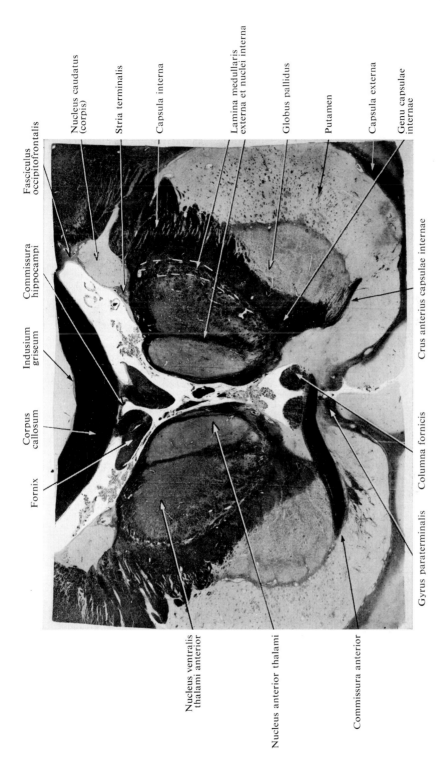

Fasciculus occipitofrontalis

Nucleus caudatus (corpis)

Stria terminalis

Capsula interna

Lamina medullaris externa et nuclei interna

Globus pallidus

Putamen

Capsula externa

Genu capsulae internae

Commissura hippocampi

Indusium griseum

Corpus callosum

Fornix

Nucleus ventralis thalami anterior

Nucleus anterior thalami

Commissura anterior

Gyrus paraterminalis

Columna fornicis

Crus anterius capsulae internae

Fig. 117. Diencephalon.

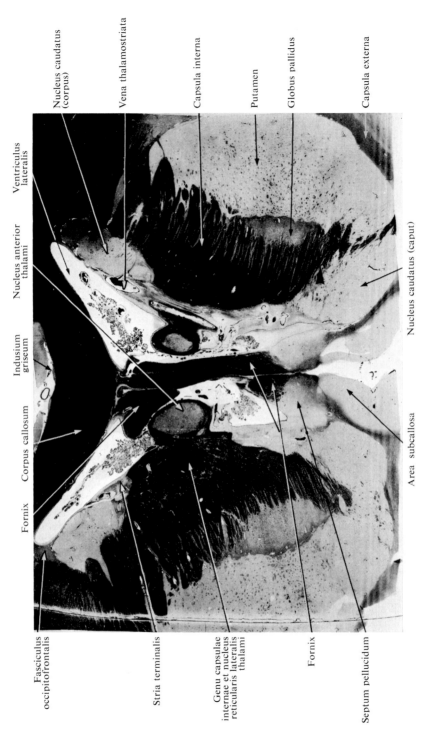

Nucleus caudatus (corpus)

Vena thalamostriata

Capsula interna

Putamen

Globus pallidus

Capsula externa

Ventriculus lateralis

Nucleus anterior thalami

Indusium griseum

Corpus callosum

Fornix

Fasciculus occipitofrontalis

Stria terminalis

Genu capsulae internae et nucleus reticularis lateralis thalami

Fornix

Septum pellucidum

Area subcallosa

Nucleus caudatus (caput)

Fig. 118. Basal nuclei.

188

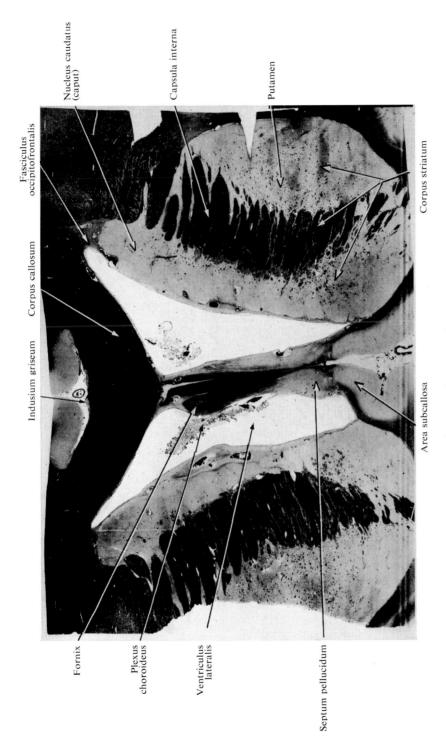

Nucleus caudatus (caput)

Capsula interna

Putamen

Fasciculus occipitofrontalis

Corpus callosum

Corpus striatum

Indusium griseum

Area subcallosa

Fornix

Plexus choroideus

Ventriculus lateralis

Septum pellucidum

Fig. 119. Corpus striatum.

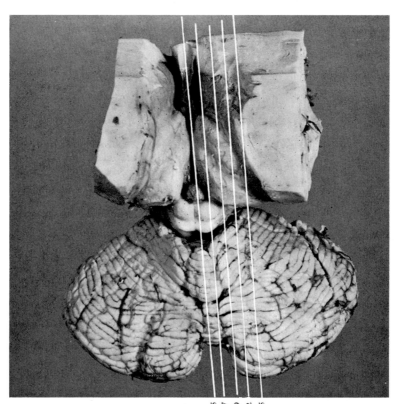

115
117
119
122
125

Fig. 120.

190

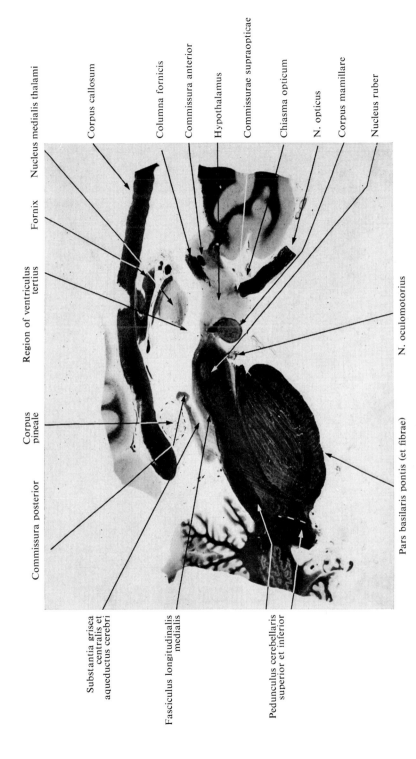

Nucleus medialis thalami

Corpus callosum

Columna fornicis

Commissura anterior

Hypothalamus

Commissurae supraopticae

Chiasma opticum

N. opticus

Corpus mamillare

Nucleus ruber

Fornix

Region of ventriculus tertius

Corpus pineale

Commissura posterior

Substantia grisea centralis et aqueductus cerebri

Fasciculus longitudinalis medialis

Pedunculus cerebellaris superior et inferior

Pars basilaris pontis (et fibrae)

N. oculomotorius

Fig. 121.

191

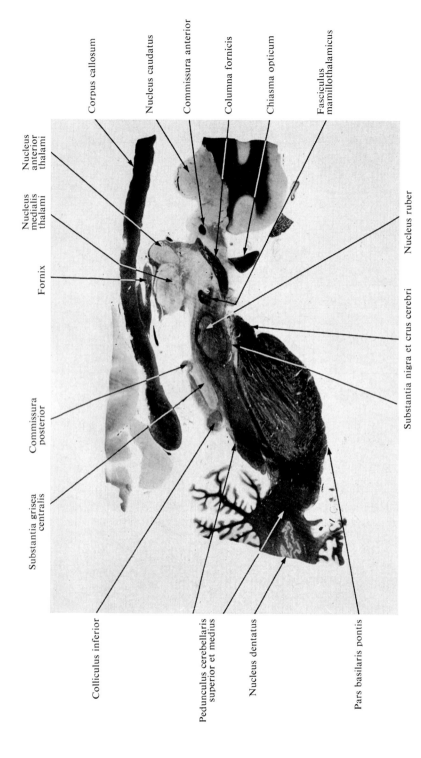

Corpus callosum

Nucleus caudatus

Commissura anterior

Columna fornicis

Chiasma opticum

Fasciculus
mamillothalamicus

Nucleus
anterior
thalami

Nucleus
medialis
thalami

Fornix

Commissura
posterior

Substantia grisea
centralis

Colliculus inferior

Pedunculus cerebellaris
superior et medius

Nucleus dentatus

Pars basilaris pontis

Substantia nigra et crus cerebri

Nucleus ruber

Fig. 122.

Nucleus anterior thalami

Fasciculus mamillothalamicus

Columna fornicis

Commissura anterior

Hypothalamus

Commissurae supraopticae

Chiasma opticum

Corpus mamillare

Nucleus ruber

Nucleus medialis thalami

Nucleus lateralis thalami

Fasciculus retroflexus

Decussatio pedunculorum cerebellarium superiorum

Pars basilaris pontis

Pyramis

Oliva

Fornix (fimbria)

Splenium corporis callosi

Pulvinar

Colliculus superior

Colliculus inferior

Tractus tegmentalis centralis

Lemniscus medialis

Fig. 123.

193

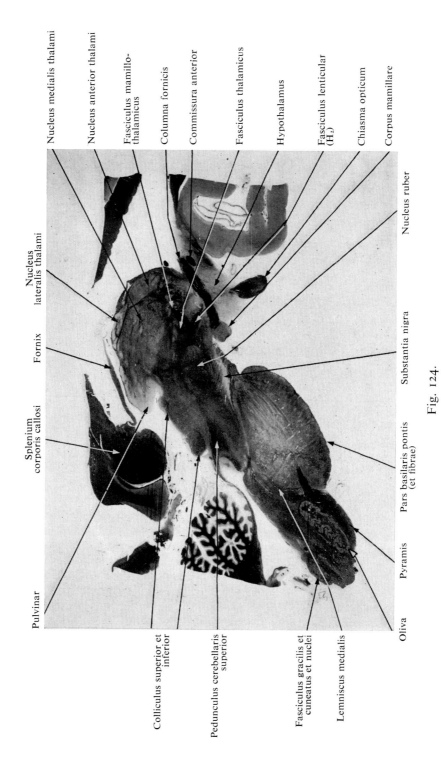

Pulvinar

Nucleus
lateralis thalami

Fornix

Splenium
corporis callosi

Nucleus medialis thalami

Nucleus anterior thalami

Fasciculus mamillo-
thalamicus

Columna fornicis

Commissura anterior

Fasciculus thalamicus

Hypothalamus

Fasciculus lenticular
(H₂)

Chiasma opticum

Corpus mamillare

Colliculus superior et
inferior

Pedunculus cerebellaris
superior

Fasciculus gracilis et
cuneatus et nuclei

Lemniscus medialis

Oliva

Pyramis

Pars basilaris pontis
(et fibrae)

Substantia nigra

Nucleus ruber

Fig. 124.

194

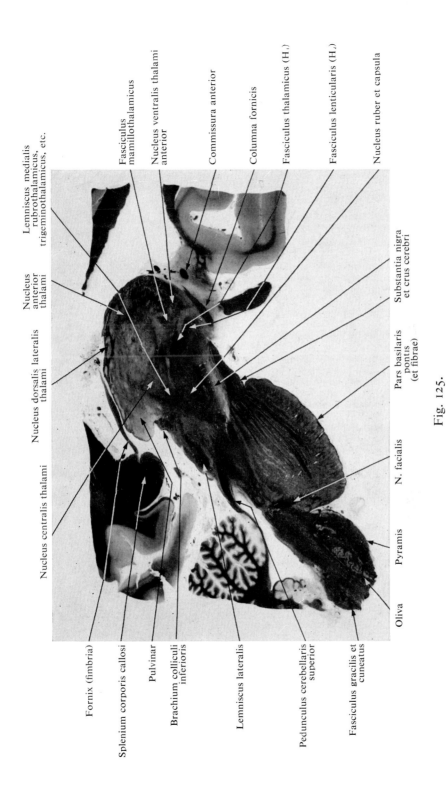

Lemniscus medialis
rubrothalamicus,
trigeminothalamicus, etc.

Fasciculus
mamillothalamicus

Nucleus ventralis thalami
anterior

Commissura anterior

Columna fornicis

Fasciculus thalamicus (H₁)

Fasciculus lenticularis (H₂)

Nucleus ruber et capsula

Nucleus
anterior
thalami

Nucleus dorsalis lateralis
thalami

Nucleus centralis thalami

Substantia nigra
et crus cerebri

Pars basilaris
pontis
(et fibrae)

N. facialis

Pyramis

Oliva

Fornix (fimbria)

Splenium corporis callosi

Pulvinar

Brachium colliculi
inferioris

Lemniscus lateralis

Pedunculus cerebellaris
superior

Fasciculus gracilis et
cuneatus

Fig. 125.

195

Capsula interna (genu)

Nucleus caudatus

Nucleus ventralis lateralis

Commissura anterior

Ansa lenticularis

Chiasma opticum

Nucleus ventralis thalami posterior (medialis et lateralis)

Nucleus centralis thalami

Nucleus subthalamicus

Lemniscus medialis

Substantia nigra et crus cerebri

Fibrae pontis transversae

Pulvinar

Fasciculi longitudinales

Fornix

Splenium corporis callosi

Brachium colliculi superioris

Corpus geniculatum mediale

Brachium colliculi inferioris

Lemniscus lateralis

Pedunculus cerebellaris superior

Lemniscus medialis

Fig. 126.

196

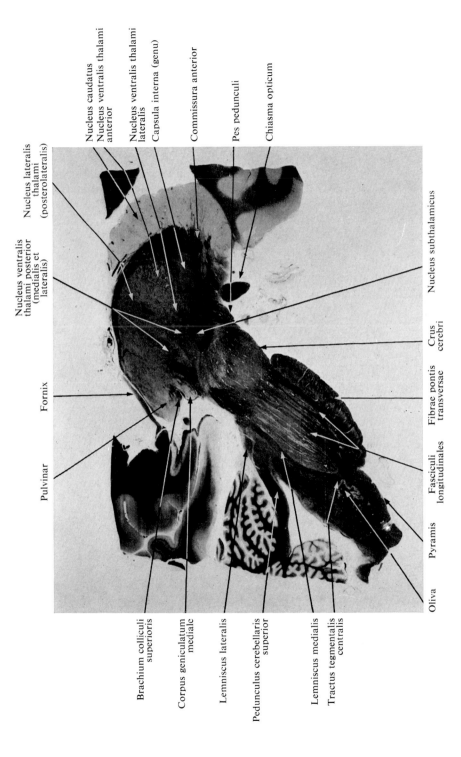

Nucleus lateralis thalami (posterolateralis)

Nucleus caudatus
Nucleus ventralis thalami anterior
Nucleus ventralis thalami lateralis
Capsula interna (genu)
Commissura anterior
Pes pedunculi
Chiasma opticum

Nucleus ventralis thalami posterior (medialis et lateralis)

Fornix

Pulvinar

Nucleus subthalamicus

Crus cerebri

Fibrae pontis transversae

Fasciculi longitudinales

Pyramis

Oliva

Brachium colliculi superioris
Corpus geniculatum mediale
Lemniscus lateralis
Pedunculus cerebellaris superior
Lemniscus medialis
Tractus tegmentalis centralis

Fig. 127.

197

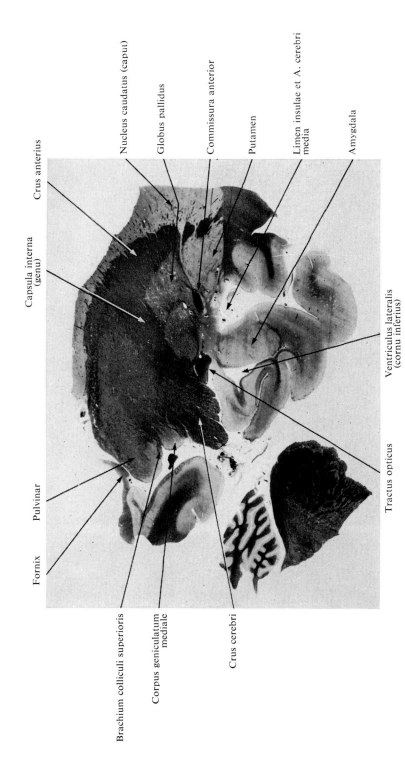

Nucleus caudatus (caput)

Globus pallidus

Commissura anterior

Putamen

Limen insulae et A. cerebri media

Amygdala

Crus anterius

Capsula interna (genu)

Pulvinar

Fornix

Brachium colliculi superioris

Corpus geniculatum mediale

Crus cerebri

Ventriculus lateralis (cornu inferius)

Tractus opticus

Fig. 128.

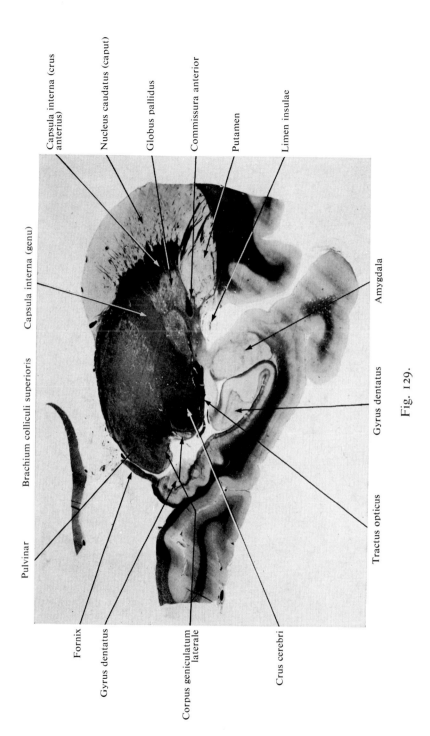

Capsula interna (crus anterius)

Nucleus caudatus (caput)

Globus pallidus

Commissura anterior

Putamen

Limen insulae

Capsula interna (genu)

Brachium colliculi superioris

Pulvinar

Amygdala

Gyrus dentatus

Tractus opticus

Fornix

Gyrus dentatus

Corpus geniculatum laterale

Crus cerebri

Fig. 129.

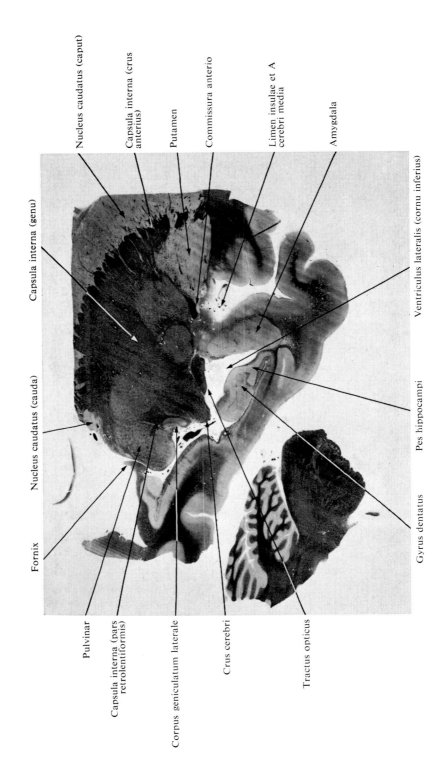

Nucleus caudatus (caput)

Capsula interna (crus anterius)

Putamen

Commissura anterio

Limen insulae et A cerebri media

Amygdala

Capsula interna (genu)

Ventriculus lateralis (cornu inferius)

Fig. 130.

Nucleus caudatus (cauda)

Fornix

Pes hippocampi

Gyrus dentatus

Pulvinar

Capsula interna (pars retrolentiiformis)

Corpus geniculatum laterale

Crus cerebri

Tractus opticus

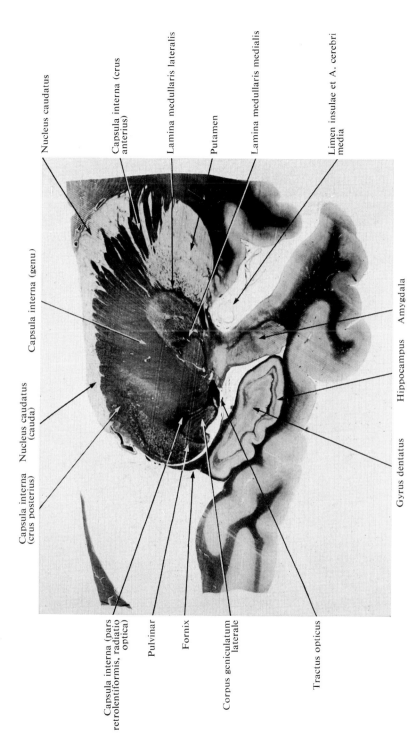

Nucleus caudatus

Capsula interna (crus anterius)

Lamina medullaris lateralis

Putamen

Lamina medullaris medialis

Limen insulae et A. cerebri media

Capsula interna (genu)

Capsula interna (crus posterius)

Nucleus caudatus (cauda)

Capsula interna (pars retrolentiformis, radiatio optica)

Pulvinar

Fornix

Corpus geniculatum laterale

Tractus opticus

Gyrus dentatus

Hippocampus

Amygdala

Fig. 131.

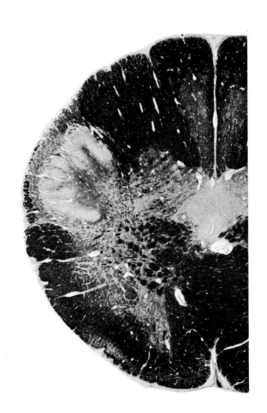

Fig. 132.

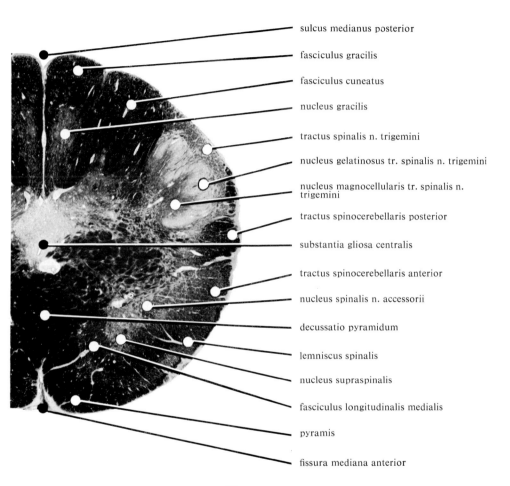

sulcus medianus posterior

fasciculus gracilis

fasciculus cuneatus

nucleus gracilis

tractus spinalis n. trigemini

nucleus gelatinosus tr. spinalis n. trigemini

nucleus magnocellularis tr. spinalis n. trigemini

tractus spinocerebellaris posterior

substantia gliosa centralis

tractus spinocerebellaris anterior

nucleus spinalis n. accessorii

decussatio pyramidum

lemniscus spinalis

nucleus supraspinalis

fasciculus longitudinalis medialis

pyramis

fissura mediana anterior

Fig. 133.

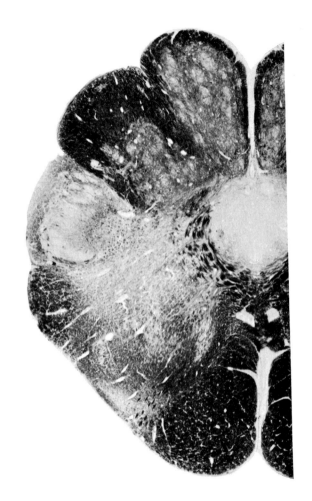

Fig. 134.

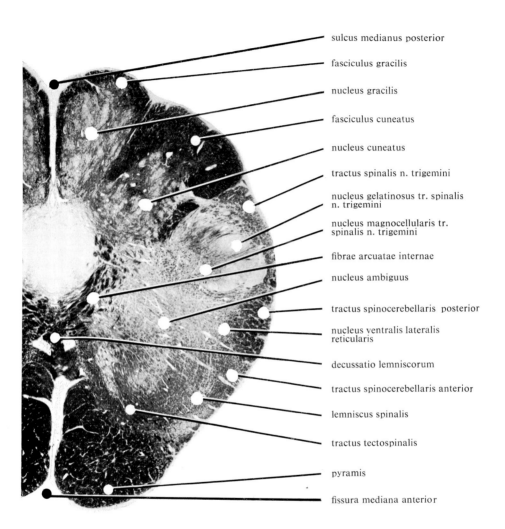

sulcus medianus posterior

fasciculus gracilis

nucleus gracilis

fasciculus cuneatus

nucleus cuneatus

tractus spinalis n. trigemini

nucleus gelatinosus tr. spinalis
n. trigemini

nucleus magnocellularis tr.
spinalis n. trigemini

fibrae arcuatae internae

nucleus ambiguus

tractus spinocerebellaris posterior

nucleus ventralis lateralis
reticularis

decussatio lemniscorum

tractus spinocerebellaris anterior

lemniscus spinalis

tractus tectospinalis

pyramis

fissura mediana anterior

Fig. 135.

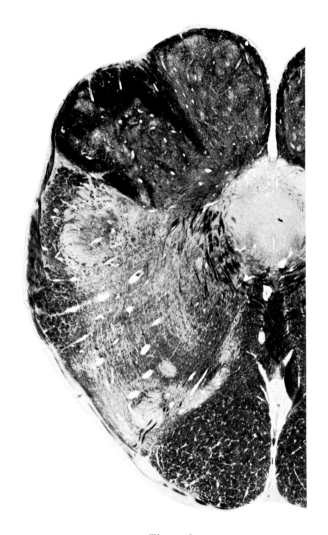

Fig. 136.

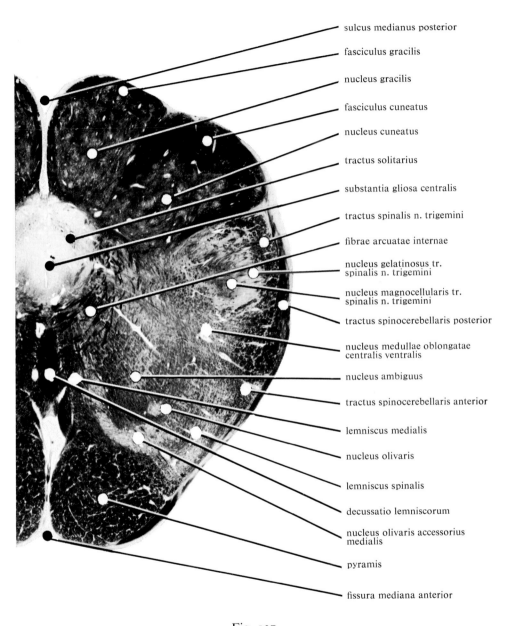

sulcus medianus posterior

fasciculus gracilis

nucleus gracilis

fasciculus cuneatus

nucleus cuneatus

tractus solitarius

substantia gliosa centralis

tractus spinalis n. trigemini

fibrae arcuatae internae

nucleus gelatinosus tr.
spinalis n. trigemini

nucleus magnocellularis tr.
spinalis n. trigemini

tractus spinocerebellaris posterior

nucleus medullae oblongatae
centralis ventralis

nucleus ambiguus

tractus spinocerebellaris anterior

lemniscus medialis

nucleus olivaris

lemniscus spinalis

decussatio lemniscorum

nucleus olivaris accessorius
medialis

pyramis

fissura mediana anterior

Fig. 137.

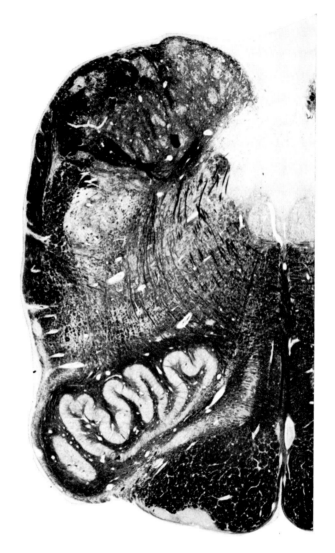

Fig. 138.

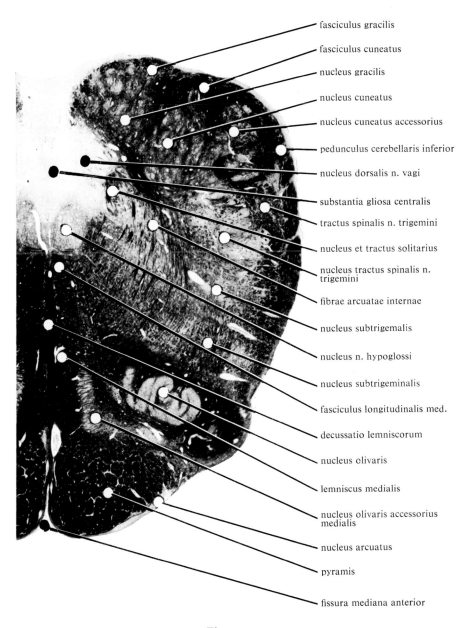

fasciculus gracilis

fasciculus cuneatus

nucleus gracilis

nucleus cuneatus

nucleus cuneatus accessorius

pedunculus cerebellaris inferior

nucleus dorsalis n. vagi

substantia gliosa centralis

tractus spinalis n. trigemini

nucleus et tractus solitarius

nucleus tractus spinalis n. trigemini

fibrae arcuatae internae

nucleus subtrigemalis

nucleus n. hypoglossi

nucleus subtrigeminalis

fasciculus longitudinalis med.

decussatio lemniscorum

nucleus olivaris

lemniscus medialis

nucleus olivaris accessorius medialis

nucleus arcuatus

pyramis

fissura mediana anterior

Fig. 139.

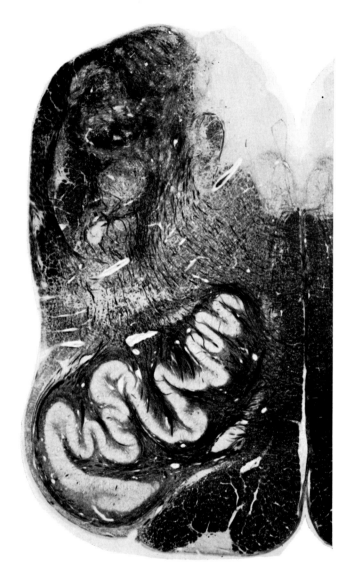

Fig. 140.

nucleus gracilis

substantia gliosa centralis

nucleus cuneatus

nucleus dorsalis n. vagi

nucleus et tractus solitarius

nucleus cuneatus accessorius

pedunculus cerebellaris inferior

tractus spinalis n. trigemini

nucleus tractus spinalis n. trigemini

nucleus n. hypoglossi

tractus spinocerebellaris posterior

nucleus subtrigeminalis

fibrae arcuatae internae

lemniscus spinalis

formatio reticularis (ventralis lateralis)

fasciculus longitudinalis medialis

tractus tectospinalis

nucleus olivaris

lemniscus medialis

nucleus olivaris accessorius medialis

pyramis

nucleus arcuatus

fissura mediana anterior

Fig. 141.

211

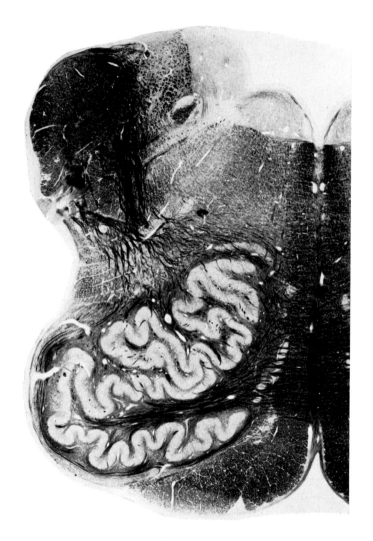

Fig. 142.

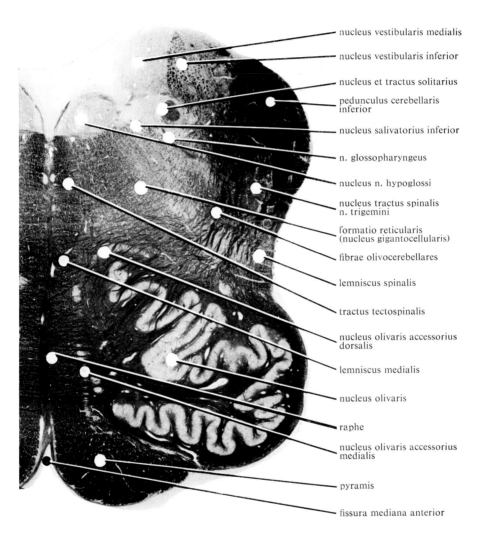

nucleus vestibularis medialis

nucleus vestibularis inferior

nucleus et tractus solitarius

pedunculus cerebellaris inferior

nucleus salivatorius inferior

n. glossopharyngeus

nucleus n. hypoglossi

nucleus tractus spinalis n. trigemini

formatio reticularis (nucleus gigantocellularis)

fibrae olivocerebellares

lemniscus spinalis

tractus tectospinalis

nucleus olivaris accessorius dorsalis

lemniscus medialis

nucleus olivaris

raphe

nucleus olivaris accessorius medialis

pyramis

fissura mediana anterior

Fig. 143.

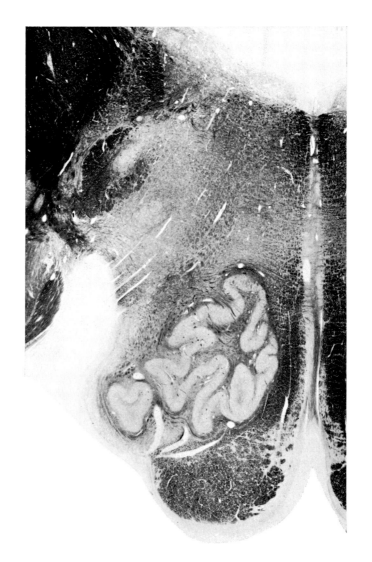

Fig. 144.

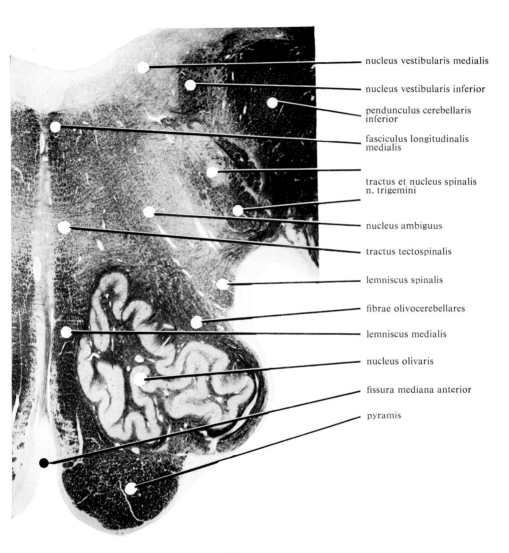

nucleus vestibularis medialis

nucleus vestibularis inferior

pendunculus cerebellaris inferior

fasciculus longitudinalis medialis

tractus et nucleus spinalis n. trigemini

nucleus ambiguus

tractus tectospinalis

lemniscus spinalis

fibrae olivocerebellares

lemniscus medialis

nucleus olivaris

fissura mediana anterior

pyramis

Fig. 145.

Annotated bibliography

The following annotated bibliography includes titles of representative atlases of the human and other mammalian species. They have been chosen to providing a guide line to further study in this field.

ANGEVINE, J. B. JR., MANCALL, E. L. and YAKOVLEV, P. I., (1961); The human cerebellum. An atlas of gross topography in serial sections. Little Brown, Boston.
  The atlas consists of 42 photographs of stained sections of adult human cerebella cut in the 3 cardinal planes. The sections in the sagittal series were prepared from the brain of a 28-year-old male, who died a few hours after fracturing his cervical spine in a fall from a scaffold. Brain weight, 1890 g. The horizontal series of sections was prepared from the brain of a 23-year-old male. There was a clinical history of encephalitis lethargica with postencephalitic parkinsonism. The cerebellum was unaffected and particularly well developed. The coronal series of sections was prepared from the brain of a 31-year-old mentally retarded female who had a clinical history of grand mal seizures and died in a mental hospital from miliary tuberculosis. The cerebellum was normal and the sections stained particularly well with hematoxylin.
  After approximately 3 months fixation in a 10% solution of commercial formalin, the brains were dehydrated in graded alcohols, embedded in celloidin and cut serially at 35 micra. Every tenth section was stained with the Loyez method for myelin sheaths, and every adjacent section was stained with the cresyl violet method of Bielschowsky–Plien for nerve cells.
  Each photograph is matched by a drawing made from the original myelin-stained section. The degree of enlargement for the drawing and the photographic material is 3 times.
  The nomenclature used is that employed by Larsell.
BRUCE, A., (1901); A topographical atlas of the spinal cord. Williams and Norgate, Oxford.
  The spinal cord employed in the investigation was obtained from a young adult female. It was the last of a series of five and was the only one of these that satisfactorily fulfilled the requirements of being free from flaw and from evidence of any morbid condition. The spinal cord was removed 24 hours after death.
  Fixation was in a chrome-alum-copper solution and the sections stained according to the Ford Robertson modification of Heller's method. In staining the nerve cells, toluidin and polychrome blue were employed.
  Photographs of 32 sections are reproduced at a magnification of 10 times actual size. For the demonstration of motor nerve cells a typical section was selected from each segment and its grey matter photographed with a magnification of 20 times actual size.
CHIRO, G. DI, (1961); An atlas of detailed normal pneumoencephalographic anatomy. Thomas, Springfield, Ill.
  The pneumoencephalographic atlas provides a detailed study *in vivo* of the intracranial structures by the combined techniques of fractional encephalography and laminography.
  Most of the encephalograms used in the present study have been obtained with the encephalographic technique *ad modum Lindgren*. All the reproductions have been done with Logetron. The roentgenograms in various planes are reproduced in the same size as the original. Explanatory sketches have been used when necessary. There are 283 reproductions.
  The nomenclature of the *Nomina Anatomica Parisiensia* (1955) was used and the equivalent English names have been added in most cases.

DAVIS, R. and HUFFMAN, R. D., (1968); A Stereotaxic Atlas of the Brain of the Baboon (Papio). Univ. of Texas Press, Austin.

A total of 15 female baboon brains was used in the preparation of this stereotaxic atlas. These were adult animals and their body weight varied from 18 to 33 pounds. These animals were captured in central East Africa (Kenya) and included both *Papio cynocephalus* and *Papio anubis*.

The brain sections included in this atlas were chosen because they encompass those areas that are of most importance to neurophysiological study. The sections presented in the atlas were obtained from a single brain and photomicrographs of both Nissl- and Weil-stained sections have been included. An abbreviated name of each structure illustrated in the photomicrographs has been labelled directly on the plates; the full designation is found in the key to abbreviations located at the bottom of each page. *Nomina Anatomica* was the main guide for the nomenclature used in this atlas.

DELMAS, A. and PERTUISET, B., (1959); Cranio-cerebral topometry in man. Masson, Paris, and Thomas, Springfield, Ill., U.S.A.

Cranio-cerebral topometry is a metric topography of the brain. Topometry defines the location and variations in position of structures in the frontal, sagittal and horizontal planes. The atlas contains both topographic and topometric documentation on the positions of intra-cerebral structures and their variations in relation to their location with stereotaxic instruments.

28 heads were used for this study. The subjects were perfused with 40% formaldehyde containing sodium chloride. The heads were kept for 5 to 6 days in formaldehyde, and then embedded in plasticine. After being placed in a freezer for 5 days at $-20°$ C, the plaster, skull and brain formed a homogeneous mass of exceptional hardness. Sectioning was accomplished by means of an electric saw.

94 life-size photographs and 94 schematic drawings are represented of whole human heads sectioned along three planes: sagittal, horizontal and frontal. These illustrations permit seeing both the cerebral structures and the bony framework. A full description of all cerebral structures charted in the atlas is given in English and French.

The nomenclature of the *Nomina Anatomica Parisiensia* (1955) was used.

DELUCCHI, M. R., DENNIS, B. J. and ADEY, W. R., (1965); A stereotaxic atlas of the chimpanzee brain. (*Pan satyrus*). University of California Press, Los Angeles.

Eight chimpanzee brains were used. The animals were equally divided between males and females with ages of from one to five years. The body weights varied from 15 to 39 pounds.

Brain number 1 was fixed in formalin-alcohol for 1 week, after which frozen sections in the frontal plane were made. Brains number 2, 3, 4, 5 and 8 were used for celloidin sectioning in frontal, sagittal and horizontal planes. These were put through alcohols, impregnated with a graded series of parlodion for 3 months. The types of staining used in this atlas are the Weil–Weigert and Nissl methods for all brains, and in addition one brain was stained by the Klüver technique.

The coordinates induced in the final atlas were used as a basis for chronic depth electrode placements in the brain of 4 living chimpanzee. A sample recording with electrode placements in the amygdala, hippocampus, mid-brain, reticular formation and parieto-occipital cortex is included for a drowsy state.

Line drawings based on tracings made directly from projections of whole brain slices are included for all sections. Horsley–Clarke reference planes are given for each drawing and photomicrograph. In this atlas the Horsley–Clarke zero plane is 10 mm above the interaural plane.

The nomenclature used in this atlas is based on the *Nomina Anatomica Parisiensia* (1955) and Walker's description of the chimpanzee thalamus (*J. Anat.*, vol. 73, 1938).

DUMITRESCU, H., (1959); Atlas citoarchitectonic al creierului de cobai. Editura Academiei Republicii Populare Romine.

The sections used represent those which would be found in a guinea pig weighing from 600 to 650 g.

The Weigert–Pal method for nerve fibers and a Nissl staining method were alternately used on sections which extend from the rostral forebrain to the level of the nucleus facialis in the hindbrain. There is then one further figure at the pyramidal decussation.

There are 41 frontal sections and 8 photomicrographs of cells in selected regions. Identification of structures is accomplished by the use of transparent overlays.

EMMERS, R. and AKERT, K., (1963); A stereotaxic atlas of the brain of the squirrel monkey (*Saimiri sciureus*). University of Wisconsin Press, Madison.

This atlas is based on the brains of 13 male squirrel monkeys weighing from 575 to 920 grams.

The atlas is divided into two parts. Part I contains 20 photographs illustrating the craniocerebral relationships with the head and the brain of the squirrel monkey viewed in relation to the stereotaxic position.

The sections used for Part II were obtained from the histological material of 8 squirrel monkey brains. The animals were sacrificed by perfusing their brains through the aorta with a small amount of normal saline solution, followed by 4% formaldehyde in 1.25% saline. Blocks from 10 to 15 mm thick were prepared. These slices were sectioned serially at 50 micra according to the frozen section method described by Marshall, and two series were mounted with albumin. Every tenth section was stained with cresylecht violet (Nissl method), while an adjacent series was stained with iron hematoxylin (Weil method).

There are photographs of 75 frontal sections in Part II which are reproduced at a magnification of 15 times actual size. A series of 75 drawings of these sections is reproduced on adjacent pages facing the photographs.

Latin nomenclature was adopted and, with a few exceptions, the *Nomina Anatomica* (Kopsch, 1957) was followed.

FRIEDE, R. L., (1961); A histochemical atlas of tissue oxidation in the brain stem of the cat. Karger, Basel, New York.

Twenty adult cats were used for this investigation without consideration of sex. The animals were killed under slight pentothal anesthesia.

The material obtained from the cats was:

One complete paraffin series, stained with chromalum gallocyanin, as a reference to the cytoarchitecture. There is one complete series for each of the enzymes investigated, while one control series establishes the relationships between incubation time and distribution of succinic dehydrogenase. Five complete series demonstrate the distribution of capillaries in the brain. Four of these series were obtained by injection with india ink; the fifth demonstrated the vessels by staining the erythrocytes by the technique of Slonimski and Chunge; maximal bloodfilling of the vessels was obtained by killing the animal by histamine shock. The data on capillarization are presented in text form. The demonstration of enzymes localization was based on frozen sections, 60 μ thick, which were cut from unfixed tissue and then transferred directly to the incubation media. Incubation was terminated with 10% formalin.

Sections were mounted with glycerin gelatin after a part of the water had been removed in a mixture of water and glycerin. Part of the material was dehydrated with alcohol and mounted with xyline and balsam.

Quantitative analyses were measured with a Welch Densichron densitometer.

Photographs of 24 frontal sections are reproduced in the atlas. The large plates of the atlas demonstrate succinic dehydrogenase and TPN and DPN diaphorase and are accompanied by drawings which show the names of the nuclei and the densitometer readings.

The *Nomina Anatomica Parisiensias* (1955) was used in this atlas.

GERGEN, J. A. and MacLEAN, P. D., (1962); A stereotaxic atlas of the squirrel monkey's brain. (*Saimiri sciureus*). U.S. Department of health, education and welfare. Public Health Service. National Institutes of Health, Bethesda, Maryland.

31 adult male animals with a mean body weight of 821 g were used for this study. 29 brains were cut in the frontal plane and 2 in the sagittal plane. Extensive measurements by the authors indicate that in carrying out stereotaxic exploration with a modified Horseley–Clarke apparatus, one would have a 50 % chance of coming within 0.5 mm of a point described by the coordinates in the atlas.

The animals were perfused through the heart with 100–200 ml of normal saline at 40° C, followed by an equal amount of a mixture of 10 % formalin–1.0 % agar agar (U.S.P.) at 40° C. Serial frozen sections were cut at approximately 50 μ and stained according to the cresyl violet and Lillie's variant of the Weil–Weigert method.

Photographs of 64 frontal sections are reproduced in the atlas at a magnification of 7 times the actual size. The cresyl violet and Weil–Weigert photographs are placed face to face. There are also photographs of 15 sagittal sections stained by the Weil–Weigert method on 7 males.

The terminology is based on that compiled by Riley.

GERHARD, L., (1968); Atlas des Mittel- und Zwischenhirns des Kaninchens. Springer, Berlin.

This atlas presents a continuation of the works of *Meessen* and *Olszewski*. Most of the plates were magnified at 20:1, several at 40:1 and some at 100:1. To fascilitate electron-microscopic studies, care was taken to point out in some parts of the brain correlations between the surface pattern and underlying nuclei and tracts. In addition to the traditionally used frontal sections, horizontal and sagittal planes were included to aid spatial orientation.

The plates are accompanied by a short legend describing the main anatomical structures to be seen. Brief descriptions giving information about individual structures, nuclei as well as tracts, then follow.

The last part of the atlas deals with efforts to present a functional correlation of nuclei and tracts as far as these are known today.

JASPER, H. H. and AJMONE-MARSAN, C., (1956); A stereotaxic atlas of the diencephalon of the cat. National Research Council of Canada, Ottawa, Canada.

50 cat brains were used for this atlas. Three photographs of the forebrain region relate the gross surface brain anatomy to the stereotaxic coordinates. Electrodes positions in the atlas series are marked by the electrolytic deposit of iron from the tip of a steel electrode when the electrode is connected to the positive pole of a 1.5 V battery. The site of iron deposit is stained by the Prussian blue reaction during preparation for histological study, as described by Hess and Marshall. Serial sections were made at 50 micra thickness and stained by the Nissl method and the Weil methods.

Photographs and drawings of 27 frontal planes are reproduced in the atlas at a magnification of 10 times actual size. Facing each drawing are microphotographs of adjacent sections at the same frontal plane, the one on the left representing the Nissl stain and one on the right the Weil stain for fibers.

The nomenclature employed was largely that used by Walker for the monkey with occasional modifications suggested by Olszewski.

KÖNIG, J. F. R. and KLIPPEL, R. A., (1963); The rat brain. A stereotaxic atlas of the forebrain and lower parts of the brain stem. Williams and Wilkins, Baltimore.

The atlas consists of both frontal and sagittal sections of female rats weighing 150 g. The axis for the rat forebrain for the frontal sections is defined as being vertically directed to an adequate base plane which comes together with the boundary plane between diencephalon and mesencephalon. The base plane is defined as the frontal plane that lies in the line drawn from the median point just behind the posterior commissure to the median rostral point of the fossa interpeduncularis. The frontal zero plane lies in the interaural line. The horizontal zero plane is situated 4.9 mm above the interaural line.

The brains were stored in 8 % formalin for one week and embedded in gelatine. Sections were cut at 10 μ and stained with Sudan black B. For the drawings, the brains were fixed in situ in 8 % neutral formalin and stored in formalin for three days. The sections from these brains were stained by tartaric acid-Thionine.

A series of 66 photographs from frontal and sagittal sections are reproduced at a magnification of 17.5 times actual size. The black stained myelin sheaths are reproduced in white and the unstained cell nuclei appear as small but distinct stipples. Brain nuclei rich in cells stand out as dark areas.

A series of 66 drawings is reproduced opposing the photographs. The photographs selected from the Sudan black B series were photographed at an enlargement of 13 times and the subsequent outlines of these photographic patterns were copied.

The nomenclature used is based on the sixth edition of *Nomina Anatomica*, revised by the International Anatomical Nomenclature Committee and approved by the Seventh International Congress of Anatomists New York, 1960.

KUSAMA, T., (1970); Stereotaxic Atlas of the Brain of Macaca Fuscata. SBN 8391–0011.6.

The continuing refinement of neurological surgery and the growing importance of sociopsychological research, especially the physiological aspects of mental disorder, have made comparative anatomical studies of the brain indispensible. This large atlas provides a detailed anatomical photographic study of the brain of *Macaca fuscata*, a monkey species of great experimental value because of the structural similarity between its brain and that of humans.

LUDWIG, E. and KLINGLER, J., (1911); Atlas cerebri humani. The inner structure of the brain, demonstrated on the basis of macroscopical preparations.

This is a photographic atlas of dissected brain preparations. In preparing the material for dissection the preparation method of Klingler was used. The brain is suspended in a fixing fluid of 5% formalin. 7 weeks later the further preparation was begun. (the brain may be stored in 5% formol, up to a year or more). In the second step the brain is washed in running water, drained and placed on a flat tray in a refrigerator for 8 days at a temperature of $-8°$ to $-10°$ C. The brain is then thawed in running water and can be stored as long as desired in 5% formol. Once dissection has started, the work may be interrupted overnight or longer and the material kept safely in 2% formol.

Photographs of 100 frontal, sagittal and horizontal sections are reproduced in the atlas.

MANOCHA, S. L., SHANTA, T. R. and BOURNE, G. H., (1968); A Stereotaxic Atlas of the Brain of the Cebus Monkey (*Cebus apella*). Oxford University Press.

This stereotaxic atlas of the brain of the Cebus monkey is designed to provide a detailed Horsley-Clarke co-ordinate type of atlas for use with various neurophysiological and neuroanatomical studies and experiments. The value of this atlas lies mainly in the fact that it provides details of all the important nuclei and fiber systems in the brain of this New World monkey, with their co-ordinates. Because of its intelligence and its more attractive personality the Cebus is an important alternative to the widely used Rhesus monkey for neurophysiological and neuroanatomical studies. It is also much cheaper to purchase and to keep than the Rhesus and does not require as strong or expensive caging. The Cebus is thus an attractive primate for many types of experimental and anatomical study.

Five animals of both sexes weighing from 2.0–2.9 kg were used for this study. The brains were perfused with formalin and stained both for nerve fiber systems (Weil method) and for cellular systems (Nissl method). Vertical sections are presented throughout the atlas.

McCORMICK, J. B and BLATT, M. B., (1961); Atlas and demonstration technique of the central nervous system. Thomas, Springfield, Ill.

This atlas is based on the human brain. The technique for removal of the brain and spinal cord at autopsy is described and illustrated. The whole brains are then fixed in a special 5% buffered formalin containing Prague powder and ascorbic acid to maintain natural tissue coloration. Brains are then embedded in a gelatin-carbowax-400 mixture which can be blocked and sliced after hardening. Then slices may be mounted in plastic envelopes.

Sketches of the intact brain provide for a gross nomenclature. Labeled drawings of 53 coronal sections provide for an atlas extending from the polus frontalis to the decussation of the pyramids.

MEESSEN, H. and OLSZEWSKI, J., (1949); A cytoarchitectonic atlas of the rhombencephalon of the rabbit. Karger, Basel–New York.

The atlas is based primarily on four rabbit brains. The first animal was killed by air-embolism, the others by Evipan narcosis.

The frontal sections made from the first brain were sectioned at 20 μ and stained with cresyl-violet and Heidenhain–Weigert, following fixation with 4% neutral formalin and paraffin embedding. In a second complete cresyl-violet series the brain was first perfused with physiological saline solution and then with 4% formalin. A third brain, prepared sagittally, was fixed in the same way. The fourth brain was cut sagittally into two halves; one was fixed in 4% formalin, the other in sublimate glacial acetic acid. The sections were stained with cresyl-violet.

Photographs of 15 frontal sections are reproduced in the atlas. The magnification of the plates is 40 times the actual size, while the partial views are 200 times the actual size and the single nerve cells are 1000 times the actual size.

The old customary names were retained in the nomenclature.

MILLER, R. A. and BURACK, E., (1968); Atlas of the Central Nervous System in Man. William & Wilkins, Baltimore.

The atlas is based on a series of slides stained according to the Weigert method. The legends attempt to develop the concept of the functional organization of the central nervous system by a running account of segmental reflex pathways and of supra-segmental fiber tracts to and from higher levels of the central nervous system. The practice of indicating both the origin and determination of each major fiber tract fascilitates the earlier conceptualisation of the nervous system.

MONNIER, M. and GANGLOFF, H., (1961); Atlas for stereotaxic brain research on the conscious rabbit. Elsevier, Amsterdam–London–New York.

Over 500 rabbits of from 2.5 to 3.0 kg weight have been used for the atlas.

In the atlas the Hess and the Horsley–Clarke techniques are used. Details for establishing the stereotaxic coordinates and implanting stereotaxic sockets are included with a chart for positioning of the sockets in relation to frontal and sagittal sections. There are also several examples of various types of EEG recordings of spontaneous brain activity, arousal, after discharge, etc.

The sections were stained by the Loyez and Weil methods. (Additional details pertaining to histologic methods may be found in the Winkler and Potter atlas of the rabbit brain, 1911, and the Messen and Olszewki atlas of rabbit hindbrain, 1949).

Photographs of 22 frontal and sagittal sections are reproduced in the atlas with the appropriate coordinates indicated.

The nomenclature of the *Nomina Anatomica Parisiensia* (1955) was used.

OLSZEWSKI, J., (1952); The thalamus of the *Macaca mulatta*. An atlas for use with the stereotaxic instrument. Karger, Basel–New York.

Twenty brains of *Macaca mulatta* weighing between 2.6 and 7.9 kg have been used in this study.

The animals were perfused with 150 ml of normal saline which was followed by an equal amount of fixative (distilled water, 40%; absolute ethanol, 50%; and formol, 10%) given through the carotid arteries. The head was then removed and additional fixing procedures followed. Various sketches relate the brain to the sterotaxic coordinates. The brains were embedded in paraffin, serially sectioned at from 30 to 50 μ in the frontal, sagittal and horizontal planes and stained according to the Nissl and Heidenhain method.

Selected sections in the atlas are shown at a magnification of 20 times and the distance between selected figures is from 10 to 20 sections. There are 92 photographic pictures based on myelin: Nissl stained material and numerous sketches.

Nomenclature is based on that of Walker (*J. Anat.*, vol. 73, 1938).

OLSZEWSKI, J. and BAXTER, D., (1954); Cytoarchitecture of the human brain stem. Karger, Basel, New York.

15 Brain stems were used for the atlas from persons aged between 15 weeks to 77 years. There is also one premature child of 7 months postconception. There were different causes of death, which are indicated in the atlas. Fixation was by immersion in 10% formalin. Blocks were embedded in paraffin and sections cut at 20 μ. The interval between mounted sections was from $\frac{1}{2}$ to 2 mm and the planes of section were transverse and sagittal.

Photographs of 19 Nissl stained cross sections are reproduced in the atlas at a magnification of 15 times actual size. The neurons were silhouetted with india ink. Various regions of the 19 representative cross sections were photographed at 40 times magnification. These appear on pages adjacent to the corresponding semischematic drawings. Part I of the atlas contains 42 major plates and provides information of the cytoarchitecture. Part II of the atlas contains photomicrographs of individual nuclei (magnification 100 to 150 times) with accompanying anatomical descriptions.

The Latin nomenclature is used in this atlas.

RILEY, H. A., (1960); An atlas of the basal ganglia, brain stem and spinal cord, based on myelin-stained material. Reprinted by Hafner, New York.

An atlas of the human brain. The method used was the standard Pal–Weigert technique.

Photographs of 157 transverse sections are reproduced at varying magnifications (22 to 40 times) through the medulla spinalis from the sacral to the cervical level. There are also 63 horizontal sections (magnifications: 2 to 5 times) and 39 sagittal sections (magnification: 2 to 4 times) through the brain stem.

The nomenclature used is based in part on that of Stieve, while in many instances old familiar terms were retained.

SCHALTENBRAND, G. and BAILEY, P., (1959); Introduction to the stereotaxic operation and an atlas of the human brain. Thieme, Stuttgart. (Three volumes, English and German text).

A most beautiful but also very expensive ($233.35) atlas of the human brain.

The first volume discusses the technical features involved in the preparation of the atlas, the general problem of stereotaxis and a number of neuroanatomical and neurophysiological problems.

The second volume consists of 57 beautifully prepared macroscopic brain sections in frontal, sagittal and horizontal planes. The magnification is twice the actual size. Transparent overlays are marked with the stereotaxic coordinates. The last 26 plates are of myelin-stained microscopic sections in each of the three planes, at a magnification of 4 times actual size.

The third volume consists of 18 plates of Nissl-stained microscopic sections taken in the frontal and sagittal planes. The photographs are enlarged by a factor 20.

SHANTA, T. R., MANOCHA, S. L. and BOURNE, G. H., (1969); A Stereotaxic Atlas of the Java Monkey Brain (Macaca irus). Karger, Basel.

Eight healthy animals of both sexes weighing 3–4 kg were used for the atlas. The brains were perfused with 10% formalin. Sections were stained with the Weil and Nissl methods The figures in the atlas were evenly magnified 9.5 times the original stained brain preparations.

The Nissl and Weil stained sections belonging to the same stereotaxic level have been arranged on opposite pages. The names of the major nuclei and fiber tracts are represented.

SINGER, M., (1962); The brain of the dog in section. Saunders, Philadelphia and London.

The brains of 3 disease-free beagle dogs, aged 5 months were used for this study. A fourth dog brain was used for the surface drawing of the whole brain. Each brain was sectioned in one of the three planes: horizontal, sagittal, and transverse and the sections cut at 35 micra.

The dogs were perfused through the heart with a physiological saline solution followed by solution of 10% formalin. The sections were stained by the iron-hematoxylin method of Loyez for myelin sheaths after mordanting in alum of iron. Alternate sections were stained for nerve cell bodies according to the cresyl violet method of Bielschowsky–Plien.

Photographs of 106 sections are reproduced, 49 in the transverse, 27 in the sagittal and 28 in the horizontal plane; there are 5 drawings of surface topography.

The approximate magnification of the sections in the atlas is as follows:

Full sagittal, 4.9 times.   Horizontal, 4.9 times.

Sagittal brain stem, 8.3 times.   Transverse, between 13.7 and 7.5 times.

The sagittal sections were taken from the left side.

The nomenclature of the *Nomina Anatomica, Parisiensia* (1955) was used.

SINGER, M. and YAKOVLEV, P. I., (1954, 1964); The human brain in sagittal section. Thomas, Springfield, Ill., 1st edition, 1954, 2nd edition, 1964.

Sections were made of a well developed dolichocephalic brain of a healthy adult male in his late twenties, who died after a fall and fracture of the neck. The brain weight was 1890 g. The brain measurements were 190 mm in the fronto-occipital plane and 125 mm in the bitemporal plane. Fixation was in 10% formalin solution followed by embedding in celloidin and sectioning at 35–40 micra. Sections were stained according to the cresyl violet method of Bielschowsky–Plien and the iron-hematoxylin method of Loyez for myelin sheaths after mordanting in alum of iron.

Photographs of 29 sagittal sections are reproduced in the atlas at a magnification of 1.5 times actual size. In the region of the brain stem, 16 of the figures for these sections are enlarged to a total magnification of 2.5 times and reproduced as separate plates to show with greater clarity the details of structure.

Basel and Jena anatomical nomenclature.

SNIDER, R. S. and LEE, J. C., (1961); A stereotaxic atlas of the monkey brain (*Macaca mulatta*). University of Chicago Press, Chicago.

This atlas, which provides stereotaxic coordinates of the monkey brain was originally started by S. W. Ranson and is based on the Horsley–Clark technical procedure introduced in 1908.

The method is based on a 3-dimensional coordinate system. Distances are measured anteriorly (A) and posteriorly (P) from a starting line through a plane which extends through the brain from one external auditory meatus to the other (the interaural plane). The sections selected in this atlas are numbered in 0.05 mm increments from this plane. The midline of the brain serves as a zero plane for sections either to the right (R) or left (L). The horizontal plane is parallel to the horizontal and 10 mm above the interaural plane. Horizontal planes (H) are expressed as negative (−) mm below and positive (+) mm above this plane. The monkeys should weigh between 4.5 kg and 3.5 kg to be used with these coordinates.

A frozen method for cutting the tissues, modified after Marshall, was used. Sections were stained with the Weil's modification of the Weigert method and the Windle, Rhines and Rankin's modification of the original Nissl stain. Since facing plates show comparable areas with the two stains, the book actually comprises two atlases.

Photomicrographs are made at a uniform magnification of 9.5 times from carefully chosen representative levels taken from 40-micra serial sections.

The nomenclature used was the *Nomina Anatomica Parisiensia* (1955).

SNIDER, R. A. and NIEMER, W. T., (1961); A Stereotaxic Atlas of the Cat Brain. University of Chicago Press, Chicago.

This atlas includes 124 photomicrographs which represent typical levels. The brains of more than 200 animals have been selected from stereotaxic experiments. Pairs of sections were selected at 0.5 mm intervals. One of each pair was stained by the Weil myelin-sheath method, the other by a Nissl method. They were then photographed at a uniform magnification of 13. This is in effect, therefore, a double atlas, combining the nuclear pattern and the fiber topography.

Each plate includes a detail legend at the side with arrows indicating the structures named. Marginal scales, corresponding to the stationary frame which is clamped to the animal's head, guide the experimenter to the exact point he wants. At the rear of the book, an index of major structures gives the localization and range of appearance of those structures most often under consideration.

TALAIRACH, J. and SZIKLA, G., (1967); Atlas d'Anatomie Stéréotaxique du Télencéphale. Masson & Cie, Paris.

This atlas is based on an exhaustive analysis of over a hundred carefully prepared human brains with more than four hundred selected angiograms and pneumencephalograms.

The first three chapters deal with the techniques used in preparation of the anatomical material; the presentation of sagittal, frontal and horizontal atlases, and detailed methods of radiological localization of principal structures utilizing positive contrast materials and air. The fourth chapter describes the statistical localization necessary for proportional representation of principal surface structures.

VERHAART, W. J. C., (1964); A Stereotaxic Atlas of the Brain Stem of the Cat. Van Gorcum, Assen.

This atlas has been produced as a successor to Winkler and Potter's Anatomical Guide to Researches on the Cat's Brain. The work is in two volumes, one of text and one of figures, allowing reference to both simultaneously. The work is primarily descriptive and must be very useful to anyone engaged in experimental work on the cat brain stem.

WINKLER, C. and POTTER, A., (1914); An anatomical guide to experimental researches on the cat's brain. Versluys, Amsterdam, 1914.

This atlas is based on a series of sections of the brain stem and cerebral hemisphere stained after the Weigert–Pal method for myelin. Figures based on Nissl and carmine or Van Gieson stained material are also included.

Sections of 15–20 micra thickness were used for the cytological preparations, though occasionally the sections were 25 micra thick. All the figures of cell and fiber structure are drawings which are enlarged 12 tot 15 times. There are also 4 photographs of the brain surface as seen from the ventral, lateral, medial and dorsal aspect (magnified about 2 times).

The nomenclature of Nissl is used.

Subject Index

226

fasciculus *(continued)*
  thalamicus, 52, 182, 183, 194, 195
  uncinatus, 28, 47, 122
fasciola cinerea, 179
fibrae
  arcuatae externae, 28, 88
    internae, 39, 205, 207, 209, 211
  corticonucleares, 171, 174, 176
  corticopontinae, 172, 174, 176
  corticospinales, 166, 168, 169, 172, 174, 176
  gustatorius, 27
  mandibularis, 41
  maxillaris, 41
  motorius, 27
  olivocerebellares, 213
  pontis transversae, 151, 153, 154, 166, 168,
    169, 172, 174, 176, 196, 197
  sensorius, 27
fimbria fornicis, 9, 10
  hippocampi, 127, 138
fields of Forel, 13
filum terminale, 22, 98
fissura
  hippocampalis, 8
  longitudinalis cerebri, 72, 73, 81
  mediana anterior, 21, 22, 33, 85, 86, 87, 88,
    160, 161, 162, 203, 205, 207, 209, 211, 213
  orbitalis superior, 24, 25
  posterolateralis, 16, 84
  postpyramidalis, 16, 84
  prepyramidalis, 15, 84
  prima, 15, 16, 84, 91, 149
flocculus, 16, 46, 82, 83, 86, 87, 88, 89, 104
folia cerebelli, 85
folium, 15, 84
foramen
  intraventriculare, 29, 30, 78, 143, 150
  jugulare, 26
  of Luschka, 25
  magnum, 3, 27, 68
  stylomastoideus, 26
forceps
  major, 124
  minor, 124
formatio reticularis, 15, 41, 44, 49, 51, 52, 211,
    213
  lateralis, 38
fornix, 9, 10, 29, 54, 55, 63, 78, 79, 111, 123,
    124, 125, 127, 136, 137, 138, 139, 143,
    144, 146, 148, 149, 150, 179, 180, 181,
    182, 183, 184, 185, 186, 187, 188, 189,
    191, 192, 196, 197, 198, 199, 200, 201
  fimbria, 193, 194, 195

fossa
  cranii anterior, 64, 65, 68
    media, 64, 65
    posterior, 68
  interpeduncularis, 33, 137, 152
  rhomboidea, 92
fovea
  inferior, 19, 90
  superior, 18, 19, 90
funiculus
  anterior, 22, 28, 160, 161, 162
  lateralis, 22, 28, 160, 161, 162
  posterior, 22, 28, 39, 160, 161, 162

ganglion, 10
  spinale, 22, 95
  trigeminale, 17, 25
genu, 5
  capsulae internae, 187, 188
  corporis callosi, 63, 76, 77, 78, 79, 131, 132,
    144, 148, 149, 150
  n. facialis, 166, 167
globus pallidus, 10, 11, 23, 34, 48, 52, 134, 135,
    136, 137, 142, 143, 146, 147, 182, 183,
    184, 185, 186, 187, 188, 189, 198, 199
griseum
  centrale mesencephali, subnucleus dorsalis,
    179
    subnucleus lateralis, 177, 178, 179
    subnucleus medialis, 177, 178, 179
  centrale pontis, 168, 169, 170, 171, 172, 173
gyri
  breves insulae, 9, 118, 119, 121
  cerebri, 70
  occipitales lateralis, 8
  orbitales, 7, 73, 78, 80, 81, 85, 131, 132, 141
  temporales transversi, 9, 118, 120
gyrus
  angularis, 7, 74
  cinguli, 5, 6, 7, 8, 28, 76, 77, 78, 79, 132, 133,
    134, 139
  dentatus, 10, 139, 145, 146, 147, 199, 200, 201
  fasciolaris, 10, 79, 142
  frontalis inferior, 6, 74, 105, 117, 131, 132
    medius, 6, 72, 74, 118, 131, 132, 133, 134
    superior, 6, 72, 74, 76, 118, 131, 132, 133,
    134
  hippocampi, 138
  lateralis olfactorius, 43
  longus insulae, 9, 118, 119, 121
  medialis olfactorius, 23
  occipitalis lateralis, 74
    medius, 140

233